1

GROWTH OF SICKNESS IN INDIAN INDUSTRIES

1.0 Introduction

In the past few decades, the accent in management literature and in research has been upon the achievement and success of companies doing business. The subject of company failure has received virtually little attention from writers, academicians and management specialists.

The failure of a business is an event which brings a lot of mental pain to entrepreneurs, managers and to their families. The society is also affected by business failure, as unemployment goes up, availability of goods and services decreases and the cost goes up. The shareholders lose their savings, creditors lose their cash and future business. Thus a coherent framework setting out the causes and symptoms of industrial sickness and developing a model predicting the potential industrial sickness is the need of the hour. Such a coherent and systematic body of knowledge about corporate sickness would serve to minimise, if not eliminate, such losses by providing ample warning in advance to those concerned.

1.1 The Dimensions of Industrial Sickness

The phenomenon of industrial sickness, both in large and small scale industry, has become alarming in recent years. About Rs. 3190 crores [1] are locked up in sick industrial units. These include both small and large scale units. According to Reserve Bank of India's report on Currency and Finance 1983-84 (the latest statistics available on industrial sickness in the country), there were 463 large industrial units availing of bank credit of Rs. 1 crore and above and 64,388 small scale industrial

units on the sick lists as at end June 1983. About Rs. 2539 crores of bank loan stands locked up in these units. This constitutes a 20 per cent increase in outstanding bank loans to sick units in just one year (Rs. 2122 crores in 1982). In just over two years since 1981, the number of sick industrial units has more than doubled and the rise of industrial sickness seems to be unabated. Although one-third of large and medium size sick industrial units belong to the textile industry, more and more units of other industries are also added to the sick list every year. No statistics are available on how many industrial units in the country are prone to sickness. If statistics were worked out on some criterion of an industrial unit being prone to sickness, it would more than likely indicate that industrial sickness has been growing at an alarming proportion.

The data availability position regarding industrial sickness is itself far from satisfactory. There are no comprehensive reviews of sick industries published by the Government except occasional statements and announcements of Government takeover of sick units. The Reserve Bank of India [2] collects data on the monetary involvement of banks in sick units. However, this data does not indicate the actual or the likely loss of employment and output arising out of the sickness of industrial units.

1.2 Industrywise Breakup

The industrywise breakup of sick large and medium industrial units is given in Table 1.1 and the yearwise progressive increase in sickness is shown in Figs. 1.1 (*a*) and (*b*).

Table 1.1 clearly points out that there were 345 large and medium scale industrial units at the end of June 1979, each of which had availed the bank credit of Rs. 1 crore and above and which had been classified by the RBI as sick. The amount of bank credit locked up in and outstanding against them at the end of June 1979 was Rs. 1101.72 crores. By the end of June 1980, the number of such sick industrial units had gone up to 389 and the amount of bank credit outstanding against these units had increased to Rs. 1232.70 crores. At the end of June 1982, Rs. 1728.95 crores of bank money was locked up

TABLE 1.1: **Number of sick industrial units and credit outstanding: Industrywise**

(*Amount in Rs. crores*)

Industry	End-June 1979		End-June 1980		End-June 1981		End-June 1982		End-June 1983	
	No. of units	Credit outstanding (Amount)	No. of units	Credit outstanding (Amount)	No. of units	Credit outstanding (Amount)	No. of units	Credit outstanding (Amount)	No. of units	Credit outstanding (Amount)
I. Large and medium scale										
1. Engineering and electricals } 2. Iron and steel	115	337.25								
1. Engineering and electricals			88	304.25	92	319.61	91	345.23	101	365.74
2. Iron and steel			42	82.36	47	105.89	39	138.33	38	142.45
3. Cotton textiles	84	287.71	89	349.56	94	406.48	111	515.55	119	579.83
4. Chemicals	23	135.04	22	146.16	26	186.12	25	194.13	27	209.24
5. Sugar	35	100.95	48	77.97	48	117.00	45	149.34	44	180.11
6. Jute textiles	33	89.75	35	86.81	35	92.26	37	111.35	37	120.53
7. Rubber	07	34.07	09	42.50	12	64.95	15	100.41	16	108.33
8. Cement	04	13.21	03	11.83	03	13.20	03	12.08	03	09.23
9. Others	44	103.74	53	131.26	65	147.78	69	162.53	78	197.64
Total (I)	345	1101.72	389	1232.70	422	1453.29	435	1728.95	463	1913.10
II. Small scale	16805	181.71	22325	292.80	22360	321.82	26973	393.67	64388	626.52
Total (I+II)	17150	1283.43	22714	1535.50	22782	1775.11	27408	2122.62	64851	2539.62

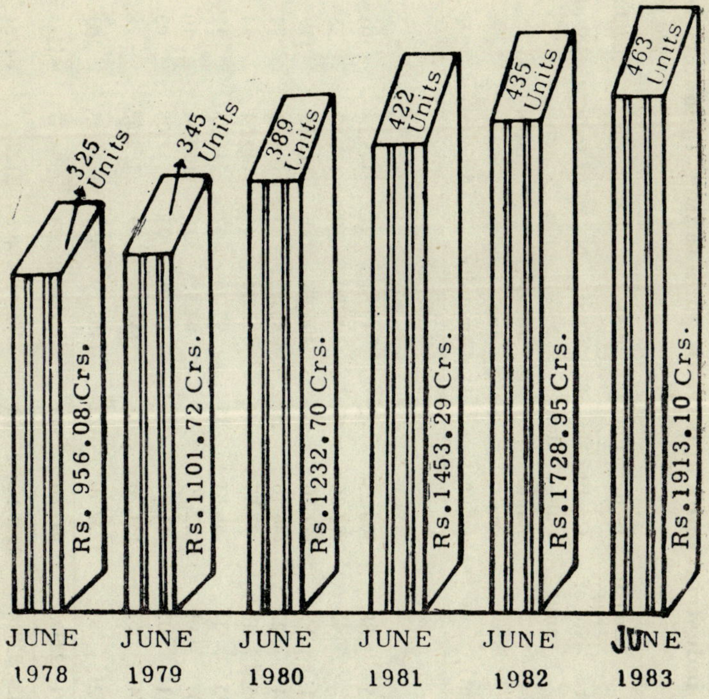

Fig. 1.1 (*a*) **Industrial sickness: Major sector enjoying credit at rupees one crore and above**

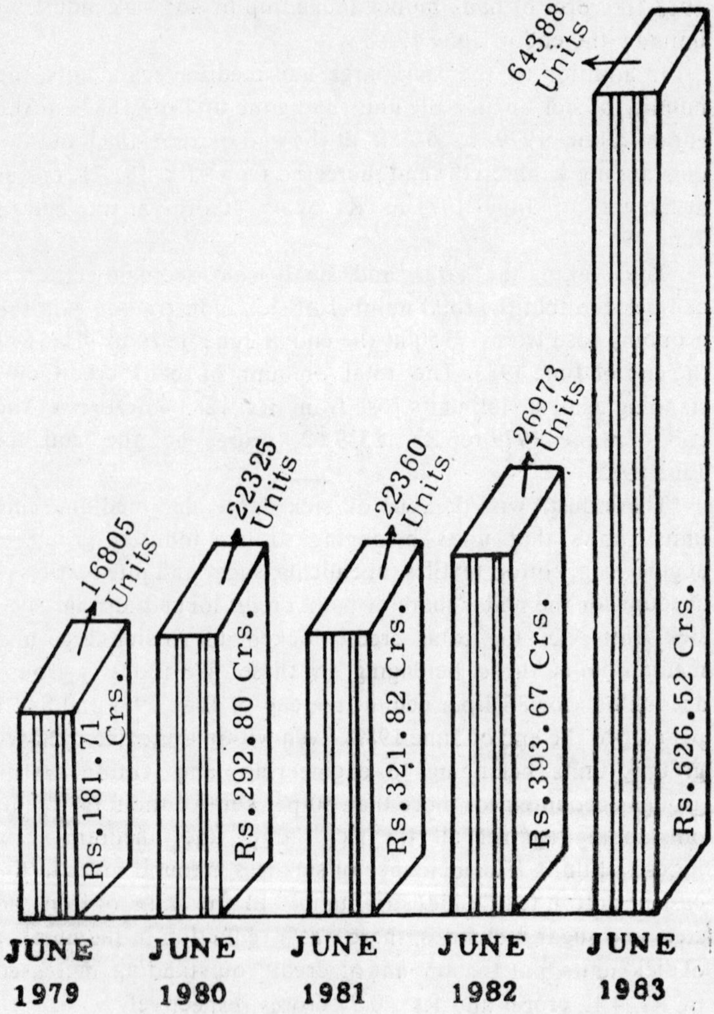

Fig. 1.1 (b) **Industrial sickness: Small scale sector**

in 435 sick industrial units which had further gone up to Rs. 1913.10 crores of bank money locked up in 463 sick industrial units by the end of June 1983.

In addition to the sick large and medium scale units, the number of sick small scale units had gone up from 16805 at the end of June 1979 to 64388 at the end of June 1983 and the outstanding bank credit had increased from Rs. 181.71 crores at the end of June 1979 to Rs. 626.52 crores at the end of June 1983.

Thus, taking the large and small scale sector together, it can be seen that the total number of sick industrial units in the economy rose from 17150 at the end of June 1979 to 64851 at the end of June 1983. The total amount of bank credit outstanding against sick units rose from Rs. 1283.43 crores at the end of June 1979 to Rs. 2539.62 crores at the end of June 1983.

The industrywise breakup of sick large and medium scale units shows that units belonging to five industry groups—engineering, cotton textiles, chemicals, sugar and jute textiles—account for the major share of bank credit locked up in such sick units. Of the total credit locked up in sick large and medium units, those belonging to these five industry groups accounted for 86.3 per cent at the end of June 1979 and 84.21 per cent at the end of June 1982. Even within these five industry groups, units belonging to engineering and cotton textile groups accounted for more than 50 per cent of the total credit outstanding against all the sick large and medium scale industrial units. The incidence of sickness is found more in the case of cotton textile industrial units. In the case of iron and steel and sugar industries, there was a reduction in the number of sick units, but the amount of credit outstanding increased by Rs. 4.12 crores and Rs. 30.77 crores respectively.

1.3 **Statewise Incidence of Sickness**

The statewise breakup of sick large and medium scale units (Table 1.2) shows that six states—West Bengal, Maharashtra, Tamil Nadu, Gujarat, Uttar Pradesh and Karnataka—account for the major share of bank credit outstanding against such units. As at the end of June 1978, June 1979, June 1981, June

TABLE 1.2: **Number of sick industrial units and credit outstanding: Statewise position**

(*Amount in Rs. crores*)

State	End-June 1978		End-June 1979		End-June 1981		End-June 1982		End-June 1983	
	No. of units	Credit outstanding	No. of units	Credit outstanding	No. of units	Credit outstanding	No. of units	Credit outstanding	No. of units	Credit outstanding
Large and medium scale										
1. West Bengal	78	229.62	84	267.13	107	345.59	111	426.17	108	423.94
2. Maharashtra	68	227.61	71	253.44	88	330.59	88	355.22	92	405.48
3. Tamil Nadu	36	15466	36	155.36	35	187.02	35	216.33	40	228.24
4. Gujarat	38	80.51	35	88.08	36	110.47	42	131.73	42	151.95
5. Uttar Pradesh	33	77.37	36	95.51	50	141.95	53	183.60	54	220.89
6. Karnataka	13	48.69	14	62.95	21	102.81	20	140.64	27	173.11
7. Others	59	137.62	69	179.25	85	234.86	86	275.26	100	309.49
Total	325	956.08	345	1101.72	422	1453.29	435	1728.95	463	1913.10

1982 and June 1983, these six states accounted for more than 80 per cent of the credit outstanding against such sick units. And even within these six states, the three states of West Bengal, Maharashtra and Tamil Nadu accounted for more than 55 per cent of outstanding credit as on these dates.

The statewise distribution of sick small scale sector units shows that at the end of December 1979, West Bengal had the highest number of such units followed by Maharashtra, Andhra Pradesh, Uttar Pradesh, Karnataka and Assam in that order (Table 1.3). Tamil Nadu, Gujarat, Bihar and Orissa also had sizeable number of sick small scale units at the end of December 1979.

TABLE 1.3: **Statewise number of sick small scale units**
(As at the end of December 1979)

State/Union territory	No. of sick small scale units
West Bengal	6948
Maharashtra	2763
Tamil Nadu	955
Uttar Pradesh	1152
Gujarat	856
Karnataka	1039
Andhra Pradesh	1323
Bihar	802
Rajasthan	323
Madhya Pradesh	525
Kerala	653
Haryana	225
Orissa	772
Punjab	403
Assam	1045
Delhi	530
Pondicherry	03
Goa	75
Himachal Pradesh	51
Jammu & Kashmir	71
Manipur	186
Nagaland	03
Meghalaya	25
Tripura	70
Chandigarh	43
Total	20841

1.4 Companies in Liquidation

The statewise distribution of companies in liquidation [3] as on March 1982 is given in Table 1.4.

As at the end of March 1982 as many as 3694 companies went into liquidation. West Bengal accounted for 26.2 per cent of the total liquidation followed by Maharashtra 18.7 per cent, Tamil Nadu 13.6 per cent, Delhi 8.4 per cent and Kerala 7.6 per cent. Out of 3694 companies, the number of companies which were asked to wind up by court were 1599 followed by members' voluntary winding up 1430, creditors' voluntary winding up 638 and subject to supervision of the court 27.

TABLE 1.4: **Statewise distribution of companies in liquidation as on March 1982**

State/Union territories	No. of companies
Andhra Pradesh	99
Assam	11
Bihar	36
Gujarat	131
Haryana	23
Himachal Pradesh	05
Jammu & Kashmir	07
Karnataka	231
Kerala	281
Madhya Pradesh	40
Maharashtra	689
Orissa	43
Punjab	83
Rajasthan	81
Tamil Nadu	502
Uttar Pradesh	136
West Bengal	966
Chandigarh	04
Delhi	310
Meghalaya	03
Pondicherry	11
Tripura	02
Total	3694

1.5 Need for a Forewarning System

The progressive increase in industrial sickness has been causing considerable concern to the Government, Financial Institutions and Banks. The common effects of such sickness are locking up of financial resources, wastage of capital assets, loss of production and decrease in employment. It has become a national problem requiring a comprehensive redress rather than inventing quick fixes to revive sick units. A coherent framework consisting of the dynamics of sickness and a forewarning system is, thus, needed to identify the incidence of sickness in different industries, so that timely action can be initiated to stem it and even overcome wherever possible. The intervention may involve change in management of the firm, grant of additional funds or funding by other organisations jointly to prevent further sickness. Appropriate remedial action will depend on the diagnosis of the causes of sickness and in the identification of the critical parameters responsible for it. Sickness in units has to be predicted and key parameters identified to monitor its incidence is, thus, very necessary so that timely and prompt action can be taken to stem further growth of industrial sickness in the country.

1.6 The Concept of Sickness

Sickness in industries has been viewed in several ways: Walter [4] and Donaldson [5-6] has termed it as technical insolvency when a firm is unable to meet its maturing obligations. Others restrict the term to the so-called real insolvency case where the total value of the firm's assets is smaller than its liabilities. Sometimes business failure is interpreted in the strict legal sense of bankruptcy or liquidation when the firm ceases its operations [7].

According to ICICI, "Sick Industry" is one whose financial viability is threatened by adverse factors present and continuing. The adverse factors might relate to management, market, fiscal burden, labour relations or any other. When the impact of these factors reaches a point when a company begins to incur cash losses leading to erosion of its funds, there is a threat to its financial viability. The Financial Bill, 1977 contained a

clause defining a sick unit as one whose 50 per cent or more of capital reserves were wiped out by the losses.

A sick unit is defined by the Reserve Bank of India [8] as a unit which has incurred cash losses for one year and in the judgement of the bank, it is likely to continue to incur cash losses for the current year as well as the following year and which has an imbalance in its financial structure such as current ratio of less than 1.1 and worsening debt equity ratio. This definition seeks to emphasize operational performance and financial position which are interrelated to each other. Keeping the above in view, there can be at least three different view-points in defining sickness:;

(*a*) At the Government level in India, corporate sickness gets recognised generally only when a unit is on the brink of closure or closes its doors, throwing a large number of people out of employment;

(*b*) At the lending institutions level, the problem gets recognised when non-payment of instalments due to money lent starts and continues for two or three intervals i.e. recovery of money lent becomes uncertain;

(*c*) From the shareholders' point of view, an enterprise is considered sick if it fails to pay reasonable dividends and the future also looks bleak and the share value tumbles down.

A review of three different view-points defining sickness brings to bear that the third view is nearer the economic sense of the term 'failure'. It is related to the earning potential of the enterprise and the second view is nearer to the business sense of the term 'failure'.

Non-payment of dividends will almost invariably precede the default on debt obligations, and the default on the latter will ordinarily precede the cessation of operations. Hence, these different view-points may be said to represent stages of sickness.

1.7 **Sickness is an Organic Process**

Sickness in an industry is an organic process in the life history of a unit. A healthy unit may grow sick temporarily and may

recover or vice-versa. Factors that cause sickness could be internal or external. The external factors usually affect all the industrial units in the same group while the internal factors may affect a particular unit only and not the whole industry. In such cases, the sickness has an origin followed by several stages of sickness. The sickness process is illustrated in Fig. 1.2. Initially a healthy unit may show good cash profit and may have positive values of net working capital and net worth. As it tends towards sickness, the first (cash profit) may become negative although the unit may continue to pay its instalments to the term lending institutions. As sickness grows more and more through other stages, two or more financial parameters may become negative. The negative values do signal sickness. It is these initial stages that require careful monitoring. For such a purpose, a forewarning system which signals the probable sickness of industrial concerns before any loss is inflicted upon the concerned parties would prove to be a great boon. It would provide a warning to all the concerned parties to reconsider their situation and take prompt and appropriate action.

It is a well established fact that earlier the trouble is detected, more easily and economically it may be countered. Early detection of sickness possibly may enable the management to take timely action to avert the crisis of such an occurrence. If there exists a forewarning system which helps in predicting corporate sickness, the attention can be focussed on those concerns which are trudging towards sickness. The Chairman of the Industrial Finance Corporation of India (IFCI) mentioned on 33rd Annual General Meeting about the importance of an effective monitoring system, "One is well aware of the sickness in industry. While it is not possible to avoid sickness in the industry entirely, it has come to be clearly recognised that (*i*) this process can be considerably controlled with effective monitoring, and timely steps to ensure prevention of sickness, and (*ii*) by rehabilitation of some of the units which have become sick, but which are potentially viable. This can be feasible only when some monitoring system is in force" [9].

Companies do not go burst 'overnight' as many people think. The process of sickness can take years and thus the

Healthy Unit Criteria		**Tending Towards Sickness Criteria**		**INCIPIENT OF SICKNESS**		Sick	
1. Cash Profit +	→	1. Cash Profit/ Loss −	→		→		→ Increasing Sickness or Closure
2. Net Working Capital +		2. Net Working Capital+					
3. Net Worth +		3. Net Worth+		2 or more—ve		All −ve	

Fig. 1.2 **The Process of Sickness**

seeds of sickness may be discernible very early in the story of a company's rise and decline. The forewarning system would help in reducing, if not completely eliminating, the irreparable loss to the interested parties caused by corporate collapse. The importance of such a forewarning system can be described in the words of Lev [10] more clearly: 'An early warning signal of probable failure will enable both management and investors to take preventive measures; operating policy changes, reorganisation of financial structure, and even voluntary liquidation will usually shorten the length of time losses are incurred and thereby improve both private and social resource allocation'.

2

CAUSES OF INDUSTRIAL SICKNESS

2.0 Introduction

Various views have been expressed by the experts and writers [11-24] on the causes of industrial sickness. Although there are different opinions about the causes of sickness, there is certainly a widespread agreement on a number of key factors causing it. Often several factors working simultaneously push the unit in the track of sickness. Some are external and others are internal to the unit.

2.1 External Factors

The external factors usually affect an industrial group as a whole and on these the industry has no direct control. Some of the external factors may include the following:

(1) Unexpected adverse market conditions for a prolonged period;
(2) Changes in Government policies in respect of excise duty, import/export restrictions and subsidies;
(3) Industrial strikes not always originated by the parent companies;
(4) Disequilibrium between demand and supply;
(5) Recessionary trends;
(6) Rise in cost of production, not compensated by corresponding increase in prices because of Government control; and
(7) Scarcity of critical resources like raw materials, power and skilled labour.

2.2 **Internal Factors**

Internal factors are those which are within the control of the management of a unit. Internally some are management related and others are function related. The internal factors contributing sickness could arise from poor financial management, poor capacity utilisation, poor operation of equipment and plant and outdated production technology. Sickness is normally caused by internal factors which are mostly related with the mismanagement in various areas of operations i.e. technical, financial, operational, marketing etc. However, a mere list of causes of sickness, no matter how comprehensive it may be, is not enough unless linked together in a mechanism leading to sickness. Hence, the dynamics of sickness—the sequencing of events that bind together all the causes and symptoms of sickness into a working model—is the need of the hour.

2.3 **Data on Sick Projects**

Data on 223 projects have been collected which were in default between June 1970 and December 1980 over a decade. All these projects had drawn their term loans from the financial institutions. These data were analysed for main weaknesses which were identified in eight main groups. The number of projects, percentage of the projects and percentage contribution of each cause is shown in Table 2.1.

TABLE 2.1: **Causewise distribution of new projects in default**

	No. of projects	% of the projects	% Contribution of the cause to default
1. Lack of good management	36	16.1	22.19
2. Poor implementation	56	25.1	21.70
3. Marketing problems	29	13.1	15.81
4. Non-availability of raw materials	53	23.8	13.45
5. Shortfall of working capital	03	01.4	07.20
6. Labour trouble	12	05.4	05.74
7. Technical/operational problems	13	05.8	05.55
8. Other causes	21	09.4	08.36

These factors, if not controlled, start creating conditions which force a unit to pass from a healthy state to one tending towards sickness and then through incipient sickness to a gravely sick state.

2.3.1 **Poor management**

In the table on causewise distribution of projects in default, lack of good management constitutes the maximum contribution to the sickness in industry. There is a widespread agreement that poor management is the prime cause of sickness in industry. Poor management is that management which lacks requisite personnel, expertise skills and adequate information and reporting systems at the top. One should be alarmed for the viability of any company exhibiting one or all of the following structural defects in top management:

(*a*) Unbalanced top management team;
(*b*) Non-participating top management;
(*c*) Lack of requisite personnel;
(*d*) Insufficient knowledge for the industry concerned.

It has been observed that top management of a company exhibiting any or all of these defects would be in grave danger of making just those decisions that often lead to sickness. If the top management does not contain expertise and requisite skills, the chances of some new threat appearing but going unnoticed are severely increased.

2.3.2 **Poor reporting**

Lack of proper information and reporting system especially accounting informations is another factor associated with poor management that contributes to sickness. Several deficiencies have been noticed relating to the information and reporting system that contribute to sickness in industry. Some of these are—(*a*) poor reporting of faults, breakdowns and sales in the industry; (*b*) no or poor cash flow planning; (*c*) no or poor costing system and (d) no or poor budgetary control. The lack of adequate information and reporting systems will preclude the management seeing the approaching disaster and thus causing sickness. The absence of reliable informa-

tion make difficult for anyone inside the company to analyse its growing problems and evaluate and suggest solutions.

2.3.3 **Inability to respond**

Poor management with poor information and reporting systems will generally result in its inability to respond to changes which then becomes a major cause of sickness. Such management either does not notice the approaching crisis or does not respond correctly. The crisis may relate to technological, competitive, economic, social and political changes taking place. A poor management with inadequate information and reporting systems and inability to respond to changes will further lead to mismangement in other areas like marketing, technical and operational performance of the industry resulting in poor production leading to poor financial position of the company.

2.3.4 **Poor implementation**

In the table on causewise distribution of new projects in default, poor implementation constitutes the second largest factor contributing to the sickness in industry. This is particularly noticeable in the lot of the 223 projects examined which were financed by the financial institutions and which later became sick resulting in non-payment of their term loan or interest or both. The process of poor implementation arises from poor planning and inability to make contingency plan when the project duration overshoots either in time or in cost and the inability of the management to curb it. The financial institutions also contribute to some element of sickness in this stage because of their insistence in getting more of paper particulars and not releasing the instalments due to the industry in time.

Poor implementation implies that with respect to time the various stages in project progress are not reached as per schedule and get delayed. For instance, the building might not have been completed in the required time frame, the plant and equipment did not arrive in time or the installation could not take place as projected in the schedule resulting in poor implementation. When major activities in the project planning

do not take place according to the schedule, the release of further instalment of loans from the financial institutions are also delayed contributing to further time and cost overshoots in project. Poor implementation is a general feature in Indian environment because of the shortage economy which sometimes is real and quite often manipulated. The management of project has to be aware of the key materials needed for the project, the lack of which can delay the project progress. Contingency planning has, therefore, to be thought of to overcome such situations when they arise or are anticipated. The same applies when equipment and components are ordered for supply. The vendor analysis should be taken before placing the order and where the size of order for components and sub-system is high, splitting the order in more than one supplier may be desirable. There has to be a constant monitoring of the key activities of project progress so that delays if any should be anticipated in the regular periodic review which is must for all projects.

2.3.5 Examples of poor implementation

Kuchhal [25] has carried out a study of 46 units drawn from a group of 12 industries, namely tractors, automobile tyres, detergents, synthetic yarns, mini-steel, steel tubes, scooter, automobile gears, fibre glass, steel strips and tools, sheet glass and hotels. These were provided assistance by the national level financial institutions. Of the 46 units studied, 61 per cent were in the private sctor, 33 per cent were in the joint sector and 6 per cent were in the public sector. Out of these 46 units, 25 units were successful and 21 units were sick. The study revealed that only 6 units (13 per cent) implemented their projects without any time or cost over-runs. Of the remaining 40 units, 26 units (57 per cent) faced both time as well as cost over-runs in varying degree averaging 57.3 per cent cost over-runs and 27 months time over-runs. Seven units (15 per cent) had only time over-runs. Seventeen of these 26 units were sick and the remaining 9 units were successful.

The major cause of poor implementation is cost and time over-runs. In the case of 46 units studied, the cost and time over-runs are given in Tables 2.2 and 2.3.

TABLE 2.2: **Cost over-runs**

Over-run	Number of units		
	Total	Successful	Sick
1—25	16	8	8
26—50	8	5	3
51—100	3	1	2
Over 100	4	—	4
Information not available	2	2	—
Total	33	16	17

TABLE 2.3: **Time over-runs**

Grouping	Number of units		
	Total	Successful	Sick
Up to 3 months	5	3	2
Over 3 months—up to 6 months	6	3	3
Over 6 months—up to 1 year	6	1	5
Over 1 year—up to 2 years	8	5	3
Over 2 years—up to 3 years	3	1	2
Over 3 years	5	—	5
Total	33	13	20

2.3.6 **Delay in disbursement by financial institutions**

Delay in receiving instalments of loans from the financial institutions also contributes to poor implementation of projects as the promoters have no funds to carry on. It has been observed while analysing the 223 projects that there are a number of terms and conditions laid down at various stages in the processing of loans by the financial institutions and also at the time of the issue of letter of intent. No distinction is drawn between terms and conditions and also among the conditions as some of these are very vital for taking disbursement decisions while others are relaxable to a large extent in the interest of project completion when it is on the verge of time overshoots. For example, if a work package or group of work packages is already reaching the latest date of completion (Fig. 2.1) and a condition for compliance is not vital, it should not be insisted upon for release of disbursement in the interest of the

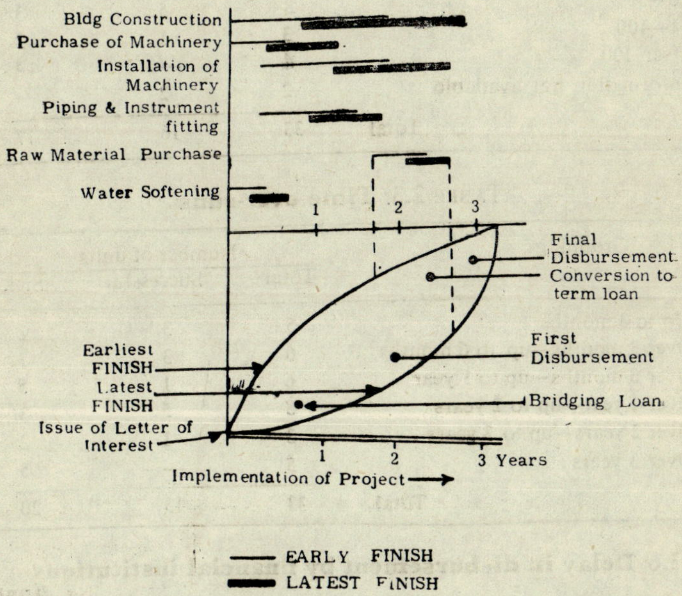

Fig. 2.1: **Project plan bar chart (earliest and latest finish)**

project; otherwise the project will overshoot in time and cost both. The loop shown in Fig. 2.1 is the slack available on any project when its activities are plotted by the critical path method in terms of early and late start of each activity.

It is, thus, desirable to evolve a disbursement plan in agreement with the promoters on the compliance of conditions which are vital for disbursement. This is possible if this aspect is made clear in the letter of intent itself so that promoters understand the importance of complying with vital conditions for getting disbursement from the financial institutions. The conditions usually laid down could be arranged in three groups—(*a*) pre-sanction stage; (*b*) pre-disbursement stage; and (*c*) post-implementation stage. Those which are considered variable can be identified. The variability is only from the point of view of granting additional time to the promoter for compliance if and when necessary so as to minimise the time overshoot in the project resulting later in the increase of pre-operating expenditure.

2.3.7 **Poor marketing management**

In the table on causewise distribution of new projects in default, poor marketing constitutes 15.81 per cent of the causes leading to industrial sickness. The main causes for sickness due to this factor are—(1) Poor market survey (2) Reliance on only one customer or one customer one product set-up (3) Lack of market penetration i.e. Inability to perceive changes in customer needs (4) Seasonal demand for products and (5) Recession.

It has been observed that in most of the sick industries due to this factor, too much reliance has been placed on the demand indicated by the only customer of that product. In fact product formulation has assumed a continuing demand of a single customer like defence requirements or those of a single firm. By the time the industry comes to the stage of production, the customer has changed the demand or the product has become obsolete. In both the cases inability of the producer in contacting more customers or carrying out market surveys before product launch have been the main

cause of failure. Periodical review of the customer's demand has not been done.

The success of an industry ultimately depends on its capacity to market its producton. This requires an intelligent and well planned market strategy. Very often the entrepreneures are quite indifferent towards demand forecast or rely on sketchy market surveys. They may take data compiled by the Planning Commission or other similar agencies. In all these cases, forecasts are found to be out-dated by the time the companies are in a position to go in production. Usually, no efforts are made to revise the estimates of the demand at the point of production.

There are examples of a few cases of detergent units in the hands of promoters with sound technical knowhow. But the projects failed in spite of the fact that there was a big demand. The failure was attributed to the stranglehold of the brand loyalty to the established manufacturer. The promoters of the new projects could not get a foothold in the market. In another case, another detergent company succeeded in spite of the stiff competition from established companies and the success was mainly attributable to its pricing policy as well as to its promotional activities.

2.3.8 Poor technical and operational management

In the table on causewise distribution of sickness of new projects the contribution of technical and operational mismanagement is 5.55 per cent which is relatively a low figure. However, the parameters are extremely important and can make a large contribution towards sickness as internal factors. Generally, both these factors when poor will contribute to low production and consequent loss of internal cash generation. These are described as under:

(*i*) **Technical factors**: Mostly the factors that contribute to technical mismanagement are (*a*) inefficient operation of plant and machinery on account of frequent breakdowns (*b*) poor maintenance and replacement of components and parts (*c*) obsolete technology (*d*) under-utilisation of capacity and (*e*) shortage of power, and, therefore, operating well below the break-even point. The state of plant and equipment

in a factory and its technical efficiency is a critical factor in determining the sickness in the industrial unit. The breakdown in the plant depends on the age and proneness to failure of components and sub-systems in the plant. This technical parameter can be measured by the ratio of the actual working hours to the total available if the plant and equipment were in perfect health. This can be called plant utilisation ratio and can be a critical parameter in several industrial groups particularly engineering, textile, paper and chemicals. The production cost ratio will also rise and can also be a second indicator of the performance of the unit.

(*ii*) **Operational factors**: The availability of critical raw materials could be an operational factor which can affect the health of the units. Non-availability of raw materials generally reduces the capacity utilisation of the company and thus becomes a critical parameter in determining the degree of sickness of the unit. In cases of newly started factories where the economic size has been determined for minimum requirement of raw materials, its non-availability can cause grave sickness in that industry. In addition to this, the other operational factors which can contribute to sickness are (*a*) lack of proper production planning and control (*b*) high material wastage and (*c*) labour unrest.

2.3.9 Poor financial management

The poorly managed company commits gross errors in the area of finance which aggravate the problem of internal cash generation contributing to deterioration in the liquidity position of a unit. Lack of working funds on continuous basis becomes a major threat to the financial viability and hence in its survival. Financial factors which contribute to financial mismanagement and consequent sickness in the industrial units are (*a*) unfavourable financial gearing i.e. noticeably high capital gearing; (*b*) overtrading i.e. increasing turnover at a faster rate than the internally generated cash flow; (*c*) deliberate diversion of funds and (*d*) poor management of working capital—poor collections, unplanned payment to creditors and high inventory (discussed in detail in Chapter 7).

(*i*) **Capital gearing**: The term capital gearing means the volume of long-term fixed interest bearing securities as a percentage of total capital employed. The sources from which funds can be raised by a company can be grouped into two categories from the charges/cost point of view (*a*) those which carry a fixed financial charge, and (*b*) those which do not carry fixed charge. The first category consists of various types of long-term debts, including bonds, debentures and preference shares. The fundamentals are that long-term debts carry a fixed rate of interest irrespective of profits which is a contractual obligation for the company, while equity dividends depend upon profits of the company. Loans are ranked before equity in case the company goes into liquidation. Both these features mean that loans are normally a cheaper source of capital than equity because the lender's both interest and capital are at less risk than the shareholder's dividend and capital. Companies, therefore, fund as much of their business as possible with loans rather than equity. But the use of loans carrying fixed rate of interest is beneficial till capital gearing/financial leverage is favourable. It is favourable when the company earns more on its total capital employed than the fixed rate of interest on loans or vice-versa. Since there is a prudent limit, though different for each business, beyond which the risk of high capital gearing outrans its advantages and pushes the company in the track of liquidity crisis and becomes more dangerous during the economic turndowns. The prudent level is determined by a number of factors such as the rate of interest expected on various forms of loans, business growth prospects and profits. Perhaps the most important determinant is the *liability* of the company's profits to extreme variations. High capital gearing contributing to liquidity crisis will force the company to borrow still more from the banks and financial institutions to finance its operations and consequently aggravate its problem of high gearing. The mismanaged companies with high capital gearing or companies trying to gear up their capital beyond the prudent level are more prone to sickness even during the normal hazards of business.

(*ii*) **Overtrading**: The term overtrading means the increase in turnover at the expense of profit margins and at a faster rate than the internally generated cash flow. When a company increases its turnover, it has to inject cash into inventories, debtors and other aspects of business at approximately the rate at which the expansion is taking place. The increasing turnover can be financed either through borrowed money or internally generated cash flow. Where the turnover increases at a rate faster than the internally generated cash flow, the company has to borrow to finance its increased turnover which will contribute further to high capital gearing. No company can continue to finance its expansion with borrowed money for long without arousing the suspicions of their bankers, who lose confidence in the company and decline to extend further credit. The companies in their attempt to increase turnover at the expense of profit margins face the problem of working funds as and when further credit is declined by the banks and the financial institutions to finance their operations. They run out of cash and hence fall sick.

3

SIGNALS AND SYMPTOMS OF INDUSTRIAL SICKNESS

3.0 **Introduction**

Sick companies start throwing up signals which need to be identified and monitored before the unit becomes gravely sick. A large number of signals are displayed by failing units initially. In the early stages of sickness, the warning signs in several functional areas are termed as signals. The persistence of these signals over a long period become symptoms of sickness. An industrial unit tends to show the signs of financial distress starting with short term liquidity problems, revenue losses, operating losses and moving in the direction of overuse of external credit until it reaches a stage where it is overburdened with debt and not being able to muster sufficient funds to meet its obligation. The signals gradually merge into symptoms and get related to plant performance, capacity utilisation, financial ratios, shares market price, practices in the area of finance, production, marketing and labour relations etc. (Fig. 3.1).

2.1 **Signals of Sickness**

Some of the important signals of sickness are as under:

(1) Frequent breakdowns of plants and equipment
(2) Decline in capacity utilisation
(3) Decline in technical efficiency
(4) Non-submission of data to banks and financial institutions
(5) Irregular bank accounts
(6) Decline in quality of product or service

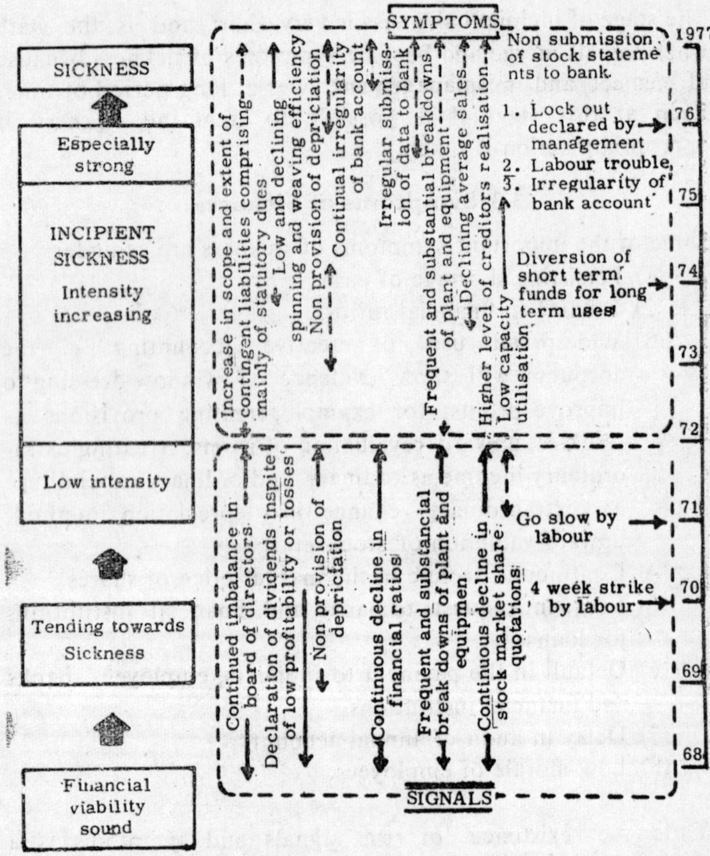

Fig. 3.1 **Signals and symptoms of sickness**

(7) Delay or default in payment of statutory dues such as provident fund, sales tax, excise duty, employees state insurance and so on

(8) Frequent turnover of personnel

3.2 Incipient Sickness

The stage of incipient sickness is very short and is the state when signals merge and become symptoms of sickness because of neglect and mismanagement over a long period of time. Even at this stage it is possible to stem the sickness if appropriate action is taken.

3.3 Symptoms of Sickness

Some of the important symptoms of sickness are as under:

(1) Persisting shortage of cash.

(2) Decline in financial ratios.

(3) Widespread use of creative accounting i.e. the accounts will show evidence of window dressing to improve profits, for example, treating provisions as reserves, upward revaluation of assets, treating extraordinary income as ordinary and ordinary expenditure as extraordinary, change in depreciation method, upward valuation of stock etc.

(4) Continuous decline in the market price of shares.

(5) Frequent requests to banks and financial institutions for loans.

(6) Default in the payment to suppliers, employees, banks and financial institutions.

(7) Delay in audit of annual accounts.

(8) Low morale of employees.

While the existence of the signals and symptoms is a ground for suspecting that the industrial unit concerned is prone to sickness, the magnitude of sickness cannot be predicted on these grounds alone. An objective analysis of units (sick vs healhy) financial condition over a time period is necessary.

3.4 Need for Predicting Sickness

In our set-up today, owners' stake in most of our industries is limited. A substantial risk of the venture many a time is taken by the commercial banks and financial institutions apart from the equity holders. This puts an additional responsibility on the banks and financial institutions to ensure an effective utilisation of credit and to prevent misutilisation by the borrowers. The rationale for prediction of sickness in advance of its occurrence is to prevent the spread of industrial sickness and by doing so, to save crores of rupees of banks, financial institutions and other investors for better use which otherwise would be locked up in sick units with little chance of recovery. It, thus, becomes necessary that sickness in units should be predicted and closely monitored to safeguard the interest of all concerned.

4

FINANCIAL RATIOS AS INDICATORS OF INDUSTRIAL SICKNESS

4.0 Significance of Ratios

Financial statements are multifunctional to meet the needs of several users, both from within and outside the company viz., managers, creditors, investors, Government and customers etc. On the basis of the information gained from these financial statements, various decisions in different areas are taken. The varied users are interested in assessing the financial viability of companies which have been in existence which is usually judged from the profitability, liquidity and solvency position of companies. These aspects are represented by profit or loss, net working capital and net worth respectively. It can be stated that solvency and liquidity are the two vital organs of financial viability of a unit and profitability is its life blood.

The three elements of financial viability are estimated normally from the financial ratios which are mostly computed from the company's balance sheet. A financial ratio is a quotient of two numbers, where both numbers consist of financial statement items. Financial ratios have been used extensively in the past. The usage of financial ratios is justified by the fact that the selection of pertinent material from a plethora of published information is more useful than wide and indiscriminate reading. Financial ratios serve this purpose by reducing the size of data disclosed in financial statements to a relatively small set of readily comprehended and economically meaningful indicators. Laurent [26] has stated that "In principle, the justification for employing financial

ratio analysis to investigate a company's financial state is highly defensible. There are certain normative relationships existing between different financial components of a company as displayed in the balance sheet and revenue and appropriation account. The extent to which a company does or does not conform to these norms for the activities (industry) that it is engaged in, is indicative of something favourable or unfavourable, depending upon relationship being examined".

If the actual relationship exhibits a significant departure from the normative relationship it acts as a precursor of some event in future. The prediction of future event is of great interest to the varied users of financial statements since prediction is necessary and prior condition for decision-making. The predictive capability of financial ratios has assumed high importance in the past few years that it is now used as a criterion for judging the usefulness of ratios [27]. The predictive capability as a criterion for judging the usefulness of financial ratios is generally justified by the fact that it circumvents the enormity of task required for a complete specification of decision settings.

4.1 Classification of Financial Ratios

Financial ratios can be classified into four major groups:

1. Profitability ratios
2. Solvency ratios
3. Liquidity ratios
4. Turnover ratios

This classification depicts different economic aspects of the company's operations. This is oriented to the needs of users. Investors are mainly concerned with profitability ratios, lenders with solvency ratios and the company with all of these.

4.1.1 Profitability ratios

Profitability ratios are designed for the evaluation of the company's operational performance. The numerator of the ratios consists of periodic profits according to a specific definition, while the denominator represents the relevant investment base. The ratios thus yield an indicator of the

company's efficiency in using the capital committed by shareholders and lenders. Some of profitability ratios in common use are:

(*a*) *Cash flow ratios*

(1) Cash flow to net sales
(2) Cash flow to total tangible assets
(3) Cash flow to net worth
(4) Cash flow to total debt

(*b*) *Income ratios*

(1) Net income to net sales
(2) Net income to total tangible assets
(3) Net income to net worth
(4) Net income to total debt
(5) Earning before interest and taxes to total tangible assets
(6) Earning before interest and taxes to net sales
(7) Net operating profit to net sales
(8) Earning before interest and taxes to interest
(9) Net income to net working capital

4.1.2 Solvency ratios

The main objective of long-term solvency ratios is to indicate the company's ability to meet its long-term obligations with regard to (*a*) periodic payment of interest during the period of the loan and (*b*) repayment of principal on maturity or in predetermined instalments when due. These measures stress the long run financial and operating structure of a company. Some of these ratios are:

(1) Total tangible assets to current debt
(2) Total tangible assets to long-term debt
(3) Total tangible assets to total debt
(4) Net worth to total debt
(5) Net worth to long-term debt.

4.1.3 Liquidity ratios

The degree to which a company can meet its current obligations is a measure of its short-term liquidity. The general objective of liquidity ratios is to indicate the company's ability

to meet its short-term financial obligations. Liquidity measures are believed to be of prime *interest* to short-term lenders such as banks and merchandise suppliers. Some of the ratios included in this category are:

(*a*) *Liquid assets to total tangible assets ratios*
  (1) Cash to total tangible assets
  (2) Quick assets to total tangible assets
  (3) Current assets to total tangible assets
  (4) Net working capital to total tangible assets

(*b*) *Liquid assets to current debt ratios*
  (1) Cash to current liabilities
  (2) Quick assets to current liabilities
  (3) Current assets to current liabilities

4.1.4 Turnover ratios

Turnover ratios usually consist of the sales figure in the numerator and the balance of an asset (e.g. inventory, debtors etc.) in the denominator. The objective of these measures is to indicate the various aspects of operational efficiency. Thus, sometimes these ratios are also called efficiency ratios. The efficiency with which the assets are used would be reflected in the speed and rapidity with which these are converted into sales. Attention is focussed here on specific assets rather than on the overall efficiency of assets utilisation measured by the profitability ratios. Following are some widely used turnover ratios:

(1) Net sales to debtors
(2) Net sales to inventory
(3) Net sales to quick assets
(4) Net sales to current assets
(5) Net sales to net working capital
(6) Net sales to total tangible assets
(7) Net sales to net worth
(8) Net sales to fixed assets
(9) Cash to total operating expenditure (cash interval ratio)
(10) Defensive assets to total operating expenditures (defensive interval ratio)

(11) Defensive assets minus current liabilities to total operating expenditures (no credit interval ratios)

4.2 Financial Ratios as Predictors
(Survey of earlier work)

The attempts made in the area of evolving financial ratios as predictors of corporate sickness can be viewed under three heads:

(*a*) Univariate empirical work
(*b*) Multivariate models
(*c*) Evaluation

4.2.1 Univariate empirical work

Patrick [28] conducted a study in 1932 to examine whether there was a significant difference in the trend of ratios for failed and non-failed firms at least three years prior to failure. He selected a sample of 19 companies which had failed during the period of 1920-29 and chose a matching sample of 19 successful companies using financial soundness, asset size, sales volume, product line and fiscal year as matching criteria. Each pair of firms was examined using a number of financial ratios for three years prior to the date of failure. The ratios of both the groups were compared with the minimum level and found that successful firms surpassed the minimum level in most of the cases, while on the other hand, the ratios of failed firms were below the minimum level in majority of the cases. The ratios of the failed firms deteriorated as the year of failure approached. It was observed that all the ratios of failed firms were persistently different from the non-failed firms at least three years prior to failure. The net worth to debt and net profit to net worth ratios were found the best indicators of failure among the ratios used.

Winakor and Smith [29] examined 183 firms which failed between 1923-1931 for ten years prior to the year of failure. Failure was defined as either entering receivership, bond default or material readjustment of rights of equities and creditors. Twenty-one ratios for each of the firms were computed and examined after the financial statements had

been standardised. The mean ratios of the middle half of all the firms were used to compare individual changes for the whole group. It was concluded that the ratios of the failed firms were frequently below the mean value used for comparison and showed deterioration as the date of failure drew near and also pointed out that the ratios of net working capital to total assets (NWC/TA) was the most accurate and steady indicator of failure, with its decline beginning ten years before the occurrence of failure.

Ramser and Foster [30] analysed eleven types of financial ratios for 173 firms whose securities were registered in the State of Illinois. It was found that firms which turned out to be less successful and those which failed tended to have ratios which were lower than the more successful firms. However, two turnover ratios—sales to net worth and sales to total assets—exhibited an opposite tendency.

The above three studies suffered some shortcomings. Patrick's sample was small and too selective to generalise the conclusions. In the study of Ramser and Foster, many of the differences were more apparent than real. Winakor and Smith's study suffered the shortcoming of lacking a contrasting control group of successful firms. However, in general the shortcomings of these three studies were outweighted by the essential importance of their contribution. They represented an extremely significant event in the development of ratio analysis because these were the first carefully developed attempts to utilise the scientific method for determining the utility of ratios for predicting the sickness of firms.

Merwin [31] using a sample of over 900 continuing and discontinuing firms corroborated the ratio differences for as far back as six years before failure. This study of the relationship between financial ratios and business failure concentrated on small corporations (under $ 2,50,000 in total assets) which failed during the period 1926-36. Two methods of comparison were used. One was to determine a high-low range for each ratio for every year, by using the companies as indicators of what the highs and lows should be. The other method was to use an estimated normal ratio reflecting the success of surviving firms. Comparing industry mean ratios of

disappearing firms against estimated normal ratios and the high-low range ratios, it was found that the ratios of the discontinuing firms were consistently below the estimated normal and out of line with the high-low range established by the surviving firms. A persistent decline from the estimated normal was also found beginning with the sixth year prior to failure. It was concluded that three ratios were sensitive predictors of failure up to as early as four to five years prior to discontinuance. These three ratios were: (1) Net working capital to total assets; (2) The current ratio; and (3) Net worth to total debt. Net working capital to total assets ratio was found to be the best 'single indicator of failure'.

Hickmen [32] found that the times interest earned ratios and the net profits to sales ratio were useful predictors of the default experience of corporate bond issues during 1900-1943. Saulinier [33] found evidence from RFC lending experience during 1934-51 that borrowing firms with poorer current ratios and net worth to debt ratios were more prone to loan default. Moore and Atkinson [34] found that the ability to obtain credit was correlated with several ratios. Seiden [35] reported that certain financial ratios (e.g. net working capital to total assets) were inversely correlated with an index of trade credit difficulties. This series of studies used ratios as variables for examining and describing economic activity, thus, further widening the empirical base of ratio analysis. Despite the various statistical shortcomings of these early studies (e.g. small and biased samples, lack of control groups), systematic differences between the ratios of failed and non-failed firms were established. However, these studies were generally descriptive and did not face directly the normative problem of predicting corporate failure.

The first pioneering attempt to predict corporate failure was made by Beaver [36] in 1966. Failure was defined as the inability of a firm to pay its financial obligations as they mature. He examined the predictive power of 30 different financial ratios and tried to predict industrial failure up to 5 years in advance. A univariate prediction model of corporate failure was developed and tested on observations of 79 failed and 79 non-failed firms, selected by the paired sample (by

industry and asset size) technique. The objective of such a sample design (paired sample) was to mitigate any effect that asset size or type of industry might have on the possibility of failure.

Beaver conducted three major empirical experiments in order to establish the predictive power of financial ratios: (*i*) a comparison of mean values, (*ii*) a dichotomous classification test, and (*iii*) an analysis of likelihood ratios. A comparison of the mean ratios of failed and non-failed firms provided substantial evidence that the financial ratios of failed firms showed deterioration and were worse than that of non-failed firms as early as five years prior to failure. Differences in ratios mean do not suggest directly the existence and extent of predictive power. To examine the predictive power of ratios, the second type of analysis (i.e. Dichotomous Classification Test was made which predicts the failure status of a unit, based solely upon a knowledge of the financial ratio. The ratio with the smallest percentage error was considered the best indicator. Dichotomous classification test indicated that the most successful predictor was the cash flow to total debt ratio followed by the net income to total assets ratio. On the basis of lowest percentage prediction error for each group over the five year period, Beaver selected the following six variables as best: (1) cash flow to total debt (2) net income to total assets (3) current plus long-term liabilities to total assets (4) working capital to total assets (5) current ratio and (6) no credit interval ratio.

However, Beaver was not satisfied with these results, because the choice was treated as dichotomous and, therefore, the magnitude of the difference between the ratios and the cut off point was not considered while predicting the probability of failure. To overcome these problems, Beaver undertook an analysis of likelihood ratios. The likelihood ratio analysis indicates the extent to which a decision-maker's assessments of the probability of failure are altered by looking at the financial ratios. The conclusion of the analysis of likelihood ratios supported that the ratios were useful indicator of failure of the firm at least five years prior to failure.

Being aware of the limitations in using only accounting data, Beaver extended his study to a comparison of the predictive power of financial ratios with that of stock market prices [37]. Using the original sample data, he found that stock market prices indeed predicted failure sooner than individual financial ratios, however, the difference was rather small. Beaver, therefore, himself cautioned against taking these results at face value because of the limited scope of his investigation.

The most important contribution of Beaver was that financial ratios or more generally accounting data have the ability to predict failure for at least five years prior to failure. However, he pointed out three important qualifications regarding the use of ratio analysis for failure prediction. First, not all ratios predict with the same degree of accuracy. Second, ratios have greater success in predicting non-failure than failure. Third, financial ratios should be complemented by frequency distributions and likelihood ratios while taking decision. Beaver's work was one of the most extensive failure-prediction study, however, it had its limitations and was criticised on the ground of being a univariate approach.

4.2.2 Multivariate models

The major feature of the multivariate approach to predict industrial sickness is the simultaneous consideration of several indicators in the prediction process. Tamari's [38] was the first multivariate study in which weighted composite of several ratios were used to indicate the possibility of failure. Few financial ratios generally accepted in the literature and practice as indicators of financial soundness were attached certain weights according to their importance in the eyes of financial analysts, economists and creditmen and combined in a subjective manner. Profit trend and equity capital and reserves to total liabilities ratios were given maximum weights relatively showing that these ratios were considered to be the best indicator of failure. Tamari pointed that ratios were only indicators and that low values were not proof of future bankruptcy. The main criticism levelled against Tamari's study was that both the ratios and relative weights used in the index

were somewhat arbitrarily chosen. The choice of ratios and relative weights were based on writer's own experience without any conceptual or empirical support. The resulting indices were, therefore, of questionable generality.

Altman's model: Altman [39] used multiple discriminant analysis (MAD) technique to assess the quality of ratio analysis as an analytical technique using corporate bankruptcy as an example. Multiple discriminant analysis is a statistical technique designed to classify an observation into one of several *a priori* groupings, dependent upon the observation's individual characteristics. This technique is primarily used to classify and/or make prediction in problems where the dependent variable appears in qualitative form e.g. male or female, bankrupt or non-bankrupt. The MDA technique derives a linear combination of various characteristics (e.g. liquidity, profitability, size etc.) that best discriminates between the groups. The discriminant function is of the form:

$$Z=V_1 X_1+V_2 X_2+\ldots\ldots\ldots V_n X_n$$

where Z=overall index

$V_1, V_2\ldots\ldots V_n$=the discriminant coefficients

$X_1, X_2\ldots\ldots X_n$=independent variables (e.g. ratios)

Altman used a paired sample consisting of thirty-three failed and thirty-three non-failed manufacturing firms where industry and size were considered as the matching criteria. Initially 22 financial ratios were considered as predictors of failure and they were classified into 5 categories e.g. liquidity, profitability, solvency, leverage and activity ratios. Only 5 ratios out of the 22 were finally selected on the basis of their relevance in predicting corporate failure. The final set of ratios was determined by F-tests and computer runs analysing the possible alternatives. The final discriminant function doing the best overall job in discriminating between the failed and non-failed firms was:

$$Z=.012X_1+.014X_2+.033X_3+.006X_4+.999X_5$$

where

X_1= Working capital/total assets

X_2= Retained earnings/total assets

X_3= Earnings before interest and taxes/total assets

X_4= Market value of equity/book value of total debt

X_5 = Sales/total assets

Z = Overall index

A cut off point for the Z-score was determined in such a way as to minimise the overlap between bankrupt and non-bankrupt firms. He concluded that Z-score of 2.675 was the best cut off point which maintained minimum misclassification. The five variable model using data of one year before bankruptcy correctly classified 95 per cent of the total sample which reduced to 36 per cent when data of five years prior to bankruptcy were used. In one [40] of the studies explaining corporate failure with new variables, Altman used MDA with both linear and quadratic structures and concluded that the newer Zeta model predicted better than his earlier model.

Deakin's model: Deakin [41] made an attempt to develop an alternative to the Beaver and Altman models. A sample of thirty-two failed firms and a matching sample of thirty-two non-failed firms was taken. The failed firms' sample included those which experienced failure between 1964-1970. Each of the failed firms was matched with a non-failed firm on the basis of industry, size and year of financial data. Deakin's original model included 14 ratios and his revised model included only 5 ratios which could best predict corporate failure in each of the five years prior to failure. Deakin conducted two major empirical experiments. First, he adopted a method of analysis similar to Beaver's study by applying the dichotomous classification test and percentage error of each ratio was ascertained. In the second test, discriminant analysis technique was applied using the same sample of data and 14 financial ratios as input to the discriminant analysis programme. It was concluded that the discriminant analysis can be used to predict business failure using ratios as prediction variables three years in advance with a fairly high degree of accuracy.

Meyer's work: Meyer and Pifer [42] developed a linear regression model for the prediction of bank failures. He selected sample of 78 banks consisting 39 failed banks which experienced failure during the period 1949-1965 and 39 solvent matching banks. The paired sample was taken on the basis of location, size, age and regulatory requirements. Thirty-two financial ratios were used as independent variables in the various

regression models tested. Financial ratios were computed for a period of six years prior to failure. A stepwise regression programme, forward selection and backward reduction was used. A classification test used by Meyer and Pifer correctly predicted 80 per cent of the initial sample banks and 72 per cent of the hold out sample with a lead time of one or two years before failure. When the lead time was three or more years, the model failed to discriminate between failed and non-failed banks. It was concluded that financial ratios were to be used along with other factors such as local and general economic conditions, quality of management, and integrity of employees to make a better prediction of failures.

Blum's model: Marc Blum [43] developed a Failing Company Model (FCM) to assess the probability of business failure. Failure was defined as inability to pay debts as they become due, entrance into bankruptcy proceedings or an explicit agreement with creditors to reduce debts. Discriminant analysis technique was applied to a paired sample of 115 failed and 115 non-failed firms to evaluate the predictive accuracy of the model. The pairing of firms was made on the basis of industry, sales, employees and fiscal year. These criteria were selected to eliminate the impact of industry, size and the year of information on the probability of business failure. A 12 variable model with emphasis upon liquidity, profitability and variability was developed. The model predicted corporate failure with an accuracy of 93-95 per cent one year before failure, 80 per cent two years before and 70 per cent thereafter up to 5 years before failure. An experiment was also conducted to test the predictive accuracy of a non-ratio model. The model is considered more reliable on account of two reasons: (*a*) the choice of each variable is justified on the basis of financial theory (i.e. cash flow framework), and (*b*) the aforementioned results are the product of a rigorous validation procedure.

Edmister's work: Edmister's [44] purpose was to develop and test a number of methods of analysing financial ratios to predict the failure of small business. A small business was defined as one with a loan from the Small Business Administration (SBA). Loss borrowers were designated as failures

and non-loss borrowers as non-failures. Nineteen ratios were tested and a 7 variable regression equation was developed. He concluded that the predictive power of ratio analysis depends upon both the choice of analytical method and the selection of ratios. Unlike Altman, Beaver and Blum who found that one financial statement is sufficient for accurate classification, Edmister concluded that three consecutive statements are required for effective analysis of small businesses.

Libby's work: Libby [45] made an attempt to evaluate jointly (*i*) the predictive power of ratio information, and (*ii*) the ability of loan officers to evaluate ratio information in a failure prediction framework. Libby's sample consisted of 60 of the 64 firms from Deakin's sample. Thirty failed firms and 30 non-failed firms drawn at random were used. Using principal components analysis, he identified five independent variable set within the Deakin's 14 variable set. Elam [46] conducted a study to determine if capitalisation of non-purchase leases enables financial statements users to predict bankruptcy more accurately than without such adjustment. He analysed 48 bankrupt firms (1966-1972) with reported lease information and a matched sample of non-bankrupt firms. Each bankrupt firm was matched with a non-bankrupt firm according to data year, industry, sales and reported leases. MDA was applied to a set of 28 ratios. Single ratio and multi-ratio predictions were made. It was concluded that models with lease data are not more accurate than ones without lease data.

Taffler's model: Taffler and Tishaw [47] developed a '*Z* Model' for the prediction of company's insolvency and the evaluation of corporate credit worthiness by banks, investment houses and credit controllers. To construct a solvency model, a statistical technique known as linear discriminant analysis was applied to a sample of 46 failed firms and 46 financially sound firms matched by size and industry. Eighty different ratios were calculated for each of the 92 companies. Extensive statistical analysis finally resulted in the following discriminant function that best discriminates between the two sets of firms:

$$Z = C_0 + C_1R_1 + C_2R_2 + C_3R_3 + C_4R_4$$

where Z = discriminant score

C_0 = a constant

$C_1 ... C_4$=the ratio weights or the coefficients
R_1=Profit before tax/current liabilities
R_2=Current assets/total liabilities
R_3=Current liabilities/total assets
R_4=No credit interval ratio (i.e. CA—CL/operating cost excluding depreciation)

It was concluded that the four ratios, taken together in the right proportions, measure the risk profile of the firm which was summarized by the single number i.e. its *Z*-score.

Ohlson's work: Ohlson [48] developed a conditional logit model which pointed out that the fundamental estimation problem can be simply reduced to the following statement: 'Given that the firm belongs to some pre-specified population, what is the probability that the firm fails within some pre-specified period'. He used a sample of 105 firms which experienced bankruptcy during the period 1970-1976 and 2058 non-bankrupt firms. Nine financial ratios were tested to form an opinion about the discriminatory power of financial ratios. Three set of estimates were computed for the conditional logit model. The results indicated that the four factors derived from financial statements were statistically significant in assessing the probability of bankruptcy. These are (1) size, (2) the financial structure as reflected by a measure of leverage (TLTA), (3) some performance measures (NITA and/or FUTL), (4) some measures of current liquidity (WCTA or WCTA and CLCA jointly).

Dambolena's model: Dambolena and Khouny [49] constructed a model using stability and level of financial ratios as explanatory variables in the derivation of discriminant function. The basic purpose of this study was to test the effect of stability of financial ratios on prediction of corporate failure. It was concluded that the inclusion of stability of ratios in the analysis improved considerably the ability of the discriminant function to predict failure.

Wilcox's approach: Wilox [50] developed a model to show how to quantify the risk of financial failure through the gambler's ruin approach. He used net liquidation value, average adjusted cash flow and the concept of 'size of bet' as important variables in predicting firm's financial health.

The 'net liquidation value' or adjusted cash position of firm is the liquidation value of assets less the liquidation value of the debts. The liquidation changes from year to year by inflows and outflows. Wilcox assumed that the change in financial state takes place always by a fixed amount labelled as size of the bet. If the probability of the firm's gaining a bet is '*p*' and that of its losing the bet is 'q' then unless '*p*' exceeds '*q*', the firm is bound to fail. He claimed great success for his prediction model on the basis of a sample study. The model is, however, neither convincing nor realistic because of the several arbitrary assumptions on which it depends.

Delton's work: Delton Chesser [51] improved the method suggested by Altman and worked out a probability function for misclassification. He also used five financial ratios and claimed a prediction accuracy of 75 per cent. Chesser's study was based upon the data collected for trade accounts of manufacturing concerns and consumer loans respectively. Frederikslust [52] made an attempt to predict business failure based on testable financial theory of corporate failure. He defined failure as a negative cash balance of the firm and pointed out that a firm will fail at a certain moment 't' when its cash balance is smaller than zero. On the basis of financial theory he identified the following observable failure prediction variables: liquidity, profitability, solvability, variability of liquidity and variability of profitability over time, industry variables and general economic variables. The model predicted correctly 92.5 per cent one year prior to failure, which reduced to 70 per cent when data of five years prior to failure were used. However, Frederikslust could achieve the object of developing a prediction model based on testable financial theory of corporate failure partially. As he defined failure as a negative cash balance, but changed this definition to bankruptcy or liquidation when the empirical work was undertaken.

Apart from the studies summarised above, there are few empirical studies--Baruch Lev [53], Aharony and Swary [54], Walker [55], John Argenti [56]—which used alternative approaches to the problem of predicting industrial sickness.

In the Indian context few studies, though scanty, have been carried out to predict industrial sickness. Kaveri [57] attempted to predict the borrower's health by using financial ratios as predictor variables. To predict the event a sample of 524 small units comprising of good, regular and sick units was taken. Ninety per cent of the units in the sample had investment up to Rs. 3.75 lakhs. Twenty-two ratios were considered for identifying the health of small scale industries. Of these only five significant ratios were selected on the basis of 'T' test. The five ratios are: the current ratio, stock/cost of goods sold, current assets/net sales, net profit before taxes/total capital employed and net worth/total outside liabilities. The multiple discriminant analysis technique was applied to assign units in the sample to one of the groups viz. good, irregular and sick. Accuracy of prediction was found to be 76 per cent in the initial sample and 69 per cent in the hold out sample for one year before the event.

Chatterjee and Roy [58] have tried to use the asset growth as an indicator for prediction of industrial sickness with a set of auto-regression equation, but the indicator has been chosen arbitrarily. NCAER [59] have also studied industrial sickness using multiple discriminant function. Rao and Sarma [60] applied multiple discriminant analysis to a sample of 60 textile firms comprising 30 failed and 30 non-failed firms. The discriminant function found to be efficient included 5 financial ratios which were: net worth to total assets, debtors turnover, working capital to total assets, retained earnings to total assets, earnings before interest and taxes to total assets. Bhattacharya and Pande [61] have also studied corporate financial strength using multiple discriminant analysis.

Gupta's work: Gupta [62] has carried out a study on 'corporate sickness' using financial ratios. He has taken a sample from homogeneous industry (cotton textile) and tried to extend it to non-textile units as well. Fifty-six ratios, classified into two broad categories of profitability ratios and balance-sheet ratios, were tested. A simple non-parametric test for measuring the relative differentiating power of the various financial ratios was used. The test was based on taking a sample of sick and non-sick companies, arraying them by

the magnitude of each ratio to be tested. A cut off point was then selected which divided the array into two classes with a minimum number of misclassifications. A percentage of misclassification error was then chosen as a deciding parameter.

The sample included 41 textile companies of which 21 were non-sick and 20 were sick. The matching was done on the basis of product or products manufactured, age and size measured in terms of paid-up capital, assets and sales. Ratios were computed and tested for each of the company in sample for each year of 13 year period i.e. 1962-1974. Five profitability ratios were finally selected which individually had shown to possess highest predictive power when applied to a homogeneous industry group. In order to minimise the classification error rates, he recommended a combination of the following four profitability ratios: (1) EBDIT/sales (2) OCF/sales (3) EBDIT/total assets plus accumulated depreciation (4) OCF/total assets plus accumulated depreciation. Ratio relating to net worth were found to be worst predictor of bankruptcy among profitability ratios. The balance sheet ratios were not so accurate as the profitability ratios. It was observed that companies with an inadequate equity base had little 'reserve strength' to weather adversities and are, therefore, sickness-prone. Another important observation was that all liquidity ratios proved to be very poor predictor contradicts the great importance traditionally attached to liquidity analysis in appraising corporate health. The current ratio, for example, showed an average classification error almost three times more than profitability ratios in case of textile companies. However, the scope of this method in predicting industrial sickness is found to be limited. In addition the financial institutions do not restrict their operations to any single group of industry.

Srivastava's approach: Srivastava [63] used a combination of operational, technical and financial parameters to discriminate between the sick and healthy units. He developed a linear discriminant function comprising seven ratio parameters—five financial, one technical and one operational. These ratios were net worth/total assets, net block/net worth, net profit/total assets, total liabilities/net worth, current assets/

current liabilities, capacity utilisation ratio and plant utilisation ratio. A computer model was built up using three financial ratios, and the predictive accuracy of the model was computed. The misclassification error was 15 per cent which reduced to 10 per cent when five financial ratios were used. It further reduced to 5 per cent when first three financial ratios were combined with technical and operational ratios. The model was enlarged to include all the seven variables which resulted in 100 per cent predictive accuracy at 1.0 per cent level of significance.

4.2.3 Evaluation

Most of the studies dealing with corporate sickness have explored a number of financial ratios as predictors of corporate sickness and incorporated a large number of ratios in their predictive models. In brief, the purpose of these studies has been:

(*i*) To investigate whether financial ratios are the significant variables to predict the survival or failure of the firms; and

(*ii*) To detect the ratio or a set of ratios taken together which are good predictors or indicators of such an event.

The evidence of these studies clearly indicates that with a few financial ratios, the survival or the failure of the firm can be predicted at least five years prior to the date of failure. Table 4.1 indicates the results of few selected studies which have pointed out that the failure of the firm can be predicted five years earlier.

TABLE 4.1: **Percentage classification error rates for predicting failure**

Year before failure	Beaver's CF/TD	Altman's discriminant function	Edward Deakin's model	Marc Blum's failing company model
1	13.0	05.0	03.0	07.0
2	21.0	28.0	04.5	20.0
3	23.0	52.0	04.5	30.0
4	24.0	71.0	21.0	N.A.
5	22.0	64.0	17.0	N.A.

Observed evidence for five years prior to failure supports the view that financial ratios can be used in the prediction of corporate sickness.

The conclusions, however, differ regarding the question of which ratio or set of ratios perform well as indicators of failures. This might be partly on account of the use of different research methodology used by the above mentioned studies, for example, Beaver used univariate approach while multivariate approach was adopted by Altman. A major criticism levelled against most of these studies is that little consideration has been given to establish the causal relationship between financial ratios and corporate failure. Secondly, on account of lack of consensus regarding the inclusion of ratios in the final profile as indicator or predictor of failure, the results of the above mentioned predictive models could not be generalised and, therefore, require further verification of their applicability. The studies, however, have the merit of having demonstrated the power of financial ratios to predict financial problems of the company. It is also evident that a relatively lesser number of ratios are sufficient to predict the chances of survival or failure of a company.

The studies conducted for predicting company failure are scanty in India [57-63]. Very little progress has been made in empirical testing of financial ratios with a view to showing which of them really reflect a company's state of health, its chances of survival or failure. Since no serious systematic attempt has been made in this direction, an attempt, therefore, is made in this book (Chapters 5 and 6) to show the way towards a more systematic and scientific financial ratio analysis for predicting the chances of survival or failure of a company.

5

PREDICTION OF INDUSTRIAL SICKNESS

5.0 Introduction

The analysis in this chapter is aimed at the empirical testing of the predictive power of a wide variety of financial ratios. The analysis and interpretation of the empirical results provide many insights into the strengths and weaknesses of different financial ratios and lead to the selection of the best set of ratios to predict corporate sickness. The corporate sickness predictive-capability of financial ratios has been judged by applying both the univariate and multivariate techniques.

5.1 Sample Selection and Data Collection

An attempt was made to identify and organise the information and the sources of data in the following way:

(*a*) A set of sick companies and matching non-sick companies in the private manufacturing corporate sector was chosen.

(*b*) Information in respect of the above identified companies was organised as under:

I. Industry
II. Size
III. Age
IV. Type of organisation

(*c*) Financial statements of companies one to six years prior to the event (i.e. sickness) was collected.

5.1.1 Selection of sick companies

The selection of sick companies for which the financial data could be obtained was the most difficult task of data collection. After discussing the nature of problem with the representatives of several institutes (i.e. The Institute of Chartered Accountants of India; The Research and Statistics Division, Department of Company Affairs. Government of India, New Delhi; practising Chartered Accountants and Academicians) who might have access to such information, it was decided to take the primary list of sick companies from the Directory of Joint Stock Companies in India—a yearly publication of the Research and Statistics Division, Department of Company Affairs, New Delhi and from the Company News and Notes—a monthly publication of the Department of Company Affairs, Government of India.

To begin with, those companies that had failed (i.e. reported to have gone into liquidation) during the period under study (1966 to 1980, both years included) were identified in the Directory of Joint Stock Companies in India and Company News and Notes and compiled in a list. The compiled list of sick companies was condensed into a list that satisfied the following four conditions:

1. The company reported had gone into liquidation during the period under study (1966 to 1980, both years included);
2. The company is classified as manufacturing unit as per the Standard Industrial Classification (SIC) system of the Department of Company Affairs, Government of India;
3. The company is a public limited company; and
4. Finally, the availability of financial data of the company for at least one year prior to sickness.

Sick company was first tested by the above mentioned four criteria and then included in the final list of initial sample of sick companies. The final list of sick companies contained 39 companies on which financial data could be obtained for first year before sickness. The frequency distribu-

tion of the financial year of sickness is given in Table 5.1.

TABLE 5.1: **The frequency distribution of sickness**

Year of sickness	No. of sick companies
1966	2
1967	1
1968	0
1969	1
1970	0
1971	1
1972	6
1973	5
1974	3
1975	5
1976	7
1977	4
1978	2
1979	2
1980	0
Total	39

Next, the sick companies were classified according to industry and size as measured by paid-up capital and capital employed. Capital employed means the funds employed in the long run i.e. capital employed=share capital+reserves and surplus+long term loans. Each company is assigned a three digit code number, that the first digit denotes its group 1 (i.e. sick companies group) and next two digits denote its serial number in the group. The industrial composition and size classification of sick companies in the sample is shown in Table 5.2.

TABLE 5.2-A: **Industrial composition of sick companies in the initial sample**

Company code No.	Industry	No. of sick companies
101, 104, 110, 119, 123, 129, 132	Cotton Textiles	7
118	Jute Textiles	1
105, 116, 125	Sugar	3
102, 107, 124	Food Products	3
109, 113, 135	Iron and Steel	3
115, 138	Electrical Equipment	2
121, 127, 130, 131, 133, 139	Machinery and Accessories	6
103, 111, 117, 120, 122	Chemicals and Pharmaceuticals	5
126	Structural Clay Products	1
106, 108, 114, 134, 136	Glass Works	5
112, 128, 137	Paper and Paper Products	3
	Total	39

TABLE 5.2-B : **Size pattern of sick companies in the initial sample**

Range (Capital employed in Rs. 000)	No. of sick companies
200— 25,00	15
25,00— 50,00	3
50,00— 75,00	2
75,00—1,00,00	8
1,00,00—1,25,00	3
1,25,00—1,50,00	4
1,50,00—1,75,00	1
2,00,00—2,25,00	2
Total	39

The size as indicated by the capital employed for each company is taken from the most recent balance sheet of the company prior to the date of sickness. The industry and size, measured in terms of capital employed, composition of sick

companies are heterogeneous. Tables 5.2-A and 5.2-B indicate that 39 sick companies were from 11 different industries and the capital employed size range is 2 lakhs to Rs. 225 lakhs and the average capital employed size is approximately Rs. 71 lakhs.

5.1.2 **Selection of non-sick companies**

Recognising the heterogeneity of sick companies sample, due to industry and size differences, a careful selection of non-sick companies was attempted on the basis of stratified sampling. The stratification of sick companies according to industry, capital employed, size and fiscal year was taken as an essential pre-requisite to the selection of non-sick companies. The companies were stratified by industry and size, with the capital employed size range restricted to between Rs. 2 lakhs to Rs. 250 lakhs. The mean capital employed size of the non-sick companies group (Rs. 80.48 lakhs approximately) is slightly greater than that of sick group, since the matching of exact size of the two groups was not feasible. The selection process of non-sick companies was based upon paired sample design i.e. for every sick company in our list of sick group, a non-sick company of the same industry, of the same financial year and of almost the same size as indicated by paid up capital and capital employed in the financial statement one year prior to sickness, was selected.

To match non-sick companies with sick companies and to reduce sampling biasness, sampling of non-sick companies was based upon three criteria, since the empirical studies [64-67] have indicated that ratio differences exist because of the variables such as size, industry and fiscal period for which the ratios are calculated:

(1) Non-sick companies were chosen from the same industry as that of the sick company;
(2) of almost the same capital employed size as that of the sick company. Capital employed and paid up capital were used as one of the matching criteria because they tend to be more stable over a period of

time compared to other measures of size such as sales, net worth and output; and

(3) the data collected were of the same financial year as that of the sick company.

The names of non-sick companies were taken from the Directory of Joint Stock Companies in India (DJSC)—a yearly publication of the Depatment of Company Affairs, Government of India and the various issues of Bombay Stock Exchange (BSE) Directory and compiled in a list possessing two convenient features:

(*a*) The companies were grouped according to industry as per the Standard Industrial Classification system of the Department of Company Affairs, Government of India; and

(*b*) Within each industry group, the companies were ranked according to size as indicated by capital employed.

The following procedure was adopted to reduce the list of non-sick companies to the final list (i.e. 39 companies) of matching sample:

(1) The industry number of a sick company was taken;
(2) That portion of the list of non-sick companies was opened where companies of that industry number were found;
(3) Within that industry group tentatively a company was selected whose size measured in terms of capital employed was closest to the size of the sick company;
(4) If the financial statement of the non-sick company for the same period as that of the sick company (i.e. preceding year before the failure) was available, it was selected as one of the non-sick companies to be studied;
(5) If the company did not satisfy condition No. 4, the list of non-sick companies was reopened and tentatively the company next closest in size was selected;
(6) This procedure was repeated until a matching non-sick company was found; and
(7) This procedure was repeated for each of the sick companies in the sample.

The paired sample design was chosen to reduce and control over the impact of other factors—industry, size and fiscal year that otherwise might have blurred the relationship between financial ratios and corporate sickness. The ratio literature indicates that industry factors must be incorporated in any complete ratio analysis [68]. It is stated in the ratio literature that the same numerical value of a ratio (e.g. current ratio of 2.00) may imply different probability of sickness in different industries. The evidence offered on behalf of industry differences is the fact that the ratio distributions differ among industries [69].

Size measured by capital employed and paid up capital was the next important criterion for matching sample design. There are certain statistical reasons for believing that size alters the relationship between financial ratios and sickness. It can be argued that smaller of the two companies will have more probability of sickness, even if the financial ratios of the two companies are identical. Secondly, the rate of return to the company will become more stable as size increases. Empirical evidence indicates that the variability of rate of return does behave in this manner [70]. It indicates that the big size companies are less prone to sickness even if the value of their financial ratios is the same as that of smaller companies. The financial ratios, therefore, of different asset size companies cannot be directly compared.

However, the use of matching sample design limits the scope of inferences in at least one respect. It is possible that the industry and size may be excellent predictors of sickness which is eliminated by the use of matching sample design. Thus, the findings will not provide any insight into the potential predictive power of industry and size when applied to the initial sample, though the model developed on the basis of initial sample has been applied on additional samples taken irrespective of industry and size in order to see the impact of these factors on sickness.

An important issue was to determine the size, as indicated by capital employed, of the sick companies to be sampled. The big size companies were excluded from the sample since the incidence of sickness in big sized companies is rare; on the

other hand, the absence of data negated the representation of too small companies. Therefore, to choose companies in initial sample of sick group in a restricted capital employed size range was not feasible, while random selection of non-sick companies irrespective of asset size seemed unwise.

Thus, the final list of the initial sample contained 78 companies i.e. 39 sick companies and 39 non-sick companies.

5.1.3 **Collection of data**

After defining the initial sample groups and selecting companies to be included in the final list for study, the next task was to collect the required data from the annual financial statements of both the sick and non-sick companies. The financial statements collected were the annual reports prepared under currently accepted reporting standards of Companies Act, 1956. The data were collected primarily from two sources:

1. Various issues of Bombay Stock Exchange (BSE) Directory; and
2. Annual Reports of Companies (i.e. Balance Sheets and Profit and Loss Accounts) from the Library of the Company Law Board, Govt. of India.

A large proportion of financial data of sick companies for six years prior to sickness were obtained from the Library of the Department of Company Law Board, Govt. of India. For some of the financial data of sick companies, various issues of Bombay Stock Exchange Directory were also consulted. A large proportion of annual reports of matching non-sick companies were taken from the various issues of Bombay Stock Exchange Directory.

The first year before sickness is defined as that year included in the most recent financial statement prior to the date of sickness of a company. The second year before sickness is the financial year preceding the first year. The years from third to six prior to sickness are similarly defined. For example, a company failed in 1978 and the most recent financial statement was prepared on 30.12.1977, the first year before sickness would include 1977 financial statement and the sixth year

would include the financial data of 1972. The financial data of the matching non-sick companies were collected for the same financial years as those of their sick mates. The financial data of the non-sick companies were also stratified into year before sickness, corresponding to the years that were assigned to their sick mates. For example, the financial statement of 1977 of a non-sick company to the matching sick company mentioned above would be assigned to the first year before sickness and the statement of 1972 would be assigned to the sixth year before sickness.

In the process of data collection, it was found that financial data were not available for each year before sickness. The number, therefore, of companies in the sample decreases as the lead time before sickness increases. Availability of data, except the first year prior to sickness, over a period of all six years was not the criterion to include a company in the initial sample. Table 5.3 indicates that the sample size is the largest in the first year before sickness (i.e. 78 companies) and is the smallest in the sixth year before sickness (i.e. 51 companies).

TABLE 5.3: **Number of observations on which financial statement data could be obtained**

Group	Year before failure					
	1	2	3	4	5	6
Sick Companies						
Group 1	39	39	37	35	29	26
Non-sick Companies						
Group 2	39	39	39	37	34	25
Total	78	78	76	72	63	51

For purposes of prediction of sickness, financial statement data were collected for the period of six years before the event (i.e. sickness). The justification for the six years as a period for prediction of sickness is provided by the fact that previous studies indicated that financial ratios beyond five years prior to sickness have very limited predictive power. Most of the studies on bankruptcy prediction (discussed in Chapter 4)

provide evidence that financial ratios are not useful for prediction beyond five years prior to bankruptcy. However, it has been extended up to six years to have the insight into the prediction of company failure prior to six years. Secondly, it is a sufficient time for testing the vibration in the profitability and liquidity reserve strength of a company to be considered. The period chosen for the study is 1966-1980. This fifteen year period is the most recent period for which the data, particularly of sick companies, were available.

5.2 Development of the Model

Selection of Variables (*i.e. Financial Ratios*): The emphasis upon financial ratios as predictor/variables does not imply that ratios are the only predictors of sickness. The concern is not with predictors of sickness, but rather with financial ratios as predictors of important event i.e. industrial sickness. Further, the primary concern is not with ratios as a form of presenting financial statement data but rather with the underlying predictive ability of financial statements themselves. The ultimate motivation is to develop a model which can verify empirically the predictability of financial ratios. Financial ratios as predictor variables for the prediction of sickness of a company are primarily selected on the basis of their ex-hypothetic capability to indicate the financial soundness or sickness of a company and on the basis of their proven performance in earlier studies (discussed in Chapter 4).

The construction of a model designed to predict the company's chances of survival or failure involves few specific problems which were classified into two categories:

1. Choosing the variables i.e. financial ratios to be included in the model;
2. (*a*) Deciding upon the mathematical relationships among the variables; and

   (*b*) Assigning relative weights to the variables.

Three specific questions were raised to answer the above problems:

1. What criteria are to be used to choose the variables i.e. financial ratios for the study?
2. Which ratios must be combined together in a specific case i.e. prediction of chances of survival or sickness of a company?
3. What weights must be attached to the ratio in a certain set of combination or combinations?

A list of 36 financial ratios was selected for the construction of a predictive model which were primarily conditioned by the objective of study and the availability of financial statement data which permitted the calculation of financial ratios.

The following guidelines were used to select the 36 ratios from the sets of all possible combinations and permutations of financial statement items:

1. The popularity in the literature i.e. the frequency of appearance of financial ratios in the literature [10, 68, 71-82].
2. The financial ratios performed well in one of the earlier studies (refer Chapter 4). However, there are certain ratios which performed well in predicting the changes of survival or failure of a company in recent empirical work, but were not included in this study on account of non-availability of relevant data e.g. Altman's Market Value of Shares/Book Value of Debt; Gupta's EBDIT/TA+Accumulated depreciation.
3. The ratios defined within the framework of cash flow concept in which the company has been treated as a reservoir of financial resources and the probability of sickness is described in terms of expected flows of these resources. Within the cash flow framework concept, other things being equal, the probability of sickness of a company is smaller:
   (*a*) the larger the reservoir;
   (*b*) the larger the net liquid flow from operations (i.e. cash in flow);
   (*c*) the smaller the amount of debt held; and
   (*d*) the smaller the fund expenditures for operations.
4. The potential relevancy of ratios for the study.

The presence of any one of the criteria was considered a sufficient condition for inclusion of a ratio in the study.

For every set of financial statement available, 36 financial ratios were computed for each of the years and classified under four groups depicting different aspect of company's operations. Financial ratios used for developing the sickness-prediction model are as under:

I. Profitability Ratios

(*a*) *Cash Flow Ratios*

V_1	Cash Flow to Net Sales	(CF/NS)
V_2	Cash Flow to Total Tangible Assets	(CF/TTA)
V_3	Cash Flow to Net Worth	(CF/NW)
V_4	Cash Flow to Total Debt	(CF/TD)

(*b*) *Income Ratios*

V_5	Net Income to Net Sales	(NI/NS)
V_6	Net Income to Total Tangible Assets	(NI/TTA)
V_7	Net Income to Net Worth	(NI/NW)
V_8	Net Income to Total Debt	(NI/TD)
V_9	Earning before Interest and Taxes to Total Tangible Assets	(EBIT/TTA)
V_{10}	Earning before Interest and Taxes to Net Sales	(EBIT/NS)
V_{11}	Net Operating Profit to Net Sales	(NOP/NS)
V_{12}	Earning before Interest and Taxes to Interest	(EBIT/Int.)
V_{13}	Net Income to Net Working Capital	(NI/NWC)

II. Solvency Ratios

V_{14}	Total Tangible Assets to Current Debt	(TTA/CD)
V_{15}	Total Tangible Assets to Long Term Debt	(TTA/LTD)
V_{16}	Total Tangible Assets to Total Debt	(TTA/TD)
V_{17}	Net Worth to Total Debt	(NW/TD)
V_{18}	Net Worth to Long Term Debt	(NW/LTD)

III. Liquidity Ratios

(a) Liquid Assets to Total Tangible Assets Ratios

V_{19}	Cash to Total Tangible Assets	(C/TTA)
V_{20}	Quick Assets to Total Tangible Assets	(QA/TTA)
V_{21}	Current Assets to Total Tangible Assets	(CA/TTA)
V_{22}	Net Working Capital to Total Tangible Assets	(NWC/TTA)

(b) Liquid Assets to Current Debt Ratios

V_{23}	Cash to Current Liabilities	(C/CL)
V_{24}	Quick Assets to Current Liabilities	(QA/CL)
V_{25}	Current Assets to Current Liabilities	(CA/CL)

IV. Turnover Ratios

V_{26}	Net Sales to Debtors	(NS/DEBTORS)
V_{27}	Net Sales to Inventory	(NS/Inv.)
V_{28}	Net Sales to Quick Assets	(NS/QA)
V_{29}	Net Sales to Current Assets	(NS/CA)
V_{30}	Net Sales to Net Working Capital	(NS/NWC)
V_{31}	Net Sales to Total Tangible Assets	(NS/TTA)
V_{32}	Net Sales to Net Worth	(NS/NW)
V_{33}	Net Sales to Fixed Assets	(NS/FA)
V_{34}	Cash to Total operating expenditures	(Cash interval ratio)
V_{35}	Defensive Assets to Total operating expenditures	(Defensive interval ratio)
V_{36}	Defensive Assets Minus Current Liabilities to Total operating expenditures	(No credit interval ratio)

Note: The financial ratios from 1-36 are denoted by V_1, V_2, V_3,............V_{36}.

5.2.1 The method of analysis

The analysis of data is grouped under two heads in order to verify predictive power of financial ratios empirically:

(*A*) Univariate Analysis
(*B*) Multivariate Analysis

(A) Univariate Analysis

The basic object of univariate approach is to compare the financial ratios of sick companies with those of non-sick companies in order to detect systematic differences which might assist in predicting the chances of survival or sickness of a company or companies. Under univariate approach, each ratio is considered individually for sick companies and non-sick companies. The analytical procedure applied for testing the predictive power of financial ratios on univarate basis is based on:

I. Comparison of Mean Values of Financial Ratios of Sick Companies and Non-sick Companies: The mean values of financial ratios are computed for the sick companies and non-sick companies in each of the years (i.e. up to a maximum of six years) prior to sickness. The comparison of mean values of ratios for the two groups—sick group and non-sick group—is undertaken in order to identify the discriminating power of ratios taken individually. It is not a predictive test. It is merely a convenient approach of sketching the general relationship between the sick and non-sick companies' financial ratios. Student's *t*-value of each ratio is also computed in order to judge whether the difference between mean values of ratios of the two groups is statistically significant or insignificant.

II. Dichotomous Classification Test: The dichotomous classification test predicts the sickness status of a company based solely upon a knowledge of financial ratios. It is a simple predictive test measuring the relative differentiating power of various financial ratios. The classification test makes a dichotomous prediction i.e. a company is either classified into sick group or non-sick group. To make predictions of sickness, the ratios of mixed sample of sick and non-sick companies are arrayed i.e. each ratio is arrayed in ascending order marking the sick company with (*x*). The array of

each ratio is inspected to find a best cut off point i.e. a point that minimises the percentage of classification error rates. The best cut off point is determined by trial and error process for each array separately. If the ratio of a company is below the cut off point, the company is classified as sick company. If the company's ratio is above the cut off point, it is classified as a non-sick company. If there are two cut off points in any array resulting in the same number of misclassification, anyone may be chosen, as our object is limited to the magnitude of classification error only. After classifying each company either in one of the two groups, the predictions are compared with the actual status of companies in the sample and the percentage of predictive accuracy is computed. The percentage of companies misclassified to the total number of companies in the array is indicative of accuracy of the dichotomous classification test, and is called a misclassification error. The ratio which shows the least percentage of misclassification over a period of six years prior to sickness and the least misclassification at the earliest possible time (i.e. sixth year in our case) has the highest predictive power. This procedure is repeated for each of the 36 ratios.

It should, however, be noted that the univariate approach is a crude technique of predicting the chances of corporate survival or sickness, because each ratio is considered individually and thus, indicates only the individual information value of a ratio. The ratios analysed and presented univariately are susceptible to faulty interpretations [39]. The main shortcomings of univariate approach, as confirmed by few empirical studies [65-67, 83-85] are as under:

(*i*) The univariate approach ignores the inter-dependencies among the various ratios over time which may exist on account of (*a*) some items in financial statements tend to move in the same direction as others, e.g. net income and dividends, sales and market costs; and (*b*) many ratios have common components e.g. total sales in various activity ratios.

If, as the sparse evidence indicates, ratio distributions are substantially correlated over time, then a smaller number of ratios taken together can convey the financial information contained in the financial statements.

(*ii*) It may result in ambiguous inferences on account of conflicting signals, for instance, a company with poor profitability ratio may be classified as a potentially sick, but, however, the situation may not be considered serious because of its high (i.e. above average) liquidity ratio.

Criticism levelled against univariate approach clearly brings out that financial ratios taken individually cannot provide the sufficient information for understanding the various economic dimensions of a company. A set of financial ratios may contain more useful information than any particular representative ratio. Therefore, the long list of ratios usually provided to users is substantially redundant.

Keeping in view the shortcomings of univariate approach, an attempt has been made to overcome its shortcomings by the use of multivariate analysis in which several ratios are combined into a model in order to predict the chances of survival or sickness of a company.

(B) Multivariate Analysis

In multivariate analysis, several ratios are considered simultaneously in order to develop an index or a meaningful predictive model. The construction of ratio index amounts to a formulation of a model designed to describe and predict industrial sickness. The formulation of sickness-prediction model involves specific problems which are to be considered:

(*a*) Which ratios are most important and must be combined together in detecting the event i.e. industrial sickness?

(*b*) What weights should be attached to the ratios in a certain combination? and

(*c*) How should the weights be objectively established?

After careful analysis of the nature and purpose of the investigation, statistical techniques known as Factor Analysis and Discriminant Analysis are applied to arrive at the final profile of ratios doing the best overall job together in the prediction of industrial sickness. With the application of statistical techniques—Factor Analysis and Discriminant Analysis—the multivariate problem is actually reduced to a simple univariate problem and assignment of companies between two groups depends upon the value of a single variable. The following steps were taken to arrive at the final best discriminant function and to ascertain its predictive accuracy:

1. Thirty-six variables (i.e. financial ratios) are screened and reduced to a smaller number of important variables having independent direction and uncorrelated with each other by using a statistical technique known as Factor Analysis.
2. Determination of relative weights to be attached to the variables determined under step 1 with the application of a statistical technique known as Discriminant Analysis.
3. Observation of predictive accuracy of various discriminant functions one year prior to the date of company's sickness.
4. Ascertaining the predictive accuracy of various discriminant functions one to six years prior to the date of company's sickness.
5. Determination of relative contributions of each independent variable to the total discriminating power of various ratio profiles with the use of scaled vector. The scaled vector is computed by multiplying corresponding variable coefficient by the square roots of the diagonal elements of the variance-covariance matrix.
6. Selecting the final best discriminant function and determining the best cut off point.

The final best discriminant function and the best cut off point is that which results in the least percentage of misclassifications. It is this figure of percentage of classification error

which forms the basis of selection of final best discriminant function. The discriminant function which results in the least percentage classification error over a period of six years prior to the date of sickness and the least percentage of misclassification at the earliest possible time (i.e. sixth year) before sickness is selected as the final discriminant function performing the best job among the alternatives which include numerous computer runs analysing different ratio-profiles or discriminant functions.

7. The Discriminant Model is applied on additional samples of companies taken irrespective of size in a homogeneous and non-homogeneous group in order to test the effectiveness of the model, as the real efficiency of the Discriminant Model lies in classifiying those companies correctly which are not used to construct the best discriminant function.

5.2.2 Statistical techniques applied for model development

The statistical techniques which have been applied to analyse data and to build up a predictive model are outlined as under:

(*i*) **Factor analysis**: Factor analyis is a statistical technique of analysing a prior set of observations from their intercorrelations to determine whether the variations represented can be accounted for adequately by a number of basic characteristics smaller than that with which the investigation was started. Thus data obtained with a large number of *a priori* measures may be explained in terms of a smaller number of variables. Factor analysis, for this study, is chosen to reduce the number of variables (i.e. 36 ratios) by describing each linearly in terms of (*n*) new uncorrelated factors. The factor provides a parsimonious description of the observed data by retaining the most important information contained in the original data. The factor model extracts the maximum variance of the data explainable by the underlying factors that described the structure and pattern of the original variables [86]. The number of factors are determined based on the criteria to extract and rotate factors with eigenvalues equal to or

greater than I. Since the eigenvalues measure the variance accounted for by a factor, this criterion assumes that the factor extracted defines a certain level of variance among the variances. Since the variance of a variable is unity, the cut off rule rejects factors that do not account for at least the variance of one variable. In addition, a minimum loading of 0.40 of a variable on a factor is used as an auxiliary criterion. Hofstede [87] chose a minimum factor load of 0.35, however, Rummel [88] chose a minimum factor load of 0.50. After careful analysis of the nature of problem, the factor analysis is chosen as an appropriate statistical technique for this study because there is evidence [65-67] to believe that some of the ratios have a high degree of correlation with each other and the factor analysis technique has the advantage of reducing the large number of variables (i.e. 36) to a smaller number of uncorrelated variables which will have the potentiality of conveying a great deal of information. Factor analysis basic assumption [89], which is found in financial ratios, is that a battery of intercorrelated variables has common factors running through it and that the scores of individual variable can be represented more economically in terms of these reference factors. Secondly, the correlation between variables can be accounted for by the nature and extent of their factor loadings.

(*ii*) **Discriminant analysis**: Discriminant Analysis is a statistical technique that classifies an observation into one of several *a priori* groupings on the basis of observation's individual characteristics under appropriate assumptions. The basic assumptions of Discriminant Analysis are as under:

(*i*) The variables are normally distributed;
(*ii*) The groups are discrete and known; and
(*iii*) Each observation in each group is described by a set of characteristics or variables.

It is used primarily for classification and/or making prediction in problems where the dependent variable appears in qualitative form e.g. good or bad; sick or non-sick; male or female. Therefore, the first step is to establish the groups explicitly as in this study two groups, namely, sick and non-sick, are

established. The number of original groups may be two or more. The purpose of discriminant function is to derive the linear combination of variables which best discriminate between the groups [90]. It attempts to determine the weight to be given to each of the original variables in order that the resulting composite score will have maximum potentiality for discriminating between the members of the two groups. In this manner, the multivariate problem is actually reduced to a simple univariate problem and the assignment of individuals between two groups depends upon the value of a single variable (i.e. combined score). To begin with, it is assumed that some unknown set of weighting coefficients exists which will define a composite score providing maximum discrimination between the two groups. The classification is done by means of a linear discriminant function and the desired discriminant function is, thus, of the form:

$$y=\lambda_1 v_1+\lambda_2 v_2+\lambda_3 v_3\dots\dots\dots\lambda_n v_n$$

where y=the discriminant score

$\lambda_1,\lambda_2,\lambda_3,\dots\dots,\lambda_n$ are the discriminant coefficients

$v_1,v_2,v_3,\dots\dots,v_n$ are discriminant variables.

The problem is to determine optimal values for the weighting coefficients such that the difference between mean scores for the two groups will be maximised relative to the variation within groups. The function to be maximised, as first defined by R.A. Fisher [91], is the ratio (i.e. F-ratio) between groups variance to the within groups variance. A test to determine the overall discriminating power of the model is the F-value which is the ratio of the sums of squares between groups to the sums of squares within groups. When this ratio of the form,

$$F=\frac{(\bar{Y}_{g1}-\bar{Y}_{g2})^2}{\sum_{i=1}^{n_{g1}}(y_i-\bar{Y}_{g1})^2+\sum_{i=1}^{n_{g2}}(y_i-\bar{Y}_{g2})^2}$$

where

$(\bar{Y}_{g1}-\bar{Y}_{g2})^2$ =sums of squares of the difference between means of the two groups

$$\sum_{i=1}^{n_{g1}}(y_i-\overline{Y}_{g1})^2+\sum_{i=1}^{n_{g2}}(y_i-\overline{Y}_{g2})^2 \quad = \text{the sums of squares within groups}$$

is maximised, it has the effect of spreading the group means of Y-scores and simultaneously reducing the dispersion of individual scores around the group means. This test is appropriate because one of the objectives of discriminant analysis is to identify and to utilise these variables which best discriminate between groups and which are most similar within groups.

After careful analysis of the nature of problem and objective of the study, Discriminant Analysis is chosen as an appropriate statistical technique to classify the companies into one of the groups—sick group and non-sick group. Multiple Discriminant Analysis has been used in a variety of disciplines [92, 93, 94] since its first application in the 1930's by Fisher [91]. More recently this method has been applied in various empirical studies successfully in the area of finance specifically to the financial problems such as consumer credit evaluation and investment classification [95, 96], classification of high and low price earnings ratio firms [97], classification of firms into standard investment categories [98], and prediction of rate of return [99]. It has also been used with proven results for prediction of corporate failure in recent years by Altman [39-40], Deakin [41] and Blum [43].

In the present study, financial ratios are used as discriminant variables and industrial sickness as the predicted or dependent variable. There are only two groups—sick and non-sick, the analysis, therefore, takes the simplest form i.e. unidimensional. The discriminant analysis determines the discriminant coefficients of a set of variables (i.e. financial ratios) which do the best job of discriminating between sick companies and non-sick companies. When these coefficients are applied to actual ratios, a basis for classification into one of the mutually exclusive groupings exists. The discriminating power of the selected variables (i.e. ratios) profile is expressed by the classification error rates computed by the application of Y-scores and actual placement of the observations.

Discriminant analysis is chosen as an appropriate technique since it has the merit of considering an entire profile of ratios common to the relevant companies, as well as the interaction of these properties. A univariate study, on the other hand, can only consider the ratios used for group assignments one at a time. Secondly, it has the merit of yielding a model with a relatively small number of selected variables (i.e. ratios which have the potential of conveying a great deal of information).

It is assumed for the application of Discriminant Analysis that financial ratios used as discriminatory variables are having normal distribution. This assumption is, however, based upon some of the empirical studies which concluded that financial ratios have normal distribution. Bird and McHugh [100] found in their study that the distribution of ratios within an industry can be approximated by a normal distribution in most of the cases, although quick asset structure ratios were often substantially non-normal at the significance level of 0.05. Horrigan [65] has also suggested that financial ratios tend to be approximately normal. Deakin [101] has also found that with the exception of TD/TA ratio, most of the ratios are normally distributed.

5.3 Accuracy and Validity of the Model

The predictive accuracy of the discriminant model is ascertained by computing the percentage of classification error over a period of six years prior to the date of sickness in the initial sample. The misclassification rates are computed by comparing the predicted results of the discriminant model with the actual status of companies in the initial sample. The predictive accuracy of the model is considered in two dimensions:

Type I—The accuracy of correctly classifying the sick companies; and

Type II—The accuracy of correctly classifying non-sick companies.

A type I error would be predicting a sick company not to fail and a type II error would be predicting a non-sick company to fail. Various statistical significance tests such as Student's *t*-test, the common *F*-ratio test are conducted in

order to judge the reliability of accuracy of the discriminant model. Student's *t*-test is applied to test the statistical significance of individual discriminating power of ratios and the common *F*-ratio, which is a transformation of the Mahalanobis measure of distance 'D^2', is applied to test the statistical significance of the overall discriminating power of the model. 'D^2' is the Mahalanobis squares distance between the centriods of the two groups. Statistical significance means that the results at a specified level, say .01 are not obtained by chance alone.

In order to test the validity and effectiveness of the model rigorously, additional samples of sick and non-sick companies were introduced and classification error rates over a period of six years were ascertained by using the parameters of the discriminant model established in the initial sample. The additional samples contain companies from both homogeneous and non-homogeneous group of industries. These samples were taken at random irrespective of size, fiscal year and age of the company. The importance of additional sample testing (i.e. validation tests) cannot be over-emphasized, since the real efficiency of the discriminant model lies in predicting the chances of survival or sickness of a company or companies not contained in the initial sample used to develop the parameters of the model.

Probabilities of misclassification of the best cut off point and the probability of individual company's belonging to each group is also computed in order to judge the predictive accuracy and validity of the discriminant model more rigorously in taking the classification decision between sick and non-sick companies with more confidence particularly in the cases of those individual companies whose discriminant scores lie near the cut off point and are more likely to be placed in the wrong group than those having extremely large or small discriminant scores.

5.4 **Empirical Findings—1: Univariate Analysis**

On univariate basis, a univariate technique, namely, the Student's *t*-test has been applied for testing the statistical significance of the difference between the mean values of the

two groups, namely sick group and non-sick group. The method involved in calculation and the findings are under the heads given below:

5.4.1 T-test of significance of difference between the mean values of ratios of sick companies and non-sick companies

The purpose of comparison of mean values of ratios is to detect the systematic differences and to judge the general relationship between the financial ratios of sick companies and non-sick companies. But the comparison of the mean values of ratios of sick companies and non-sick companies does not reflect the statistical significance of the mean difference. Student's *t*-test, therefore, has been applied to measure whether the difference between the mean values of 36 financial ratios of sick companies and non-sick companies is statistically significant and thus, to test the individual discriminating power of financial ratios between the state of financial health of sick companies and non-sick companies. The '*t*' values of 36 financial ratios have been computed by the Statistical Analysis System (SAS) of IBM 360/44 computer at the Delhi University Computer Centre, Delhi. The '*t*' value of each ratio is computed by a formula given below:

$$T = \frac{\bar{V}_{g_{1i}} - \bar{V}_{g_{2i}}}{S} \times \sqrt{\frac{n_1 n_2}{n_1 + n_2}}$$

where

$\bar{V}_{g_{1i}}$ = mean of ith variable of group 1

$\bar{V}_{g_{2i}}$ = mean of ith variable of group 2

n_1 = number of observations in group 1

n_2 = number of observations in group 2

S = combined standard deviation

The value of S is calculated as follows:

$$S = \sqrt{\frac{\Sigma(V_{g_{1i}} - \bar{V}_{g_{1i}})^2 + \Sigma(V_{g_{2i}} - \bar{V}_{g_{2i}})^2}{n_1 + n_2 - 2}}$$

where

$(V_{g_{1i}} - \bar{V}_{g_{1i}})^2$ = squares of deviation of the original scores (ith variable) from the mean of ith variable of group 1.

$(V_{g2i} - \bar{V}_{g2i})^2$ = squares of deviation of the original scores (ith variable) from mean of ith variable of group 2.

If the calculated value of 't' is greater than the table value at .05 (.01) level of significance [i.e. 't' $> t_{0\cdot05}$ ($t_{0\cdot01}$)], the difference between the ratios of group mean will be considered significant at 5% (1%) level of significance.

The mean values of 36 ratios of both the groups, their respective mean differences, combined standard deviations and finally t-values were worked out with the help of computer and presented in Table 5.4.

TABLE 5.4: **Mean and t-values of ratios for the two groups one year prior to sickness**

Ratio	Group 1 Means	Group 2 Means	t-values
I. Profitability Ratios			
(a) Cash Flow Ratios			
V_1–CF/NS	–0.7752	0.0538	2.24*
V_2–CF/TTA	–0.1315	0.0746	7.72
V_3–CF/NW	–0.9399	0.2347	3.57
V_4–CF/TD	–0.0867	0.1477	5.59
(b) Income Ratios			
V_5–NI/NS	–0.9693	0 0447	2.39*
V_6–NI/TTA	–0.1476	0.0449	6.32
V_7–NI/NW	–0.9991	0.1317	3.05
V_8–NI/TD	–0.9646	0.0941	1.25**
V_9–EBIT/TTA	–0.0938	0.1198	9.34
V_{10}–EBIT/NS	–0.5465	0.0870	2.37*
V_{11}–NOP/NS	–0.6586	0.0767	1.99**
V_{12}–EBIT/Int.	–2.2888	3.3656	5.04
V_{13}–NI/NWC	–0.9024	0.3157	4.38
II. Solvency Ratios			
V_{14}–TTA/CD	3.5222	2.1097	2.12*
V_{15}–TTA/LTD	2.0688	5.7535	2.37
V_{16}–TTA/TD	1.3202	1.6479	1.21**
V_{17}–NW/TD	0.3710	0.6427	0.96**
V_{18}–NW/LTD	0.3108	1.7095	2.43*

TABLE 5.4 (*Contd.*)

Ratio	Group 1 Means	Group 2 Means	*t*-values
III. Liquidity Ratios			
(*a*) *Liquid Assets to TTA Ratios*			
V_{19}—C/TTA	0.0710	0.0002	0.98**
V_{20}—QA/TTA	0.2907	0.3229	0.63**
V_{21}—CA/TTA	0.5563	0.7198	3.12
V_{22}—NWC/TTA	0.0630	0.1605	1.03**
(*b*) *Liquid Assets to CD Ratios*			
V_{23}—C/CL	0.9476	0.1319	1.26**
V_{24}—QA/CL	0.6935	2.7311	1.25**
V_{25}—CA/CL	1.4426	3.3969	1.22**
IV. Turnover Ratios			
V_{26}—NS/Debtors	7.0704	11.5271	1.31**
V_{27}—NS/Inv.	1.5309	4.6512	3.94
V_{28}—NS/QA	4.8542	6.7260	1.33**
V_{29}—NS/CA	1.9696	2.5870	0.87**
V_{30}—NS/NWC	0.3593	12.0122	5.77
V_{31}—NS/TTA	0.6128	1.8591	4.43
V_{32}—NS/NW	1.9334	6.4914	2.92
V_{33}—NS/FA	2.5254	8.9768	3.77
V_{34}—C/TOE (Cash interval ratio)	0.4762	0.0284	1.27**
V_{35}—DA/TOE (Defensive interval ratio)	0.2821	0.8171	1.49**
V_{36}—DA-CL/TOE (No credit interval ratio)	−1.5597	−0.1996	1.46**

Notes:

V_{1-36} denotes the variables
Group 1 represents the sick companies
Group 2 represents the non-sick companies
$t_{1,76}$ (.01)=2.64
$t_{1,76}$ (.05)=1.99
*denotes insignificant at .01 level
**denotes insignificant at .05 level

The analysis of Table 5.4 clearly indicates that the difference between the mean values of 21 ratios given below is significant at .05 level of significance:

I. Profitability Ratios

V_1—CF/NS
V_2—CF/TTA
V_3—CF/NW
V_4—CF/TD
V_5—NI/NS
V_6—NI/TTA
V_7—NI/NW
V_9—EBIT/TTA
V_{10}—EBIT/NS
V_{11}—NOP/NS
V_{12}—EBIT/Int.
V_{13}—NI/NWC

II. Solvency Ratios

V_{14}—TTA/CD
V_{15}—TTA/CD
V_{16}—NW/LTD

III. Liquidity Ratios

V_{21}—CA/TTA

IV. Turnover Ratios

V_{27}—NS/Inv.
V_{30}—NS/NWC
V_{31}—NS/TTA
V_{32}—NS/NW
V_{33}—NS/FA

The '*t*' value of the above mentioned 21 ratios is greater than the tabulated *t*-value (i.e. 1.99) for $t_{1,76}$ (.05) level of significance. It is, therefore, contended that the 21 financial ratios can discriminate between the financial state of health of two groups namely sick group and non-sick group.

The above results lead to conclude that the solvency, liquidity and liquidity turnover ratios' mean differences are not significant at $t_{1,76}$ (.01) and $t_{1,76}$ (.05) level of significance, hence, not significant variables to discriminate between the two groups. Profitability ratios and turnover ratios (except liquidity turnover) are significant variables in discriminating between the two groups on univariate basis. Among profitability ratios V_9 i.e. EBIT/TTA is the most significant ratio followed by CF/TTA and NI/TTA in discriminating between the two groups on individual basis.

Liquidity variables are the least significant variables in discriminating between the financial health of two groups, namely, sick group and non-sick group. There can be several explanations for the poor showing of liquidity ratios e.g. to some extent it could be attributed to 'Window-dressing' by management as the company approaches towards sickness.

The Student's *t*-test indicates the difference and the statistical significance of difference between the mean values of ratios of sick companies and non-sick companies, but does not speak anything about the predictive power of ratios. To test the predictive capability of ratios on univariate basis a technique known as 'Dichotomous Classification Test' has been applied.

5.4.2 Dichotomous classification test

To test the predictive power of financial ratios univariately a technique called 'dichotomous classification test' has been applied which predicts the health status of a company based solely upon a knowledge of the financial ratios. Under the dichotomous classification test, an optimal cut off point for each ratio is established which classifies the observations with minimum error of classification. In this study, thirty-six ratios were computed and arrayed in ascending order for each of the six years prior to sickness for each company in the sample (i.e. 39 sick companies and 39 non-sick companies). The percentage classification error for each of the 36 financial ratios for six years before sickness is shown in Table 5.5.

TABLE 5.5: **Percentage error for 36 financial ratios on dichotomous classification test**

Ratio	Year before sickness					
	1	2	3	4	5	6
I. Profitability Ratios						
(*a*) *Cash Flow Ratios*						
V_1—CF/NS	11	22	18	27	30	31

TABLE 5.5 (*Contd.*)

Ratio	Year before sickness 1	2	3	4	5	6
V_2—CF/TTA	10	16	19	23	28	28
V_3—CF/NW	11	15	19	24	28	29
V_4—CF/TD	13	18	18	23	29	30
(*b*) *Income Ratios*						
V_5—NI/NS	14	19	18	30	32	31
V_6—NI/TTA	13	17	18	23	29	29
V_7—NI/NW	13	16	17	24	31	33
V_8—NI/TD	13	19	17	25	33	34
V_9—EBIT/TTA	10	17	17	24	29	29
V_{10}—EBIT/NS	15	19	20	25	31	35
V_{11}—NOP/NS	16	22	23	27	28	32
V_{12}—EBIT/Int.	14	16	17	25	29	31
V_{13}—NI/NWC	14	21	24	27	30	33
II. Solvency Ratios						
V_{14}—TTA/CD	41	40	55	53	52	53
V_{15}—TTA/LTD	15	19	21	28	32	35
V_{16}—TTA/TD	18	23	26	31	33	36
V_{17}—NW/TD	18	26	30	35	38	42
V_{18}—NW/LTD	14	21	22	28	32	35
III. Liquidity Ratios						
(*a*) *Liquid Assets to Total Tangible Assets Ratios*						
V_{19}—C/TTA	35	46	49	48	46	47
V_{20}—QA/TTA	37	35	38	42	45	46
V_{21}—CA/TTA	32	33	32	37	39	41
V_{22}—NWC/TTA	35	41	40	45	47	48
(*b*) *Liquid Assets to Current Debt Ratios*						
V_{23}—C/CL	36	46	51	50	52	49
V_{24}—QA/CL	35	38	43	45	46	47
V_{25}—CA/CL	33	37	39	45	44	46
IV. Turnover Ratios						
V_{26}—NS/Debtors	29	27	33	35	37	39
V_{27}—NS/Inv.	19	17	25	29	31	35
V_{28}—NS/QA	26	27	33	36	37	39
V_{29}—NS/CA	23	22	32	35	36	37
V_{30}—NS/NWC	13	22	29	31	32	32

TABLE 5.5 (*Contd.*)

Ratio	Year before sickness					
	1	2	3	4	5	6
V_{31}—NS/TTA	20	21	24	26	33	35
V_{32}—NS/NW	13	17	21	37	31	33
V_{33}—NS/FA	23	22	23	28	32	35
V_{34}—Cash Interval Ratio	36	46	51	55	58	49
V_{35}—Defensive Interval Ratio	41	47	45	48	49	51
V_{36}—No Credit Interval Ratio	35	34	41	42	45	49

The empirical results in Table 5.5 clearly illustrate the superiority of profitability ratios in predicting the corporate sickness. From Table 5.5 it is evident that the cash-flow to total tangible assets ratio possesses the highest predictive power followed by earning before interest and taxes to total tangible assets ratio. In the first year before sickness, the classification error of V_2 (CF/TTA) and V_9 (EBIT/TTA) is 10 per cent and 10 per cent respectively, while in the sixth year, the error percentages are 28 and 29 respectively. Both error percentages are much smaller than would be expected from a random prediction model, where the expected percentage error wou'd be approximately 50 per cent. The turnover ratios show somewhat inferior results than the profitability ratios in predicting corporate health.

The predictive accuracy of all solvency and liquidity ratios is found to be much less than that of profitability and turnover ratios. Among the solvency and liquidity ratios, solvency ratios are found more reliable predictor of corporate health than the liquidity ratios. The solvency ratios directly or indirectly measure the reliance of a company on debt. The empirical results indicate that companies with heavy debt and inadequate equity base are more prone to sickness. The classification error of solvency ratios clearly show that there is a definite association between the incidence of sickness and inadequacy of equity base.

The classification error shown in Table 5.5 clearly indicates that the predictive power of all the liquidity ratios is quite

poor. The current ratio (V_{25}) and the quick ratio (V_{24}) result in almost three and a half times more classification error than the best profitability ratio. These empirical results contradict the considerable importance traditionally attached to liquidity ratios in appraising corporate health. And hence the great importance attached to the liquidity ratios, especially to the current ratio and quick ratio seems to be ill-founded. All other liquidity ratios also show poor results. This implies that the liquidity ratios are not of much use in detecting the corporate sickness.

The above analysis leads to conclude that the financial ratios possess predictive power and can predict the potential corporate sickness used on univariate basis. But not all ratios predict equally well. There is a relative difference in the predictive power of financial ratios. The cash flow to total tangible assets ratio has the ability to correctly classify both the sick and non-sick companies to a much greater extent throughout the six year period before sickness than would be possible through random prediction. However, the predictive power of liquidity ratios is much lower. Secondly, the net cash flow supplied to the reservoir is the most crucial factor, while the size of the reservoir is the least important factor in detecting the potential corporate sickness.

6

PREDICTION OF INDUSTRIAL SICKNESS—MDA MODEL

6.0 Introduction

After analysis and recognition of the discriminating and predictive power of financial ratios on univariate basis and its limitations to predict corporate sickness (refer Chapter 5), an attempt has been made to test the predictive capability of financial ratios on the basis of multivariate analysis which attempts to derive a linear combination of financial characteristics (i.e. ratios) which best discriminate between the groups, namely, sick group and non-sick group of companies.

In multivariate approach, several financial ratios are taken simultaneously and an index or a model is developed which measures both (*a*) an operational aspect which is highly sensitive to changes in the general health of the enterprise, and (*b*) the company's reserve strength available to bear shocks arising from unexpected setbacks, managerial errors or external factors. Both the aspects i.e. operational and reserve strength of a company are analysed by taking profitability and balance sheet ratios simultaneously in different combinations explaining the event of corporate sickness.

6.1 Development of MDA Model

From the original list of 36 financial ratios, four variables are selected as the ones which have better discriminating power and thus contribute most towards the prediction of chances of survival or failure of a company. In order to arrive at a best discriminant function consisting of four variables, the following steps have been taken.

I. Reduction of variables to a smaller number of variables having independent direction and uncorrelated or least correlated with each other by the use of a statistical technique known as factor analysis;

II. Evaluation of intercorrelations between the relevant variables;

III. Formation of various profiles of ratios and observation of the predictive accuracy measured in terms of classification error rates of the various ratio-profiles by the use of a statistical technique known as discriminant analysis; and

IV. Observation of the overall predictive accuracy i.e. accuracy over a period of six years prior to sickness of the various discriminant functions and selecting the best discriminant function (i.e. the discriminant function which discriminates between sick group and non-sick group with least classification error rates).

First of all, 36 variables (financial ratios) were computed for each of the sick and non-sick companies in the initial sample from the financial statements one year prior to sickness. The inter-correlations between the 36 variables of both the groups, namely sick group and non-sick group were factorially analysed using the principal components method of Factor Analysis. Factor Analysis was carried out on IBM 360/44 Computer system available at Delhi University Computer Centre, Delhi.

The solution produced:

(*i*) the factor matrix before rotation;

(*ii*) the rotated factor matrix;

(*iii*) the eigenvalues of each factor and the percentage of total variance in the data explained by each factor, and

(*iv*) the factor loading of each variable on a factor. Factor loading is equal to the correlation coefficient between a variable and a factor. In factor analysis, factor loadings indicate the cluster of variables on a factor.

From the rotated matrix, ten factors in group 1 and eight factors in group 2 accounting for 84.2 per cent and 86.1 per

cent respectively of the total variance in the data were extracted. The variables found to load 0.40 or higher on a factor were selected as its domain in both the groups There was no evidence of a single general factor accounting for a large percentage of variations in the data. The contribution of each factor ranged from 21.9 per cent to 2.9 per cent in group 1 and 30 per cent to 2.9 per cent in group 2. The factors, the variables clustered on each factor and their loading are shown in Table 6.1.

TABLE 6.1: **Rotated factor loading (0.40 and above) pattern of variables extracted from the rotated factor matrix**

Group 1			Group 2		
Factor	Variable	Loading	Factor	Variable	Loading
F_1	V_{16}	.797	F_1	V_2	.741
	V_{17}	.843		V_4	.957
	V_{18}	.647		V_6	.655
	V_{23}	.971		V_8	.923
	V_{24}	.970		V_9	.488
	V_{25}	.969		V_{14}	.633
				V_{16}	.923
F_2	V_{26}	.832		V_{17}	.925
	V_{27}	.494		V_{19}	.895
	V_{28}	.716		V_{23}	.957
	V_{31}	.794		V_{24}	.789
	V_{32}	.774		V_{25}	.707
	V_{33}	.866		V_{29}	.707
				V_{31}	.591
F_3	V_2	.907	F_2	V_1	.860
	V_4	.649		V_{10}	.929
	V_6	.897		V_{11}	.870
	V_9	.873		V_{21}	—.515
	V_{13}	.459		V_{29}	—.459
				V_{30}	—.479
F_4	V_{15}	—.413		V_{31}	.545
	V_{19}	.906		V_{32}	.780
	V_{34}	.948		V_{33}	.457
	V_{35}	.951		V_{35}	.473
F_5	V_1	.558	F_3	V_2	.535
	V_5	.700		V_3	.863
	V_{10}	.958		V_4	.626

TABLE 6.1 (*Contd.*)

Group 1			Group 2		
Factor	Variable	Loading	Factor	Variable	Loading
	V_{11}	.958		V_6	.619
				V_7	.843
F_6	V_{15}	.465		V_9	.584
	V_{18}	.509		V_{13}	.671
	V_{20}	.638		V_{30}	.442
	V_{21}	.773	F_4	V_{20}	.707
	V_{22}	.719		V_{21}	.515
	V_{28}	—.440		V_{26}	—.695
	V_{29}	—.703		V_{28}	—.665
	V_{36}	.506		V_{35}	.448
F_7	V_3	.886	F_5	V_{12}	.779
	V_7	.875		V_{27}	.830
				V_{29}	.449
F_8	V_{14}	.806	F_5	V_{12}	.779
	V_{36}	.440		V_{33}	.583
F_9	V_1	.783	F_6	V_{15}	.925
	V_5	.670		V_{18}	.937
	V_{12}	.929	F_7	V_{14}	.538
F_{10}	V_8	.646		V_{22}	.809
	V_{30}	.497		V_{24}	.481
				V_{25}	.696
				V_{36}	.832
			F_8	V_{13}	—.476
				V_{34}	.620
				V_{35}	.497

Notes: 1. Group 1 represents sick companies
Group 2 represents non-sick companies
2. *F* denotes Factor
V denotes Variables

Fifteen variables clustering around five factors were extracted from Table 6.1 based on the criterion:

(*a*) Factor loading of a variable;
(*b*) a variable or variables loaded on the same factor in both the groups, and
(*c*) the observation of correlation within the variables clustering around a factor.

The number of factors, the variables clustered on each factor and their loading are presented in Table 6.2.

TABLE 6.2: **Factor loading pattern of variables extracted from Table 6.1**

Factor	Variable	Loading	
		Group 1	Group 2
F_1	V_{16}	.797	.923
	V_{17}	.843	.925
	V_{23}	.970	957
	V_{24}	.971	.789
	V_{25}	.969	.622
F_2	V_{31}	.794	.595
	V_{32}	.774	.780
	V_{33}	866	.457
F_3	V_2	.907	.535
	V_4	.649	.624
	V_6	.897	.619
	V_9	.873	.584
	V_{13}	.459	.671
F_4	V_{35}	.951	.448
F_6	V_{15}	.465	.925

The analysis of the factors given in Table 6.2 showed that (*a*) two factors (F_4 and F_6) are loaded with only one variable on each, (*b*) one factor i.e. F_2 is loaded with three variables; and the remaining two factors i.e. F_1, F_3 are loaded with five variables on each.

Initially seventy-five ratio-profiles consisting of five variables each were formulated and their predictive accuracy one year prior to sickness was ascertained by the use of a statistical technique known as discriminant analysis. Apart from the above, twenty-four ratio-profiles were also formulated by adding or deleting variables in the list of fifteen variables loaded on five factors and their predictive accuracy was computed. The discriminant functions were carried out on IBM 360/44 Computer available at the Computer Centre, University of Delhi. The variables in various discriminant functions and their predictive accuracy i.e. percentage of correctly classifying the companies in sample are shown in Table 6.3.

TABLE 6.3: **Predictive accuracy of 99 discriminant functions one year prior to sickness**

S. No.	Variables	Number of variables	Percentage correctly classified
1	V_2 V_{15} V_{16} V_{31} V_{35}	5	90
2	V_2 V_{15} V_{16} V_{32} V_{35}	5	91
3	V_2 V_{15} V_{16} V_{33} V_{35}	5	86
4	V_4 V_{15} V_{16} V_{31} V_{35}	5	82
5	V_4 V_{15} V_{16} V_{32} V_{35}	5	65
6	V_4 V_{15} V_{16} V_{33} V_{35}	5	63
7	V_6 V_{15} V_{16} V_{31} V_{35}	5	90
8	V_6 V_{15} V_{16} V_{32} V_{35}	5	86
9	V_6 V_{15} V_{16} V_{33} V_{35}	5	82
10	V_9 V_{15} V_{16} V_{31} V_{35}	5	94*
11	V_9 V_{15} V_{16} V_{32} V_{35}	5	91
12	V_9 V_{15} V_{16} V_{33} V_{35}	5	90
13	V_{13} V_{15} V_{16} V_{31} V_{35}	5	82
14	V_{13} V_{15} V_{16} V_{32} V_{35}	5	65
15	V_{13} V_{15} V_{16} V_{33} V_{35}	5	58
16	V_2 V_{15} V_{17} V_{31} V_{35}	5	91
17	V_2 V_{15} V_{17} V_{32} V_{35}	5	86
18	V_2 V_{15} V_{17} V_{33} V_{35}	5	75
19	V_4 V_{15} V_{17} V_{31} V_{35}	5	67
20	V_4 V_{15} V_{17} V_{32} V_{35}	5	60
21	V_4 V_{15} V_{17} V_{33} V_{35}	5	56
22	V_6 V_{15} V_{17} V_{31} V_{35}	5	91
23	V_6 V_{15} V_{17} V_{32} V_{35}	5	86
24	V_6 V_{15} V_{17} V_{33} V_{35}	5	74
25	V_9 V_{15} V_{17} V_{31} V_{35}	5	93*
26	V_9 V_{15} V_{17} V_{32} V_{35}	5	85
27	V_9 V_{15} V_{17} V_{33} V_{35}	5	73
28	V_{13} V_{15} V_{17} V_{31} V_{35}	5	74
29	V_{13} V_{15} V_{17} V_{32} V_{35}	5	63
30	V_{13} V_{15} V_{17} V_{33} V_{35}	5	57
31	V_2 V_{15} V_{23} V_{31} V_{35}	5	87
32	V_2 V_{15} V_{23} V_{32} V_{35}	5	82
33	V_2 V_{15} V_{23} V_{33} V_{35}	5	73
34	V_4 V_{15} V_{23} V_{31} V_{35}	5	59
35	V_4 V_{15} V_{23} V_{32} V_{35}	5	51
36	V_4 V_{15} V_{23} V_{33} V_{35}	5	51
37	V_6 V_{15} V_{23} V_{31} V_{35}	5	91
38	V_6 V_{15} V_{23} V_{32} V_{35}	5	86
39	V_6 V_{15} V_{23} V_{33} V_{35}	5	74

TABLE 6.3 (*Contd.*)

S. No.	Variables	Number of variables	Percentage correctly classified
40	V_9 V_{15} V_{23} V_{31} V_{35}	5	93*
41	V_9 V_{15} V_{23} V_{32} V_{35}	5	90
42	V_9 V_{15} V_{23} V_{33} V_{35}	5	74
43	V_{13} V_{15} V_{23} V_{31} V_{35}	5	70
44	V_{13} V_{15} V_{23} V_{32} V_{35}	5	68
45	V_{13} V_{15} V_{23} V_{33} V_{35}	5	62
46	V_2 V_{15} V_{24} V_{31} V_{35}	5	92
47	V_2 V_{15} V_{24} V_{32} V_{35}	5	86
48	V_2 V_{15} V_{24} V_{33} V_{35}	5	78
49	V_4 V_{15} V_{24} V_{31} V_{35}	5	80
50	V_4 V_{15} V_{24} V_{32} V_{35}	5	64
51	V_4 V_{15} V_{24} V_{33} V_{35}	5	64
52	V_6 V_{15} V_{24} V_{31} V_{35}	5	91
53	V_6 V_{15} V_{24} V_{32} V_{35}	5	86
54	V_6 V_{15} V_{24} V_{33} V_{35}	5	83
55	V_9 V_{15} V_{24} V_{31} V_{35}	5	93*
56	V_9 V_{15} V_{24} V_{32} V_{35}	5	90
57	V_9 V_{15} V_{24} V_{33} V_{35}	5	81
58	V_{13} V_{15} V_{24} V_{31} V_{35}	5	82
59	V_{13} V_{15} V_{24} V_{32} V_{35}	5	60
60	V_{13} V_{15} V_{24} V_{33} V_{35}	5	62
61	V_2 V_{15} V_{25} V_{31} V_{35}	5	94*
62	V_2 V_{15} V_{25} V_{32} V_{35}	5	86
63	V_2 V_{15} V_{25} V_{33} V_{35}	5	85
64	V_4 V_{15} V_{25} V_{31} V_{35}	5	85
65	V_4 V_{15} V_{25} V_{32} V_{35}	5	69
66	V_4 V_{15} V_{25} V_{33} V_{35}	5	67
67	V_6 V_{15} V_{25} V_{31} V_{35}	5	94*
68	V_6 V_{15} V_{25} V_{32} V_{35}	5	87
69	V_6 V_{15} V_{25} V_{33} V_{35}	5	82
70	V_9 V_{15} V_{25} V_{31} V_{35}	5	95*
71	V_9 V_{15} V_{25} V_{32} V_{35}	5	88
72	V_9 V_{15} V_{25} V_{33} V_{35}	5	83
73	V_{13} V_{15} V_{25} V_{31} V_{35}	5	85
74	V_{13} V_{15} V_{25} V_{32} V_{35}	5	60
75	V_{13} V_{15} V_{25} V_{33} V_{35}	5	60
76	V_2 V_{15} V_{17} V_{22} V_{31} V_{35} V_{36}	7	51
77	V_3 V_{15} V_{17} V_{22} V_{31} V_{35} V_{36}	7	50
78	V_4 V_{15} V_{17} V_{22} V_{31} V_{35} V_{36}	7	54
79	V_2 V_{15} V_{22} V_{24} V_{31} V_{35} V_{36}	7	50
80	V_3 V_{15} V_{22} V_{24} V_{31} V_{35} V_{36}	7	51
81	V_4 V_{15} V_{22} V_{24} V_{31} V_{35} V_{36}	7	52

TABLE 6.3 (*Contd.*)

S. No.	Variables	Number of variables	Percentage correctly classified
82	V_2 V_{15} V_{17} V_{27} V_{31} V_{36}	6	58
83	V_3 V_{15} V_{17} V_{22} V_{31} V_{36}	6	54
84	V_4 V_{15} V_{17} V_{22} V_{31} V_{36}	6	60
85	V_2 V_{15} V_{22} V_{24} V_{31} V_{36}	6	52
86	V_3 V_{15} V_{22} V_{24} V_{31} V_{36}	6	55
87	V_4 V_{15} V_{22} V_{24} V_{31} V_{36}	6	54
88	V_2 V_{12} V_{15} V_{22} V_{24} V_{31} V_{35} V_{36}	8	56
89	V_4 V_{12} V_{15} V_{22} V_{24} V_{31} V_{35} V_{36}	8	49
90	V_9 V_{25} V_{35}	3	91
91	V_6 V_{31} V_{35}	3	90
92	V_2 V_{31} V_{35}	3	87
93	V_9 V_{31} V_{35}	3	92
94	V_2 V_{35}	2	80
95	V_2 V_{31}	2	90
96	V_9 V_{31}	2	90
97	V_9 V_{35}	2	87
98	V_6 V_{31}	2	77
99	V_6 V_{35}	2	80

Note: The predicted results marked with (*) are selected for further analysis.

After screening the predictive accuracy of various discriminant functions shown in Table 6.3, seven sets of variables predicting corporate sickness to an accuracy of 93 per cent and above one year prior to the event i.e. sickness were chosen for further analysis. The seven ratio-profiles and their predictive accuracy are shown in Table 6.4.

TABLE 6.4: **Predictive accuracy of seven discriminant functions one year prior to sickness**

S. No.	Variables	No. of variables	Percentage correctly classified
10	V_9 V_{15} V_{16} V_{31} V_{35}	5	94
25	V_9 V_{15} V_{17} V_{31} V_{35}	5	93
40	V_9 V_{15} V_{23} V_{31} V_{35}	5	93
55	V_9 V_{15} V_{24} V_{31} V_{35}	5	93
61	V_2 V_{15} V_{25} V_{31} V_{35}	5	94
67	V_6 V_{15} V_{25} V_{31} V_{35}	5	94
70	V_9 V_{15} V_{25} V_{31} V_{35}	5	95

To arrive at the final profile of variables doing the best overall job together in the prediction of industrial sickness, 17 new combinations of variables shown in Table 6.4 were formulated and the predictive accuracy of each profile for each of the years before sickness (i.e. six years) was ascertained by the use of discriminant analysis. The discriminant functions and the predicted results of each function for the period of one to six years prior to sickness are shown in Table 6.5.

Any function which satisfies the two conditions given below was selected as the best discriminant function:

I. The discriminant function which results in the least percentage classification error over a period of one to six years prior to the date of sickness; and
II. The least percentage of misclassification at the earliest possible time (6th year in this study) before company's sickness.

From Table 6.5, it is clear that the discriminant function-4 satisfies the above mentioned two conditions for selecting the best profile of ratios in predicting corporate sickness. The discriminant function-4 results in the least percentage error rates in classification of companies in the sample in one of the groups over a period of six years prior to sickness and also the least percentage of classification error in the 6th year prior to sickness. Though the predictive accuracy of discriminant functions 1, 2, 3, 4, 5, 6, 7, 11 in Table 6.5 one year prior to sickness is equivalent to the predicted results of discriminant function-4 (i.e. 95%), but it falls rapidly compared to discriminant function-4 as the lead period before the company failure increases. The predicted results of discriminant function-4 over a period of six years prior to sickness are more consistent and better as compared to the predictive accuracy of all other discriminant functions shown in Table 6.5. Thus the discriminant function-4 has been chosen as the best profile of ratios in predicting the chances of survival or failure of a company. The discriminant model so developed is not claimed to be optimal, since the process is iterative, it, however, does the best job among the alternatives which include numerous

TABLE 6.5: **Predictive accuracy of seventeen discriminant functions for the period of six years prior to sickness**

(*in percentages*)

Discriminant function	Cut-off point	Year prior to failure					
		1st	2nd	3rd	4th	5th	6th
1. $Y=17.0684V_2-.5872V_{17}+.7802V_{35}$	0.501	95	81	82	68	62	73
2. $Y=20.3118V_9+.0073V_{25}+.6586V_{31}$	1.0604	95	85	84	82	78	75
3. $Y=22.0264V_9-.6613V_{16}+.8178V_{31}+.9530V_{35}$	0.7515	95	84	84	80	73	75
4. $Y=19.8927V_9+.0047V_{25}+.7141V_{31}+.4860V_{35}$	1.425	95	87	86	82	79	78
5. $Y=19.4533V_9+ 0931V_{15}+.8120V_{31}+.5532V_{35}$	1.750	95	70	71	65	68	61
6. $Y=14.0754V_2+.0902V_{15}+.9626V_{31}+.8499V_{35}$	2.200	95	86	83	69	68	73
7. $Y=10.0671V_6+.0097V_{25}+.8622V_{31}+.7024V_{35}$	1.750	95	79	80	68	67	69
8. $Y= 9.7910V_6+.0951V_{15}+.9555V_{31}+.7611V_{35}$	1.750	94	78	76	65	68	83
9. $Y=14.5166V_2+.0015V_{25}+.8715V_{31}+.7914V_{35}$	1.500	94	82	86	75	71	76
10. $Y=22.3105V_9-.0679V_{17}+.8075V_{31}+.9385V_{35}$	1.500	94	83	79	80	75	76
11. $Y=19.5975V_9+.0939V_{15}+.0112V_{25}+.8085V_{31}+.5455V_{35}$	1.803	95	85	84	80	76	75
12. $Y=14.1613V_2+.0907V_{15}+.0073V_{25}+.9610V_{31}+.8462V_{35}$	1.960	94	87	84	67	70	76
13. $Y= 9.7554V_6+.0949V_{15}+.0035V_{25}+.9563V_{31}+.7633V_{35}$	1.500	94	82	79	68	71	71
14. $Y=21.7631V_9+.1003V_{15}-.7044V_{16}+.9280V_{31}+1.0518V_{35}$	0.800	94	83	80	78	70	71
15. $Y=20.1804V_9+.0909V_{15}+.5836V_{23}+.8843V_{31}+.8788V_{35}$	1.350	93	83	80	78	70	71
16. $Y=22.0508V_9+.1007V_{15}-.7202V_{17}+.9169V_{31}+1.0344V_{35}$	1.300	93	82	79	78	68	75
17. $Y=20.5628V_9+.0976V_{15}+.4058V_{24}+.8658V_{31}+.9180V_{35}$	1.730	93	86	83	78	75	75

computer runs and analysis of various ratio-profiles. The final best discriminant function is as under:

$$Y = 19.8927V_9 + 0.0047V_{25} + 0.7141V_{31} + 0.4860V_{35}$$

where

Y=overall discriminant score

V_9=Earning before Interest and Taxes/Total Tangible Assets

V_{25}=Current Assets/Current Liabilities

V_{31}=Net Sales/Total Tangible Assets

V_{35}=Defensive Assets/Total Operating Expenditure

The variables in the above discriminant function are independent and least correlated with each other in both the groups, namely, sick group and non-sick group and thus each variable provides additional information about the financial health of the company. The contribution of each variable is additional towards the predictive power of the discriminant function. The correlation matrix given in Table 6.6 indicates the inter-correlations between the variables in the discriminant model.

TABLE 6.6: **Correlation matrix of variables in the discriminant function**

	V_9	V_{25}	V_{31}	V_{35}
V_9	1.00	.189	—.208	.095
		(.174)	(.391)	(—.165)
V_{25}	.189	1.00	—.176	—.016
	(.174)		(.443)	(.196)
V_{31}	—.208	—.176	1.00	—.254
	(.391)	(.443)		(—.421)
V_{35}	.095	—.016	—.254	1.00
	(—.165)	(.196)	(—.421)	

Note: Top row of numbers indicates the inter-correlations between variables of group 1; the bottom row of numbers, enclosed in parentheses, represents the inter-correlations between variables of group 2.

V_9—Earning before Interest and Taxes/Total Tangible Assets

This ratio is a measure of the true productivity of the company's assets, abstracting from any tax or leverage

factors. It is expressed as:

$$V_9 = \frac{\text{Earning before Interest and Taxes}}{\text{Total Tangible Assets}}$$

It indicates how effectively the operating assets are being employed in generating profits. The ratio attempts to reflect all the consequences of operations of the company as well as the external events that might have affected it. This is a real test of economic success or failure of the firm [102]. Since the survival of a company is based on the earning power of its assets, this ratio appears to be appropriate particularly for the studies dealing with the prediction of chances of survival or failure of a company. A smaller EBIT/TTA ratio of a company is claimed to provide premonition of financial crisis in the future. Therefore, a negative relationship is understood to exist between this ratio and the probability of company's sickness.

V_{25}—Current Assets/Current Liabilities (CA/CL)

This measure is defined as the ratio of current assets to current liabilities:

$$\text{Current Ratio} = \frac{\text{Current Assets}}{\text{Current Liabilities}}$$

Current assets include cash and those assets which are converted into cash within a year such as marketable securities, debtors and inventories. All obligations maturing within a year are included in current liabilities. Thus, current liabilities include creditors, bills payable, accrued expenses, bank overdrafts, and income tax liability. It indicates the availability of current assets in rupees for every one rupee of current liability. Current ratio provides an idea about the cushion available with the firm to meet its short-term liabilities. It represents a margin of safety for short-term creditors. If an enterprise cannot meet its short-term obligations as they become due, its continued existence becomes doubtful and that renders all other measures of performance irrelevant. Therefore, the liquidity crisis generally leads to solvency crisis. Current ratio, therefore, aids in the prediction of future company's sickness. Since current assets are generally regarded as the reservoir from which maturing obligations

can be paid, it seems reasonable to assume that larger the current ratio, smaller the probability of sickness.

V_{31}—*Net Sales/Total Tangible Assets*

This ratio is calculated by dividing net sales by total tangible assets of the firm:

$$\text{Total Tangible Assets Turnover Ratio} = \frac{\text{Net Sales}}{\text{Total Tangible Assets}}$$

The total assets turnover ratio is a significant ratio since it shows the company's ability of generating sales from all the financial resources committed to the firm. As this ratio increases, there is more revenue generated per rupee of total investment in assets. A higher ratio of net sales/total tangible assets gives an indication of a higher degree of efficiency in the utilisation of assets. Higher the ratio, more efficient the utilisation of resources and, therefore, smaller the probability of financial problems. The higher turnover brings forth fair return and even if the profit margin is small, the total return on investment shall be large enough to overcome any financial difficulties. Therefore, a lower turnover of total assets is generally treated as a precursor of financial crisis and thus an indicator of corporate sickness.

V_{35}—*Defensive Assets/Total Operating Expenditure*

This measure indicates the defensive position of the firm [103-104]. This calculates the interval of time for which the company can finance its continuing operations (without acquiring additional assets or paying down liabilities) from its liquid assets without resorting to cash flows from sales or from other short term sources of finance. This ratio, known as 'Defensive interval ratio' is calculated by dividing the defensive assets by daily operating expenditures of the firm. In this study it is calculated by dividing the defensive assets by total operating expenditures in order to determine it in terms of times instead of days. Defensive assets or quick assets include cash, marketable securities and receivables; the denominator of the ratio consists of operating expenses minus depreciation, depletion and amortization. Depreciation, depletion and amortization are excluded from operating expenses, because they are not current drain on cash and its

equivalent. This ratio is relatively new to the accounting literature. It indicates the liquidity position of a firm more clearly. A smaller ratio of a firm indicates that the firm can operate on existing liquid assets for a shorter period as compared to the firm having high ratio, if all other sources of short term finances are cut off. Therefore, a smaller defensive interval ratio is considered a sign of liquidity crisis and thus an indicator of corporate sickness. A negative relationship is understood to exist between this ratio and corporate sickness.

6.2 Determination of Discriminant Coefficients

The coefficients of discriminant function and the cut off point which tend to minimise errors of classification of sick companies and non-sick companies are worked out as under:

To begin with, it is assumed that some unknown set of weighting coefficients exist which would define a composite score providing maximum discrimination between the two groups, namely sick group of companies and non-sick group of companies. The simplest form which the desired discriminant function can take is the linear one:

$$Y=\lambda_1V_1+\lambda_2V_2+\lambda_3V_3 \quad \ldots\lambda_nV_n$$

where Y is the composite score or index that is desired, $V_1, V_2, V_3 \ldots, V_n$ are the variables measured and $\lambda_1, \lambda_2, \lambda_3, \ldots \lambda_n$ (lamdas are the corresponding weighting coefficients). The immediate task is to determine optimal values for the weighting coefficients ($\lambda_1, \lambda_2, \ldots\lambda_n$) such that the difference between mean scores for the two groups is maximised relative to the variation within groups. The optimum weighting coefficients providing maximum discrimination between the two groups, namely, sick group and non-sick group are obtained by multiplying the inverse of the within groups variance-covariance matrix by the vector of mean differences. It can be presented in a matrix notation form:

$$\lambda=c^{-1}d$$

where c^{-1} is the inverse of the within groups variance-covariance matrix, d is the vector of mean differences; and λ represents the weighting coefficients defining the best discriminating linear combination of the original V_n scores. The mean values of the four finally selected variables (i.e. financial

ratios) of both the groups; the difference between the mean values; and the inverse of the within groups variance-covariance matrix are shown in Table 6.7.

TABLE 6.7-A: **Means of original variables selected for the discriminant model**

Variables	GR-1	GR-2	(*d*)
V_9 — EBIT/TTA	—0.09389	0.11989	0.21378
V_{25} — CA/CL	1.44268	3.39694	1.95426
V_{31} – NS/TTA	0.61282	1.85912	1.24630
V_{35} — DA/TOE	0.28210	0.48379	0.20169

Notes:

GR-1: represents sick companies

GR-2: represents non-sick companies

d: denotes the vector of mean differences

TABLE 6.7-B: **Within groups variance-covariance inverse matrix of variables in the discriminant model**

Variables	V_9	V_{25}	V_{31}	V_{35}
V_9	104.21127	—0.27278	−1.08841	—2.46642
V_{25}	—0.27278	0.02560	0.00802	0.01509
V_{31}	−1.08841	0.00802	0.69423	0.32648
V_{35}	—2.46642	0.01509	0.32648	2 86029

From the row-by-column rule matrix multiplication, this is equivalent to setting each unknown λ_i equal to a weighted sum of the elements in one row of the inverse matrix, each being weighted by the appropriate mean difference:

$$\lambda_i = d_1c^{i1} + d_2c^{i2} + d_3c^{i3} + \ldots\ldots + d_Jc^{iJ}$$

where c^{iJ} is the element in the *i*th row and *j*th column of the inverse matrix and d_J is the difference between mean values for the two groups on *J*th variable. This multiplication results in the following equations:

$$\lambda_9 = .21378(104.21127) + 1.95426(-.27278) + 1.24630(-1.08841) + .20169(-.46642)$$

$$\lambda_{25} = .21378(-\ .27278) + 1.95426(\ .02560) + 1.24630(\ .\text{\textsubscript{c}}0802) + .20169(\ .01509)$$

$$\lambda_{31} = .21378(-1.08841) + 1.95426(\ .00802) + 1.24630(\ .69423) + .20169(\ .32648)$$

$$\lambda_{35} = .21378(-2.46642)+1.95426(\ .01509) +1.24630(\ .32648)+ .20169(\ 2.86029)$$

Solution of these equations yields the following values of discriminant coefficients:

$$\lambda_9 = 19.8927$$
$$\lambda_{25} = 0.0047$$
$$\lambda_{31} = 0.7141$$
$$\lambda_{35} = 0.4860$$

To test the statistical significance of overall discriminating power of the discriminant function (i.e. $Y=19.8927V_9+0.0047V_{25}+0.7141V_{31}+0.4860V_{35}$), multivariate F-ratio is worked out. F-value is the ratio of the sums of squares i.e. variances between groups to the sums of squares within groups. If this ratio is maximised, it has the effect of separating the means of the two groups and similarly reducing the dispersion of the individual points about their group means.

Symbolically:

$$F=\frac{(\bar{Y}_{g_1}-\bar{Y}_{g_2})^2}{\sum_{i=1}^{n_{g_1}}(Y_i-\bar{Y}_{g_1})^2+\sum_{i=1}^{n_{g_2}}(Y_i-\bar{Y}_{g_2})^2}$$

where

$\bar{Y}_{g_1}-\bar{Y}_{g_2}$ = sums of variance between the group means

$(Y_i-\bar{Y}_{g_1})^2+(Y_i-\bar{Y}_{g_2})^2$ = sums of variance within groups

g = Number of groups

n_g = Number of observations in group g

Y_i = Score of individual observation

$\bar{Y}$ = Group mean

Mean discriminant function values i.e. $\bar{Y}_{g_1}$ and $\bar{Y}_{g_2}$ of the sick group and non-sick group are computed by applying the weighting coefficients to the group means of the original variables (i.e. V_9, V_{25}, V_{31}, V_{35}):

$$\bar{Y}_{g_1} = 19.8927(-.09389)+.0047(1.44268) + .7141(\ .61281)+.4860(\ .28210)$$

$$\bar{Y}_{g_2} = 19.8927(\ .11989) + .0047(3.39694) + .7141(1.85912) + .4860(\ .48379)$$

Solution of the above equations and F-ratio formula yields the following values:

$$\bar{Y}_{g_1} = 1.2862$$

$$\bar{Y}_{g_2} = 3.9635$$

$$F = 24.4976$$

$$F_{1,\ 76}(.01) = 6.98$$

The values given above were worked out on IBM 360/44 Computer available at Delhi University Computer Centre.

6.3 Ranking of Variables

The significance test of the overall discriminating power of the discriminant function rejects the null hypothesis that the observations come from the same population. It is, therefore, concluded that *a priori* groups are significantly different from each other and it leaves no doubt as to the discriminating power of the discriminant function.

The relative contribution of each variable to the total discriminating power of the function is also determined on the basis of scaled vector of each variable which is computed by multiplying corresponding elements by the square roots of the diagonal elements of the variance-covariance matrix. The scaled vector for each variable (ratio) is worked out by taking the following steps:

(*a*) Square root of diagonal elements of each of the variables in the variance-covariance matrix is obtained; and
(*b*) discriminant coefficient of each of the variables is multiplied by the concerned square root of the diagonal element in the variance-covariance matrix.

Since the actual variable measurement units are not comparable to each other, simple observation of the discriminant coefficients may mislead. The adjusted coefficients (i.e. scaled vectors), therefore, are computed and presented in Table 6.8. These adjusted coefficients enable us to evaluate the relative contribution of each variable towards discriminant index.

TABLE 6.8: **Scaled vectors indicating relative contribution of the variables**

Variable	Scaled vector	Ranking
V_9—EBIT/TTA	2.009	1
V_{25}—CA/CL	0.033	4
V_{31}—NS/TTA	0.885	2
V_{35}—DA/TOE	0.298	3

The scaled vectors presented in Table 6.8 clearly indicate that the profitability ratio (i.e. EBIT/TTA) contributes the most followed by the turnover ratio (i.e. NS/TTA) towards the discriminating power of the discriminant function.

6.4 Determination of Cut off Point

Once the values of the discriminant coefficients are determined, it is possible to calculate discriminant scores for each observation in the sample or any new company and to assign the observation to one of the groups based on this score. The essence of the procedure is to compare the score of an individual company with that of the alternative groups. In this manner the company is assigned to the group it most closely resembles.

Having selected the final best discriminant function, discriminant scores (*y*-scores) of each of the individual observations are calculated one year prior to the event (i.e. sickness) and presented in Table 6.9.

TABLE 6.9: **Y-Score values of 78 companies in the initial sample one year prior to sickness**

Co. code number	*Y*-Score (Discriminant Score)	Co. code number	*Y*-Score (Discriminant Score)
101	0.322516	102	—0.183123
103	—7.479732	104	2.062744
105	—1.625042	106	—4.121619
107	0.695223	108	0.778460
109	—0.124596	110	—0.099117
111	—1.092987	112	1.866842
113	—2.998042	114	—3.139478
115	0.363427	116	0.621903

TABLE 6.9 (*Contd.*)

Co. code number	*Y*-Score (Discriminant Score)	Co. code number	*Y*-Score (Discriminant Score)
117	—0.076411	118	—0.629480
119	—0.306769	120	—0.650435
121	—3.019234	122	1.313031
123	3.367076	124	3.932187
125	—0.012189	126	—8.045675
127	—0.789917	128	—2.921009
129	—1.018811	130	—0.355697
131	—3.111678	132	—2.515463
133	—4.084116	134	—6.108268
135	—1.275113	136	—2.468291
137	—2.816355	138	—1.257897
139	0.148498	140	5.972725
241	5.835010	242	6.760247
243	1.804542	244	2.807704
245	2.246477	246	9.849155
247	4.040750	248	3.325727
249	3.880880	250	3.299144
251	3.168562	252	3.920242
253	2.363754	254	2.449077
255	3.491007	256	2.774686
257	3.763230	258	3.389658
259	4.316798	260	2.450748
261	3.067127	262	3.437861
263	4.336874	264	4.489725
265	3.267273	266	3.954998
267	4.852349	268	2.713541
269	3.587265	270	4.451972
271	4.658970	272	3.209098
273	3.910942	274	3.190253
275	1.705799	276	3.437982
277	2.130720	278	1.526115

Note: First digit of the code number denotes the group; and next two digits denote the observations' serial number in the sample.

The discriminant model will have more practical applicability for investors, bankers, credit managers and executives if an attempt is made to extend the model for general application, which is possible only if a cut off point is selected for general applicability. Cut off point is an optimum value which results

in minimum number of misclassification. The cut off point makes predictions possible without computer support which is not easily accessible to bankers, credit managers, executives and potential investors at all levels. A question, therefore, of more concern than mere statistical significance in most discriminant function analysis is the selection of a "cut off" point and assignment of individuals to one of the two groups.

In this case, it is observed that each individual is certain to belong to one of the two groups, no other alternatives are available. If there is no basis for assuming that one group should contain substantially more observations than the other and if the seriousness of errors of misclassification is about equal, the logical "cut off" point lies halfway between the two group means $\bar{Y}_{g1}$ and $\bar{Y}_{g2}$ [90]

$$Y_c = \frac{\bar{Y}_{g1} + \bar{Y}_{g2}}{2}$$

where

Y_c = Cut off point
$\bar{Y}_{g1}$ = Group-1 discriminant mean value
$\bar{Y}_{g2}$ = Group-2 discriminant mean value

If the individual discriminant score is below Y_c, the individual should be classified in group-1 and if above Y_c, it should be assigned to group-2. It can be presented in a equation form by adding the constant $-Y_c$ to the discriminant function:

$$Y = -Y_c + \lambda_1 V_1 + \lambda_2 V_2 + \lambda_3 V_3 + \ldots\ldots + \lambda_n V_n$$

where Y_c = cut off point

$V_1, V_2, V_3, \ldots\ldots\ldots, V_n$ are variables measured and $\lambda_1, \lambda_2, \lambda_3, \ldots\ldots\ldots \lambda_n$ are the corresponding weights.

The decision rule then becomes: 'assign to group-2 if the individual's discriminant score is positive and to group-1 if negative.' This is known as a maximum likelihood procedure, because each individual is assigned to the group in which the occurrence of his particular discriminant score is most likely.

In this study, the discriminant cut off point (i.e. the value lying half-way between the two group means) is:

$$Y_c = \frac{\bar{Y}_{g1} + \bar{Y}_{g2}}{2}$$

$$Y_c = \frac{-1.2862 + 3.9635}{2} = 1.3386$$

But an empirical method is adopted for determining the value to minimise total classification error rather than defining Y_c arithmetically. Table 6.9 indicates that all companies having a Y-score greater than 3.9322 clearly fall into the non-sick group while those companies having a Y-score below 1.5261 are all sick companies. Thus, the area between 1.5261 and 3.9322 discriminant scores is defined as the 'Zone of Ignorance' because of susceptibility to error classification. Since errors are observed in this range of values, there will be uncertainty about a new company whose Y-score falls within the 'zone of ignorance'. Hence, it is desirable to minimise this range of uncertainty and to establish a guideline for classifying companies falling in the 'zone of ignorance'.

The process begins by identifying companies which fall within the overlapping range. The companies falling within the 'zone of ignorance' are shown in Table 6.10.

TABLE 6.10: **Companies whose Y-score falls within the 'zone of ignorance'**

Non-sick co. code No.	Y-Score (Y_c=1.33)	Sick co. code No.
278	1.52	
275	1.70	
243	1.80	
	1.86	112
	2.06	104
277	2.15	
245	2.24	
253	2.36	
254	2.44	
260	2.45	
268	2.71	
256	2.77	
261	3.06	
274	3.19	
272	3.20	
265	3.26	
248	3.32	
	3.36	123
258	3.38	
262	3.43	

TABLE 6.10 (*Contd.*)

Non-sick co. code No.	Y-Score $Y_c=1.33$	Sick co. code No.
276	3.43	
255	3.49	
269	3.58	
257	3.76	
273	3.91	
	3.93	124

Note: The first digit of the co. code number represents its group with the last two digits locating the company within the group.

By starting with a *Y*-score towards the minimum and maximum score of the overlaping area, the range of *Y*-scores that results in the minimum number of misclassifications is determined. In the analysis, *Y*'s between the indicated values produce the following misclassifications, shown in Table 6.11.

TABLE 6.11: **Number of misclassifications using Y-score criterions**

Range of Y-Scores	Number misclassified	Companies
1.33—1.52	4	112, 104, 123, 124
1.52—1.70	5	278, 112, 104, 123, 124
1.70—1.80	6	278, 275, 112, 104, 123, 124
1.80—1.86	6	278, 275, 243, 104, 123, 124
1.86—2.06	6	243, 275, 278, 104, 123, 124
2.06−2.13	5	243, 275, 278, 123, 124
2.13—2.24	6	277, 243, 275, 278, 123, 124
2.24—2.36	7	245, 277, 243, 275, 278, 123, 124
2.36—2 44	8	253, 245, 277, 243, 275, 278, 123, 124
2.44—2.45	9	254, 253, 245, 277, 243, 275, 278, 123, 124
2.45—2.71	10	260, 254, 253, 245, 277, 243, 275, 278, 123, 124
2.71—2.77	11	268, 260, 254, 253, 245, 277, 243, 275, 278, 123, 124
2.77—3.06	12	256, 268, 260, 254, 253, 245, 277, 243, 275, 278, 123, 124
3.06—3.19	13	261, 256, 268, 260, 254, 253, 245, 277, 243, 275, 278, 123, 124

TABLE 6.11 (*Contd.*)

Range of Y-Scores	Number misclassified	Companies
3.19—3.20	14	274, 261, 256, 268, 260, 254, 253, 245, 277, 243, 275, 278, 123, 124
3.20—3.26	15	272, 274, 261, 256, 268, 260, 254, 253, 245, 277, 243, 275, 278, 123, 124
3.26—3.32	16	265, 272, 274, 261, 256, 268, 260, 254, 253, 245, 277, 243, 275, 278, 123, 124
3.32—3.36	17	248, 265, 272, 274, 261, 256, 268, 260, 254, 253, 245, 277, 243, 275, 278, 123, 124
3.36—3.38	16	248, 265, 272, 274, 261, 256, 268, 260, 254, 253, 245, 277, 243, 275, 278, 124
3.38—3.43	17	258, 248, 265, 272, 274, 261, 256, 268, 260, 254, 253, 245, 277, 243, 275, 278, 124
3.43—3.49	19	262, 276, 258, 248, 272, 274, 265, 261, 256, 268, 260, 254, 253, 245, 277, 243, 275, 278, 124
3.49—3.58	20	255, 262, 276, 258, 248, 265, 272, 274, 261, 256, 268, 260, 254, 253, 245, 277, 243, 275, 278, 124
3.58—3.76	21	269, 255, 262, 276, 258, 248, 265, 272, 274, 261, 256, 268, 260, 254, 253, 245, 277, 243, 275, 278, 124
3.76—3.91	22	257, 269, 255, 262, 276, 258, 248, 265, 272, 274, 261, 256, 268, 260, 254, 253, 245, 277, 243, 275, 278, 124
3.91—3.93	23	273, 257, 269, 255, 262, 276, 258, 248, 265, 272, 274, 261, 256, 260, 254, 253, 245, 277, 268, 243, 275, 278, 124

It is observed from Table 6.11 that the best critical value (i.e. cut off point) falls between 1.33—1.52 since this range of Y-scores results in minimum number of misclassifications. Therefore, 1.425, the mid-point of the range (i.e. $\left(\frac{1.33+1.52}{2}\right)$, is taken as the Y_c-value (i.e. cut off point)

that discriminates best between the sick companies and non-sick companies. Of course, the real test of this 'optimum' Y_c-value lies in its discriminating power not only with the initial sample, but also with the additional samples and population (companies) in general.

6.5 Estimating Probabilities of Misclassification in Assignment of Individual Companies

Probabilities of misclassification of cut off point (i.e. Y_c) and of each company are computed in order to judge the predictive accuracy of discriminant function more rigorously in the problem of classification between sick companies and non-sick companies and to take the classification decision with more confidence. While it is important in the development of a discriminant function classification procedure to evaluate the long run probabilities of misclassification for all members of each group, it is recognised that such probabilities are not uniform for all possible discriminant scores. Individual firms whose discriminant scores lie near the best cut off point are more likely to be placed in the wrong group than those having extremly large or small discriminant scores. Therefore, it becomes a matter of importance to estimate the probability of misclassification of cut off point and of each company, which is obtained by computing the Z-scores of cut off point (i.e. Y_c) and discriminant scores of each company in the initial sample.

Z-scores or Y_c are computed as follows:

$$Z_{g_1}=\frac{Y_c-\bar{Y}_{g_1}}{\sqrt{V(Y)}}$$

$$Z_{g_2}=\frac{Y_c-\bar{Y}_{g_2}}{\sqrt{V(Y)}}$$

where Z_{g_1}=standard score deviation about the group 1 mean score

Z_{g_2}=standard score deviation about the group 2 mean score

Y_c =cut off point

$\bar{Y}_{g_1}$=Group 1 discriminant mean score

$\bar{Y}_{g_2}$=Group 2 discriminant mean score

$V(Y)$=Within group variance of the discriminant scores

In this study

$$Y_c = 1.425$$
$$\bar{Y}_{g_1} = 1.2862$$
$$\bar{Y}_{g_2} = 3.9635$$
$$V(Y) = 5.0540$$

Putting these values in the above formula of Z-scores:

$$Z_{g_1} = \frac{1.425 - (-1.2862)}{\sqrt{5.0540}}$$

$$Z_{g_2} = \frac{1.425 - 3.9635}{\sqrt{5.0540}}$$

Solution of the above equations yields the following values:

$$Z_{g_1} = 1.21$$
$$Z_{g_2} = 1.13$$

Having obtained the values of Z_{g_1} and Z_{g_2}, the associated probability density values $f(Y_{g_1})$ and $f(Y_{g_2})$ as ordinates of the normal curve are taken from [90, pp. 470-79] Table A.1—Areas and ordinates of the normal curve in terms of x/σ. The table values indicate that the probability of misclassification is $P_{g_1} = .1131$ and $P_{g_2} = .1292$ for sick companies and non-sick companies respectively, where P_{g_1} represents the probability of misclassification for companies in group 1 and P_{g_2} represents the probability of misclassification for companies in group 2. The term 'misclassification' in this context means that assignment of companies to sick or non-sick group on the basis of the best discriminant function is expected to disagree with the actual or *a priori* classification in 11.31 per cent and 12 92 per cent cases in group 1 and group 2 respectively. It confirms the predictive accuracy of the discriminant model and indicates that further investigation may be required only in 11.31 per cent companies in group 1 and 12.92 per cent companies in group 2 in order to classify them correctly.

The following steps are to be taken to calculate the probability of errors of each company and its probability of belonging to each group:

(1) The discriminant scores of each company are transformed to *Z*-score deviations about the two group means. Symbolically:

$$Z_{g1i} = \frac{Y_i - \bar{Y}_{g1i}}{\sqrt{V(Y)}}$$

$$Z_{g2i} = \frac{Y_i - \bar{Y}_{g2i}}{\sqrt{V(Y)}}$$

where

Z_{g1i} = *Z*-score deviation of ith company discriminant score about group 1 mean

Z_{g2i} = *Z*-score deviation of ith company discriminant score about group 2 mean

Y_i = discriminant score of ith company

$\bar{Y}_{g1}$ = group 1 mean discriminant score

$\bar{Y}_{g2}$ = group 2 mean discriminant score

$V(Y)$ = within group variance of the discriminant scores.

(2) The associated probability-density values of *Z*-score deviations of companies of each group are taken from Table A.1—[Areas and ordinates of the normal curve in terms of x/σ [90, pp. 470-79] and denoted by

$f(Y_{g1i})$ = the probability-density value of ith company in group 1.

$f(Y_{g2i})$ = the probability-density value of ith company in group 2.

The ratios of these ordinate values provide the required estimates or probability of the individual company's belonging to each group:

$$P_{g1i} = \frac{f(Y_{g1i})}{f(Y_{g1i}) + f(Y_{g2i})}$$

$$P_{g2i} = \frac{f(Y_{g2i})}{f(Y_{g1i}) + f(Y_{g2i})}$$

where

P_{g1i} = the probability of ith company's belonging to group 1

P_{g2i} = the probability of ith company's belonging to group 2.

For example, the probability of ith company's belonging to group 1 is estimated to be $P_{g_{1i}}=.12$ and the probability of belonging to group 2 is estimated to be $P_{g_{2i}}=.88$. Following the rule of assigning the ith company to the more probable group i.e. group 2 results in an estimated probability of error of $P_e=.12$ i.e. the probability that the ith company will be incorrectly classified is $P_e=.12$.

The probability of misclassification particularly of those companies whose discriminant scores fall within the zone of uncertainty (1.33 – 1.52) is to be evaluated before assigning them into either of the two groups, because the companies whose discriminant scores lie within the area of uncertainty are more likely to be placed in the wrong group than those falling beyond the area of uncertainty. Unless the probability of individual company's belonging to either of the two groups is clearly high, one should refrain from making a definite classification pending examination of additional information. Thus, the probability of individual company's belonging to each group should be used as an additional aid along with the discriminant scores in predicting the chances of survival or sickness, especially for those companies whose discriminant scores lie close to cut off point.

6.6 Empirical Results

Empirical results are presented in a format, called Membership Classification Chart or Accuracy Matrix. The classification error for each sample is computed and presented in a matrix form.

Membership classification matrix
or
Accuracy matrix

Actual group membership	Predicted group membership		
	GR-1	GR-2	Total
GR-1	C	M_1	—
GR-2	M_2	C	—
Total	—	—	—

The actual group membership is equivalent to the *priori* groupings and the model attempts to classify the given companies correctly. The nature of the model which is explanatory at this stage, becomes predictive when new companies are classified.

In the Accuracy Matrix, C stands for correct classification and M stands for misclassification. On the basis of the accuracy matrix, percentage of correct classification and error rates are computed. M_1 represents a Type I error and M_2, a Type II error. The sum of diagonal elements equals the total correct (C) and when divided into the total number of companies classified (e.g. seventy-eight in the case of initial sample), yields the measure of success of the Discriminant Model in classifying companies correctly. Accuracy of classification is the important factor in discriminant analysis [105]. Accuracy is considered in two dimensions:

Type I is the accuracy of correctly classifying the sick companies and type II is the accuracy of correctly classifying non-sick companies. Type I error would be predicting a sick company not to fail, and a Type II error would be predicting a non-sick company to fail. These two types of accuracy and error rates are presented in a format as under:

	Number Correct	Total No.	% Correct	Number Incorrect	% Error
Type I	—	—	—	—	—
Type II	—	—	—	—	—
Total	—	—	—	—	—

The two types of error usually do not produce equal penalty costs. For example, creditors might be more concerned to avoid Type I because the magnitude of loss in capital may exceed expected return from interest payments. The cost of Type II error is the opportunity cost of not lending to a debtor who would have been a good risk. In the anti-trust decision, a type II error might be more costly than type I. Allowing non-sick companies to go for complete merger because of predicting non-sick companies to fail, may do more harm to the interests of public than predicting sick

companies not to fail. Therefore, the accuracy of the Discriminant Model is also to be assessed in the light of magnitude of type I and type II error.

A series of tests are performed on the initial sample in order to judge the accuracy of the Discriminant Model in predicting corporate sickness.

6.6.1 Results one year prior to sickness

In this sample 39 companies in each of the two groups are examined using financial data one year prior to sickness. In this case a high degree of successful classification is expected, because the discriminant function used for classification is derived from this sample. The predictive accuracy of the model for the initial sample is computed from *Y*-scores shown in Table 6.10 and presented in Table 6.12 in the form of accuracy matrix.

TABLE 6.12-A: **Membership classification or accuracy matrix one year prior to sickness**

Actual membership	Predicted membership		
	GR-1	GR-2	Total
GR-1	35	04	39
GR-2	00	39	39
Total	35	43	78

TABLE 6.12-B

	Number correct	Total number	% Correct	% Error
Type I	35	39	90	10
Type II	39	39	100	00
Total	74	78	95	5

It is observed from the Accuracy Matrix that the model proves to be very accurate in predicting the event. Its accuracy is 95 per cent in classifying the initial sample into GR-1 and GR-2. The model is more accurate in classifying the non-sick companies (GR-2) where the accuracy is 100 per cent than

GR-1 where the error rate is 10 per cent. It further strengthens the predictive power of the model. Though, the results are encouraging but the bias (sample and search bias) should not be overlooked. And, therefore, further validation tests are to be conducted using the Discriminant Model to a set of companies not used in the model building.

6.6.2 Results two years prior to sickness

The second test is made to observe the discriminating ability of the model for companies using financial data two years prior to sickness. With the help of discriminant model parameters, *Y*-scores of individual companies (seventy-eight companies) are calculated and shown in Table 6.13.

TABLE 6.13: **Y-Score values of companies in the initial sample two years prior to sickness**

Code No.	*Y*-Score	Code No.	*Y*-Score
101	0.2998	102	9.7321*
103	—9.0991	104	2.3244*
105	0.2829	106	1.2907
107	0.9845	108	0.2504
109	0.0575	110	—0.3760
111	−8.8074	112	1.8263*
113	1.5942*	114	0.3819
115	—7.0799	116	—1.9465
117	−4.5808	118	4.5493*
119	0.0440	120	−3.9136
121	−3.0298	122	1.2812
123	4.5096*	124	4.8189*
125	−0.1528	126	—6.4537
127	1.0324	128	−4.6645
129	—1.2085	130	—0.5413
131	3.2514	132	0.0411
133	—1.9163	134	—2.8810
135	—2.2119	136	3.7099
137	−1.6136	138	—2.8984
139	—1.3015	240	4.8104
241	7.5506	242	4.8959
243	8.1700	244	2.0655
245	1.9867	246	7.7861
247	1.9207	248	3.2972

TABLE 6.13 (*Contd.*)

Code No.	*Y*-Score	Code No.	*Y*-Score
249	2.8026	250	3.0606
251	3.3012	252	3.4007
253	2.7245	254	3.6447
255	6.7874	256	2.9462
257	1.4505	258	8.9810
259	7.1452	260	2.4824
261	3.8822	262	3.8865
263	4.4963	264	4.1428
265	1.7714	266	4.5922
267	4.3252	268	0.7029*
269	1.7030	270	3.8879
271	3.5975	272	3.0974
273	3.9792	274	3.6765
275	1.5225	276	3.6300
277	6.7759	278	1.5609

Note: The misclassified companies are marked with (*).

Applying the cut off point ($Y_c = 1.425$), determined on the basis of initial sample data one year prior to sickness, the predictive accuracy of the model is calculated and presented in Table 6.14.

TABLE 6.14-A: **Accuracy matrix**

To years prior to sickness

Actual membership	Predicted membership		
	GR-1	GR-2	Total
GR-1	30	09	39
GR-2	01	38	39
Total	31	47	78

TABLE 6.14-B

	Number correct	Total number	% Correct	% Error
Type I	30	39	77	23
Type II	38	39	97	03
	68	78	87	13

Table 4.16 indicates that 30 companies out of 39 in Group 1 and 38 companies out of 39 in Group 2 are correctly classified. This means that 68 companies out of 78 are correctly classified which amounts to 87 per cent predictive accuracy of the model two years prior to sickness. The reduction in accuracy of the model in classifying the companies two years prior to sickness is understandable and it was expected, because impending sickness is more remote and the indications are less clear. Nevertheless, 87 per cent assignment of companies into respective groups is the evidence that sickness can be predicted two years prior to the event. Further tests are also performed to determine the long range predictive accuracy of the model in predicting corporate sickness.

6.6.3 **Results three to six years prior to sickness**

The predicted results of the model two years prior to the date of event (i.e. sickness) are quite encouraging and justify its extension in the prediction of corporate sickness beyond two years. Moreover, several studies (refer Chapter 4) exhibited sickness tendencies as much as five years prior to failure. Thus an attempt has been made to ascertain the predictive accuracy of the model up to 6 years prior to the event. The data were collected for the 78 companies in the initial sample for third, fourth, fifth and sixth year separately prior to sickness. The reduced sample of companies in the above mentioned years prior to the event is on account of non-availability of financial statements for the more remote years. With the help of parameters of discriminant function, the *Y*-scores of individual companies are computed for each year before sickness and presented in Table 6.15.

TABLE 6.15: **Y-Score values of companies in the initial sample three to six years prior to sickness**

Co. code number	Year prior to sickness 3	4	5	6
101	0.6244	—1.5799	—2.7379	—0.5654
102	—0.8929	—2.4083	1.2738	3.9452*
103	—2.3840	—4.2674	—1.3083	—0.8348
104	3.1050*	2.6699*	NA	NA
105	—0.8790	—1.1065	0.2778	NA
106	0.3167	0.0162	1.8518*	2.005*
107	1.5223*	0.7820	NA	NA
108	—6.1263	—0.9651	—3.5874	—2.5654
109	NA	NA	NA	NA
110	—0 3850	—0.5242	NA	NA
111	—9.4767	NA	NA	NA
112	2.2666*	2.9240*	2.9590*	—0.3704
113	3.1905*	4.4739*	3.2997*	3.1013*
114	0.3150	2.1247*	5.4462*	2.5996*
115	—1.8240	0.4242	1.3756	2.1038*
116	—2.7101	—0.3170	NA	—1.4245
117	—8.8976	—4.1930	—3.1448	—2.9714
118	—0.3572	0.4805	3 6796*	0.2787
119	0.2248	0.1123	0.5167	NA
120	—0.3897	—5.1537	—2.1824	—1.7318
121	—3.5823	—1.1611	—1.4617	—1.4556
122	—1.8570	—1.6874	—0.6489	—0.5094
123	0.7791	—0.9227	—0.1220	NA
124	2.7999*	5.2811*	5.4043*	0.0617
125	—0.7708	1.3148	NA	NA
126	—7.9896	—1.8373	NA	NA
127	0.7237	—1.0995	1.2552	0.9166
128	—1.8844	3.2009*	—0.1040	—0.3171
129	—0.8272	—1.2325	—0.6205	0.2411
130	0.8671	—0.0297	—5.3698	NA
131	2.5183*	—0.8381	0.3442	5.5352*
132	1.7879*	5.3232*	4.0715*	2.6589*
133	—3.3862	NA	NA	NA
134	—1.0404	—0.0132	—2.5454	0 4298
135	1.3995	1.0149	—0.1653	0.3261

TABLE 6.15 (*Contd.*)

Co. code	Year prior to sickness			
number	3	4	5	6
136	4.0696*	2.9525*	2.0751*	1.2560
137	0.4865	1.2167	1.1313	0.8379
138	NA	NA	NA	NA
139	0.5957	1.9430*	1.8107*	1.8192*
240	4.6236	4.0383	3.1961	NA
241	1.5731	3.0026	3.6834	1.9083
242	5.6137	6.7232	5.6591	NA
243	2.9276	—1.1196*	NA	NA
244	2.5411	4.3074	2.3278	2.6856
245	1.8685	1.9450	1.6278	1.6992
246	5.1511	4.8190	3.0447	4.7289
247	1.5607	2.9489	3.8496	2.3477
248	3.8490	NA	NA	NA
249	4.5885	0.0072*	4.1027	3.8495
250	0.6881*	1.9708	2.2692	2.5363
251	0.1744*	2.1101	2.7372	NA
252	3.2540	6.8127	5.5771	4.1122
253	2.9133	2.3401	2.5148	NA
254	2.2166	2.0927	1.7056	1.7962
255	3.9265	2.7302	1.8121	6.6372
256	2.0543	—0.6369*	—0.4299*	0.3505*
257	2.5215	3.7921	2.5886	NA
258	3.9379	2.4517	NA	NA
259	6.1546	7.8454	8.7813	5.5526
260	2.1118	NA	NA	NA
261	4.7570	3.3488	4.1172	NA
262	2.8708	3.3042	2.3460	2.0771
263	5.6573	5.7375	6.0583	6.9574
264	5.4862	2.6735	—0.7089*	—2.7253*
265	1.9586	1.4881	1.5617	NA
266	4.5550	2.3550	0.3666*	NA
267	3.2412	4.2996	3.6741	3.6220
268	2.7629	3.0372	2.5538	1.7074
269	2.9196	3.3699	2.5568	1.1595*
270	3.6141	3.3230	1.9780	2.7848
271	4.8721	3.8555	4.2476	3.1532
272	3.8620	5.3793	5.4078	4.9157
273	2.9133	1.5485	1.9124	2.5614

TABLE 6.15 (*Contd.*)

Co. code number	Year prior to sickness			
	3	4	5	6
274	4.3529	4.4577	3.9732	5.3442
275	1.7193	3.1422	3.5615	NA
276	2.8503	2.2126	NA	NA
277	2.9827	4.3640	0.5591*	2.0396
278	0.6890*	—0.2012*	4.0578	4.5663

Notes: (1) The first digit of the co. code number denotes the group and the next two digits denote the serial number of the company.
(2) The misclassified firms are marked with (*).
(3) Non-availability of data of a firm is denoted by NA.

The predictive accuracy of the model three to six years prior to sickness is ascertained and presented in Table 6.16.

TABLE 6.16-A: **Accuracy matrix**
Three to six years prior to sickness

Year prior to sickness	Actual membership		Predicted membership	
			GR-1	GR-2
3	GR-1	37	29	08
	GR-2	39	03	36
4	GR-1	35	26	09
	GR-2	37	04	33
5	GR-1	29	20	09
	GR-2	34	04	30
6	GR-1	26	18	08
	GR-2	25	03	22

TABLE 6.16-B

Year prior to sickness	Total no. of companies	Number correct	% Correct	% Error
3	76	65	86	14
4	72	59	82	18
5	63	50	79	21
6	51	40	78	22

From Table 6.16 it is evident that 65, 59, 50 and 40 companies are correctly classified out of 76, 72, 63 and 51 companies respectively in the sample three to six years prior to sickness. It amounts to 86 per cent, 82 per cent, 79 per cent and 78 per cent predictive accuracy of the model three to six years prior to the event (i.e. sickness) respectively. The reduction in the accuracy of the model is logically understandable because as one goes back from the date of the event, the indicators (ratios) about the health of the unit become less and less clear.

6.7 Overall Performance of the Model

The predictive power of the model has been examined up to 6 years prior to the date of sickness for initial sample and summarised in Table 6.17.

TABLE 6.17: **Summary of six years predictive accuracy of the discriminant model**

Year prior to sickness	Number of companies	Number correctly classified	Number misclas-sified	% of correct classi-fication
1	78	74	04	95
2	78	68	10	87
3	76	65	11	86
4	72	59	13	82
5	63	50	13	79
6	51	40	11	78

Table 6.17 clearly illustrates that it is possible to classify companies into either potentially sick or potentially non-sick groups up to six years prior to sickness, though with decreasing probability. The fall in the accuracy of the model gradually increases as the lead time prior to the date of sickness increases. The fall in accuracy of the model is logically understandable taking into account the long period that elapses because the indications of the ratios become less and less clear as the lead time from the date of the event increases. It is also clear from Table 6.17 that the model predicts well for the short period as compared to the long period. If it is

presumed that the period up to three years from the date of the event as a short period and from fourth year to sixth year as a long period, the fall in the accuracy of prediction is higher in the longer period than the short period as shown in Table 6.18.

TABLE 6.18: **Comparison of predictive accuracy of the model (short period and long period)**

Year prior to sickness		% Accuracy of the model	Fall in the accuracy
1st	Short period	95	—
2nd		87	8
3rd		86	9
4th	Long period	82	13
5th		79	16
6th		78	17

It is clear from Table 6.18 that the predictive accuracy of the model is higher in the short run than the long run. A higher degree of accuracy is quite possible in the shorter period because the indications of sickness from the study of ratios are more clear in the short run than in the long run.

6.8 Predictive Accuracy of the Model

The model is applied to a new set of samples consisting of a cross-section of companies in order to judge its validity and effectiveness, since the efficiency of the model lies in predicting the chances of survival or falling in the trap of sickness of companies not used to develop the parameters of the model. Samples have also been drawn from a homogeneous group which means all companies in the group manufacture the same type of product.

6.8.1 Homogeneous group of companies

The model is empirically tested with reference to homogeneous industry group on a sample of 38 sick textile companies. There is no doubt that the prediction of sickness of a company can be done with greater confidence and reliability within a homogeneous industry group than across industry groups on

account of similarities in financial, technological and marketing characteristics.

Thirty-eight sick textile companies were chosen from the list of sick cotton textile companies coming under the National Textile Corporation Limited. Availability of data for the latest year before takeover of a company was taken as the main criterion of including a company in the sample for investigati n. Financial data for a period of six years from the date of takeover of a company were collected from the Company Law Board Library, New Delhi and the Bombay Stock Exchange Directory. The sample size is reduced due to non-availability of data as the period prior to takeover of sick companies increases. The number of sick companies for a period of six years before takeover is shown in Table 6.19.

TABLE 6.19: **The number of sick textile companies on which financial statement data could be obtained**

Year prior to the event (Takeover)	Number of companies
1	38
2	36
3	35
4	33
5	33
6	31

Using the parameters of the discriminant model (i.e. $Y = 19.8927V_9 + 0.0047V_{25} + 0.7141V_{31} + 0.4860V_{35}$), the discriminant scores were calculated for each company for a period of six years prior to takeover as shown in Table 6.20.

TABLE 6.20: **Y-Score values of sick textile companies one to six yearsp rior to takeover**

Co. code number	Year prior to takeover 1	2	3	4	5	6
ST—01	1.2166	—6.8637	—2.0467	—0.3729	—2.5474	0.6436
ST—02	—7.6316	—1.9633	—0.6038	1.3416	0.2008	0.9670
ST—03	0.1803	—2.1468	—6.4561	—2.6889	—2.3429	0.9947
ST—04	1.0959	—0.1193	—1.2450	—2.0545	0.7369	1.3235
ST—05	0.4470	0.3902	0.2628	—0.5251	1.6287*	2.3704*
ST—06	1.1824	0.6016	—2.1739	—9.8847	—1.2972	NA
ST—07	—3.0095	—6.5169	—2.2430	—1.4930	NA	NA
ST—08	—1.2783	—0.3950	0.1658	1.7373*	1.3460	2.1597*
ST—09	—0.8945	—3.2510	—1.5399	0.9658	0.9500	—3.5729
ST—10	0.0618	—1.6071	0.1028	—1.1044	1.2657	2.1199*
ST—11	—1.3410	—3.6682	—4.0519	—4.8438	—2.0001*	—3.1846
ST—12	1.0434	1.2849	—1.7376	—7.7432	—1.3229	—2.1883
ST—13	—0.1128	—0.5732	—0.1374	1.2422	0.2935	—0.8559
ST—14	—5.0412	—0.8338	—0.9388	—1.0388	2.2331*	2.0723*
ST—15	—0.4906	—6.4633	—0.0780	0.8154	0.6778	0.4975
ST—16	—3.2008	—19.8089	—0.3989	—2.8612	—2.2191	0.8825
ST—17	0.8464	—0.4674	—0.4594	—1.2216	1.1535	—0.9123
ST—18	—0.7255	—0.3938	0.2828	0.8508	0.6381	—0.8301
ST—19	0.2671	0.6280	0.5205	NA	NA	NA
ST—20	0.3325	—1.8967	0.9308	—0.2656	—2.6646	NA
ST—21	—2.4570	0.6358	0.5907	0.6357	—0.2851	—0.6337
ST—22	—1.1527	—2.6968	—1.7032	—0.4417	0.4992	—0.1690
ST—23	—1.6844	0.5228	—0.8196	—2.8837	1.1727	0.9703
ST—24	0.9611	—0.2294	0.0709	—0.9072	0,7078	0.3532
ST—25	0.2704	0.0510	—2.2755	0.7777	—1.6217	1.0073
ST—26	—1.3805	—0.4260	—12.6780	1.1916	—1.0636	1.3412
ST—27	—2.0109	0.3556	0.3839	NA	NA	NA
ST—28	—0.1143	—0.3615	—0.9477	0.4131	1.2071	0.3427
ST—29	—4.0762	—2.5933	—2.0907	—1.1872	—1.5634	—1.0396
ST—30	—2.0447	—1.5483	—1.5459	—1.1468	1.0835	0.9656
ST—31	—4.2002	—2.4259	—0.8758	0.3582	1.3983	1.3535
ST—32	—4.3839	—2.2403	0.2369	—3.5289	0.2109	1.3075
ST—33	0.4904	3.1340	3.6222*	2.7632*	0.8852	0.0285
ST—34	—1.2415	NA	NA	NA	—0.3370	—0.7038
ST—35	0.0943	0.5132	—0.9965	—4.5785	—8.6916	—8.8215
ST—36	—2.1788	1.0576	NA	0.0311	—1.3139	—1.0530
ST—37	—0.7592	—1.0610	1.2665	NA	NA	NA
ST—38	—2.9090	NA	NA	NA	NA	NA

Notes: (*i*) ST represents sick textile unit and the digit 1-38 denotes the serial number of units in the sample.

(*ii*) The misclassified companies are marked with (*).

(*iii*) Non-availability of data of a company is denoted by (N.A.).

The predictive accuracy of the model is estimated by using the discriminant score with cut off point (Y_c=1.425) and presented in the form of accuracy matrix in Table 6.21.

TABLE 6.21-A: **Accuracy matrix of sick textile companies one to six years prior to the event (i.e. take-over)**

Year prior to the event (Takeover)	Actual membership GR-1	Predicted membership GR-1	Predicted membership GR-2
1	38	38	00
2	36	35	01
3	35	34	01
4	33	31	02
5	33	30	03
6	31	27	04

TABLE 6.21-B

Year prior to the event (Takeover)	Type of Error	N	Number Correct	Per cent Correct	Per cent Error
1	Type 1	38	38	99.00	0.01
2	Type 1	36	35	97.22	2.78
3	Type 1	35	34	97.14	2.86
4	Type 1	33	31	93.94	6.06
5	Type 1	33	30	90.91	9.09
6	Type 1	31	27	87.09	12.91

Notes: (*i*) Type 1 represents type 1 error.
(*ii*) N=Total number of observations in the sample.
(*iii*) GR-1=Sick group.
(*iv*) GR-2=Non-sick group.

The analysis of the results in Table 6.21 reveals that 38 units out of 38 in the sample are correctly classified which amounts to a very high degree of accuracy of the model in predicting sickness of textile companies one year prior to takeover. The percentage classification error rates are

.01, 2.78, 2.86, 6.06, 9.09 and 12.91 respectively one to six years prior to takeover (i.e. sickness) which shows that the model is very accurate in predicting sickness of textile companies up to six years prior to takeover. However, the performance of the model is relatively better in 1-3 years than 4-6 years prior to takeover of companies.

6.8.2 Non-homogeneous group of companies

A sample of 24 sick units consisting of a cross-section of companies was taken irrespective of size, industry, age and fiscal year. Financial data of six years prior to sickness were collected from the Library, Company Law Board, New Delhi and Bombay Stock Exchange Directory. Using the parameters of the discriminant model i.e. $Y=19.8927V_9+0.0047V_{25}+0.7141V_{31}+0.4860V_{35}$, the discriminant scores are computed for each of the companies for each year prior to sickness as presented in Table 6.22.

TABLE 6.22: **Y-Score values of sick companies in the additional sample of non-homogeneous group one to six years prior to sickness**

Co. code	Year prior to sickness					
number	1	2	3	4	5	6
S—01	—12.6245	—1.0141	0.3184	—2.2773	N.A.	N.A.
S—02	0.5364	—1.3105	—3.8558	N.A.	N.A.	N.A.
S—03	—1.0958	—2.9167	N.A.	N.A.	N.A.	N.A.
S—04	—0.3345	0.9020	—3.4637	—2.3452	2.1567*	0.4173
S—05	1.0057	—0.8221	—1.0965	0.2213	0 0371	0.4954
S—06	—5.9403	1.3376	2.0031*	N.A.	N.A.	2.0551*
S—07	0.6960	1.6830*	N.A.	N.A.	N.A.	N.A.
S—08	—0.5686	0.7339	0.0665	—2.8003	1.3957	—0.1145
S—09	1.0180	1.0423	0.6931	0.1991	0.5385	1.0519
S—10	0.5537	—3.2015	—3.3602	—0.8491	3.5479*	—2.3707
S—11	—2.1357	0.1668	—3.0095	—1.0929	—3.5479	—0.6577
S—12	—0.8505	—1.4613	—1.9525	—1.9891	—1.1075	—0.6405
S—13	—0.2250	—0.4535	—0.1466	—1.5752	—1.1165	—1.1166
S—14	—6.4120	—6.9283	—1.7723	—0.6622	—12.2258	—4.7829
S—15	—16.5161	—16.0449	N.A.	N.A.	—8.5389	—15.3251

TABLE 6.22 (*Contd.*)

Co. code number	Year prior to sickness					
	1	2	3	4	5	6
S—16	—7.4280	—5.6212	—5.9058	N.A.	N.A.	N.A.
S—17	—0.5052	0.6920	0.1587	N.A.	N.A.	N.A.
S—18	3.7326*	0.5208	0.4785	0.8278	0.7916	N.A.
S—19	0.6960	1.1112	0.6672	N.A.	N.A.	N.A.
S-20	—1.4614	—3.9501	—2.3711	0.4722	—1.7349	0.9570
S—21	0.9978	—0.0315	4.0191*	3.0132*	N.A.	N.A.
S—22	—4.7567	—1.4533	0.5282	0.5389	—0.6148	1.0970
S—23	—0.9771	—4.4510	—0.7439	0.8126	0.3581	1.6710 *
S—24	—1.3685	0.5489	—0.2651	—2.5014	—0.9568	—0.2248

Notes: (*i*) S represents the sick unit and digit 1-24 denotes the serial number of companies in the sample.
(*ii*) The misclassified companies are marked with (*).
(*iii*) Non-availability of data of a company is denoted by (N.A.).

On the basis of the cut off point (Y_c=1.425) as determined in the initial sample, the predictive accuracy of the model is estimated and presented in Table 6.23.

TABLE 6.23-A: **Accuracy matrix of sick companies in the additional sample of non-homogeneous group one to six years prior to sickness**

Year prior to sickness	Actual membership GR-1	Predicted membership GR-1	Predicted membership GR-2
1	24	23	01
2	24	23	01
3	21	19	02
4	16	15	01
5	15	13	02
6	15	13	02

TABLE 6.23-B

Year prior to sickness	Type of Error	N	Number Correct	Per cent Correct	Per cent Error
1	Type 1	24	23	95.83	04.17
2	Type 1	24	23	95.83	04.17
3	Type 1	21	19	90.48	09.52
4	Type 1	16	15	93.75	06.25
5	Type 1	15	13	86.67	13.33
6	Type 1	15	13	86.67	13.33

Notes: (*i*) Type 1 represents type 1 error.
(*ii*) N=Number of observations in the sample.
(*iii*) GR-1=Sick group.
(*iv*) GR-2=Non-sick group.

Table 6.23 clearly indicates that out of 24 units in the sample, 23 units are classified correctly one year prior to the event. The discriminant model maintains 95.83 per cent accuracy in the classification of units one year prior to sickness. In case of two to six years prior to sickness, the predictive accuracy of the discriminant model amounts to 95.83 per cent, 91.48 per cent, 93.75 per cent, 86.67 per cent and 86.67 per cent respectively. The predictive accuracy of the model is reduced to 86.66 per cent in the sixth year prior to sickness from 95.83 per cent in one year prior to sickness. It indicates that the accuracy of the discriminant model reduces as the lead period before sickness increases. This is logically acceptable because as one goes back from the date of the event, the indicators (ratios) of the health of the unit become less and less clear.

A comparison of the predictive accuracy of the model in homogeneous group and non-homogeneous group of companies in the initial sample and test samples is made and presented in Table 6.24.

TABLE 6.24: **Percentage classification error in predicting sickness in homogeneous group and non-homogeneous group of companies**

Year prior of sickness	In non-homogeneous group		In homogeneous group
	Initial sample of sick and non-sick companies	Test sample of sick companies	Test sample of sick textile companies
1	05	04.17	00.01
2	13	04.17	02.78
3	14	09.52	02.86
4	18	06.25	06.06
5	21	13.33	09.09
6	22	13.33	12.91

Table 6.24 reveals that the overall performance of the model in predicting sickness of homogeneous group of companies is better compared to non-homogeneous group of companies. The better results in case of homogeneous group compared to non-homogeneous group of companies must be, in some measure, due to the homogeneity of the industry group (cotton textiles) to which the model is applied.

6.9 Enlarged MDA Model

The poor financial state of a company is very often the outcome of mismanagement in technical and operational areas. Thus the prediction of sickness has to take into the total mismanagement of a company's working which includes technical, operational and financial parameters. A combination of technical, operational and financial parameters may prove a better discriminator between sick and the healthy units for early detection of sickness when it is just setting in an industry.

6.9.1 The choice of non-financial parameters

Non-financial parameters are chosen on the basis of availability and consistency of data for particular group of industry and also their sensitivity towards the state of health in industry. A large number of non-financial factors are given in

Chapter 3, which do significantly contribute to sickness. For instance, non-availability of raw materials affects the capacity utilisation and thus becomes an operational parameter in determining the degree of sickness in a unit. In case of a newly started factory, where the economic size has been determined for a minimum requirement of raw materials, its non-availability can cause grave sickness in that industry. Hence, one of the important operational parameters is the capacity utilisation. Examining the cases of a number of sugar mills and engineering industries, it was discovered that poor capacity utilisation due to non-availability of raw materials considerably affected the health of the units.

Another equally important variable is the plant utilisation ratio. The state of plant and equipment in a unit and its technical efficiency is one of the important parameters in determining the degree of sickness in the industrial unit. The breakdown in the plant and equipment depends on the age and proneness to failure of components and sub-systems in the plant. The technical parameters can be measured by the ratio of the actual working hours to the total available if plant and equipment were in perfect health for the season the unit was in operation. Thus, plant utilisation is a critical parameter. There are also a few other important technical parameters like the production cost ratio. The production cost ratio rise may also become significant for some industries in these days of rising prices. Thus each industrial group has to be scanned for a number of critical ratios and their net contribution determined towards the health of the units in that group.

6.9.2 Construction of the model

The use of MDA model has been enlarged to include not only financial parameters, but technical and plant operational ratios. A combination of operational, technical and financial parameters is chosen and the technique of multiple discriminant analysis (refer Chapter 5) is used to develop the discriminant model which can best discriminate a sick from healthy unit in an industry group. Discriminant models are built for each of the industries separately. The choice of possible

ratios, depending upon the availability of the data, has been increased as each ratio in its own way may not be a strong discriminator initially, but the cumulative effect of several can be. Each financial and non-financial ratio is tested for its sensitivity and '*F*' tests are made. Contributions of each parameter are estimated. Finally, the following variables were chosen as significant predictor variables to be used in the discriminant model:

X_1=Net Worth/Total Assets
X_2=Net Block/Net Worth
X_3=Net Profit/Total Assets
X_4=Total Liabilities/Net Worth
X_5=Current Assets/Current Liabilities
X_6=Capacity Utilisation Ratio
X_7=Plant Utilisation Ratio
X_8=Net Sales/Total Assets
X_9=Gross Profit/Net Sales
X_{10}=Operating Profit/Net Sales
X_{11}=Net Profit/Net Sales

A computer programme was written using MDA technique. A computer model has been used to determine the values of coefficients for sick and healthy units by using data for at least five years of a number of units in each group of industries. Equations have been developed for discriminant score '*Z*' for sick and healthy units separately in a single industrial group. The coefficients have been standardised and a difference equation obtained which gets over the necessity of a cut off point. Positive values of '*Z*' score in case of a new unit whose variables may be available will indicate it is healthy and negative values, it is sick. The model has been tested for the historical data of available units and also of totally new units when declared sick.

6.9.3 Case of homogeneous group of companies

The value of discriminant score '*Z*' has been developed for nine industrial groups separately. The nine industrial groups studied were sugar, paper, textile, cement, electricals, engineering, chemicals, jute and steel. In the MDA model of

industrial groups, some or all of the variables already listed above have been used depending upon the availability and consistency of the data for the sick and healthy units and their contribution to discriminant score 'Z'. The data of best 15 to 20 units was selected in each group for which the historical background was available over a period of six years and sick and healthy stages were identifiable. When sick and healthy units were put on a continuum scale in the computer model, the misclassification error was found to be zero. Computer results of misclassification errors and 'Z' equations are shown below in respect of each case.

(1) **Case of Paper Industry**: Observations over 5 year period of 15 sick and 15 healthy paper units were collected. Only six predictor variables were used in this case. The group mean differences of the contributing ratios and their percentage contribution to the best 'Z' score are given in Table 6.25.

TABLE 6.25: **Significant parameters (standardised values) (paper industry)**

Significant ratios	Paper	
	Group mean difference	% contribution
X_1	1.21223	2.3
X_2	1.63448	48.1
X_3	0.16415	19.1
X_4	—	2.2
X_5	1.60906	2.2
X_6	1.62216	26.1

The 'Z' equation obtained for paper industry is given as follows:

$$Z = 0.44345X_1 + 0.42551X_2 + 9.23696X_3 - 3.65928X_4 + 0.43364X_5 + 5.01243X_6 + 0.00003$$

(2) **Evaluation of classification function for each observation**: The computer model permitted scanning of each observation and determining the probability associated with largest discriminant function. The results are given in Table 6.26.

TABLE 6.26: **For the best discriminant function**

No. of observation	Sick unit probability	Healthy unit probability
1	0.99864	1.00000
2	1.00000	1.00000
3	1.000C0	1.000.0
4	0.99316	0.99999
5	1.00000	0.99998
6	1.00000	0.99984
7	0.93049	0.99999
8	0.99979	1.00000
9	0.99999	1.0:000
10	1.00000	1.00000
11	1.0)C00	1.00000
12	1.00000	1.00000
13	1.00000	0.99965
14	0.99998	0.86879
14	0.99984	0.99959

Note: The best discriminant function is one for which the misclassification error is zero.

(3) **Case of Sugar Industry**: The data for sugar industry was collected over a longer period and there were 40 observations—20 sick and 20 healthy units. Seven predictor variables were used including 5 financial ratios, one capacity utilisation ratio and one plant utilisation ratio. The significant parameters and their contribution are given in Table 6.27.

TABLE 6.27: **Significant parameters (standardised values) (sugar industry)**

Significant ratios	Sugar	
	Group mean difference	% contribution
X_1	1.57747	27.0
X_2	1.51875	11.6
X_3	0.74619	4.7
X_5	0.67845	11.6
X_6	0.28518	9.2
X_7	0.67870	32.8

'Z' equation obtained for sugar industry is given as follows:

$$Z=4.98575X_1-0.57694X_2+2.15407X_3-0.85760X_4 -2.14385X_5-1.69167X_6+6.04837X_7-0.00026$$

(4) **Evaluation of classification function for each observation**: Data for both sick and healthy units spread over a period of 5 years was carefully scanned for consistency. The computer model permitted scanning of all the 40 observations and determining the probability associated with the largest discriminant function. The result for this scanning is given in Table 6.28.

TABLE 6.28: **For the best discriminant function**

No. of observation	Sick unit probability	Healthy unit probability
1	0.99925	0.86361
2	0.99988	0.96181
3	0.99988	0.96585
4	1.00000	0.99996
5	1.00000	0.99958
6	0.90082	0.94859
7	0.95300	0.99609
8	0.98145	0.98665
9	0.89190	0.96674
10	0.99998	0.99721
11	0.55642	0.99221
12	0.81843	0.99824
13	0.89570	0.99789
14	0.62707	0.99787
15	0.97348	0.99966
16	0.97914	0.99988
17	0.91629	0.99928
18	0.99868	0.99719
19	0.99952	0.99377
20	0.99985	0.99455

Note ; The misclassification ratio is zero.

(5) **Case of Textile Industry**: The 'Z' score of textile industry is given below. In the textile group technical and operational parameters were not found to be consistent and reliable. Only financial ratios were considered significant

ratios and their contribution to the group mean difference is given in Table 6.29.

TABLE 6.29: **Significant parameters (standardised values) (textile industries)**

Significant ratios	Textile Group mean difference	% contribution
X_4	−0.53404	10.0
X_8	−1.55507	16.8
X_9	1.43412	7.0
X_{10}	1.41818	29.8
X_{11}	1.16024	26.2

'Z' equation obtained for textile industry is given as follows:

$$Z = 0.73665X_1 - 0.48324X_2 + 1.83649X_3 + 4.41901X_4 + 1.47705X_5 - 5.39149X_8 + 3.09541X_9 + 13.12446X_{10} + 11.54411X_{11} - 0.19117$$

(6) **Validation of historical data**: In the textile group 2 units were randomly selected and the ratios listed above were calculated for them. These are given in Table 6.30 below with the calculated value of 'Z' score from the equation given for the textile group. In all these cases the negative scores indicated the contribution made towards the sickness of the industry.

TABLE 6.30: **'Z' Score for textile group**

Ratios	Unit No. 1 1978	Unit No. 1 1979	Unit No. 1 1980	Unit No. 2 1978	Unit No. 2 1979	Unit No. 2 1980
X_1	−1.53	−1.31	−1.51	−0.13	−0.07	−0.06
X_2	−0.12	−0.24	−0.27	−3.81	−6.48	−8.43
X_3	−0.56	−0.19	−0.15	−0.01	0.02	0.01
X_4	−1.65	−1.76	−1.66	−8.81	−16.13	−18.44
X_5	0.32	9.32	0.26	0.78	0.83	0.73
X_8	2.18	1.89	1.87	1.11	1.23	0.91
X_9	−0.14	−0.08	−0.03	0.06	0.05	0.05
X_{10}	−0.27	−0.13	−0.10	−0.05	−0.05	−0 06
X_{11}	−0.26	−0.10	−0.08	−0.01	0.02	0.01
Calculated 'Z' Score	−25.10185	−28.50385	−23.25278	−1.775872	−4.51894	−4.05193

6.9.4 MDA model for other industrial groups

Data was collected for six other industrial groups from the publications of Bombay Stock Exchange. These groups were engineering, jute, cement, electrical machinery, chemicals and steel. Data for several years of distinctly identifiable sick and healthy units was carefully screened for consistency and use in the MDA Model. However, the values of the predictor ratios have not been standardised as in the previous three cases. The 'Z' score has been worked out for each group and the results are given below:

(*a*) *Engineering Group of Industries*

$$Z=-0.027X_1+0.029X_2+0.009X_3-0.015X_4+0.28X_5-27.36$$

(*b*) *Jute Group of Industries*

$$\begin{aligned}Z=106.0926X_1+3.28912X_2-1.17725X_3-56.90491X_4\\+13.83340X_5+107.98044X_6+554.57300X_7+0.91805X_8\\-313.78394X_9-0.68446\end{aligned}$$

(*c*) *Cement Group of Industries*

$$\begin{aligned}Z=2.22668X_1-1.25901X_2+0.47247X_3+1.65317X_4\\+3.67195X_5+7.97531X_6+3.40517X_7-15.84832X_8\\+24.88625X_9-6.56549\end{aligned}$$

(*d*) *Electrical Machinery Group of Industries*

$$\begin{aligned}Z=27.39612X_1+3.15156X_2-1.23843X_3+27.88280X_4\\-7.86577X_5+8.02935X_6+137.15733X_7-130.36533X_8\\+36.92044X_9-29.83594\end{aligned}$$

(*e*) *Chemical Group of Industries*

$$\begin{aligned}Z=26.21385X_1-0.09739X_2+25.71431X_3+0.12588X_4\\-6.17478X_5+12.64996X_8+79.49493X_9-15.51630X_{10}\\-29.03839X_{11}-27.54945\end{aligned}$$

(*f*) *Steel Group of Industries*

$$\begin{aligned}Z=-10.39435X_1-3.16780X_2+59.13895X_3+2.36225X_4\\+18.97404X_5+1.95261X_8-30.67305X_9+23.62997X_{10}\\-20.56725X_{11}-14.97050\end{aligned}$$

6.9.5 Predictive accuracy of englarged MDA model

The model has been successfully used to predict sickness in 9 industrial groups comprising of over 20 units each. The prediction reliability has been found to be 95 per cent. The equations developed for '*Z*' score for different industrial groups are very sensitive. These have been validated taking the historical data of new units from different industrial groups. In respect of paper and sugar industries, the data for the units declared sick in 1980 was taken from the financial institutions. Units were declared sick because of non-payment of interest or principal or both for the first time. '*Z*' score calculations indicated that the units had become sick much earlier i.e. in 1978-79 as shown in Table 6.31.

TABLE 6.31: **Predictive accuracy of the enlarged MDA model**

Unit	Amount outstanding (in lakhs)	Declared sick in	State of health '*Z*' (—ve)
Sugar	32.49	1980	1978 Sick
			1979 Sick
			1980 Sick
Paper	38.33	1980	1978 Sick
			1979 Sick
			1980 Sick

The units both in Sugar and Paper had become sick 2 years earlier but were paying the instalments to the financial institutions by borrowing money till the sickness became so grave that defaults started. Thus the '*Z*' score method as developed above is a positive indicator of the state of health of industrial units. The ability of the model to scan historical data and in determining the onset of sickness is very high. It has been possible to investigate the lapses that have occurred in various units, due to poor or mismanagement. Predictions can also be made a year or six months in advance with high accuracy by studying the trends of the selected variables both financial and operational. Once the health of units is estimated, appropriate managerial actions can be initiated to stem further sickness in the industry.

7

MANAGEMENT OF WORKING CAPITAL

7.0 Introduction

The two crucial determinants of corporate health—liquidity and profitability—are in part influenced by the way working capital is managed. And, therefore, it is important for the management to pay particular attention to the planning and control of working capital.

7.1 Concepts of Working Capital

There are two general concepts of working capital—gross and net. The 'gross working capital' also known as current capital or circulating capital refers to the sum total of firm's investment in current assets. Current assets are the assets which, in the ordinary course of business, can be converted into cash within an accounting year or within the normal operating cycle of the business. These include cash, marketable securities, receivables and inventories. The 'net working capital' at any point is the difference between current assets and current liabilities at that point. Current liabilities are those liabilities which are expected to fall due or mature for payment within a year. These include creditors, bills payable, bank overdraft and outstanding expenses. These represent a short-term source of funds.

The gross and net working capital concepts present two distinct and important facets of working capital management. The gross working capital is a quantitative definition that focusses attention on the level of current assets for a given activity. It focusses attention on two aspects of current assets management: (*i*) determining the level of investment in

current assets and (*ii*) financing of current assets. The first should determine the optimum investment—neither excessive nor inadequate—in current assets. Because the excessive investment in current assets impairs the firm's profitability, while inadequate working capital can be a threat to its solvency. Second aspect points out the sources of financing the current assets.

The net working capital is a qualitative concept which highlights the character of sources from which the funds have been obtained to support the excess of current assets over current liabilities. It indicates the liquidity position of the firm and the extent of financing the working capital needed by permanent sources of funds.

There is no standard and precise way to determine the exact amount of gross or net working capital and their financing for each firm, because each firm has its own constraints and plans of activities. Hence, data and problems of each firm should be identified and analysed to determine the level and financing mix of working capital.

7.2 The Need for Working Capital

There is hardly any business unit which does not require any amount of working capital. However, the amount required for working capital by the firms differs from each other. As we know, sufficient profits should be generated from the business operations in order to maximise shareholders' wealth. Earning a steady and sufficient amount of profit depends upon a successful sales programme which requires investment in current assets. Current assets needed due to conversion of sales into cash is not instantaneous. There is always an operating cycle involved in the conversion of sales into cash. The continuing flow from cash to suppliers, to inventory, to accounts receivable and back into cash is called the operating cycle [106]. The operating cycle is a continuous process and its pattern has a bearing on the nature of the business. The service and financial firms have the shortest operating cycle as shown in Fig. 7.1. A trading unit has a rather extended operating cycle as shown in Fig. 7.2.

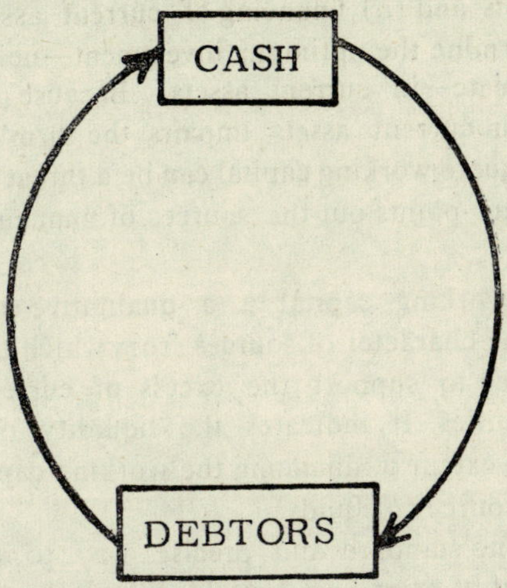

Fig. 7.1 **Operating cycle of service and financial firms**

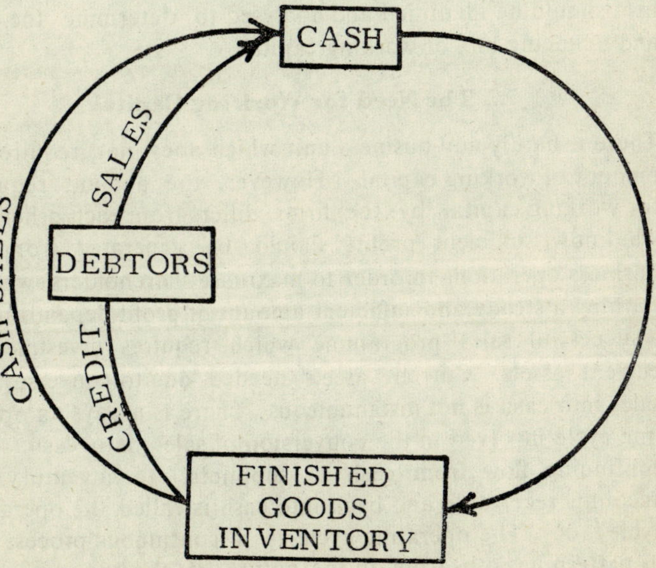

Fig. 7.2 **Operating cycie of a trading unit**

The manufacturing concern involves more stages resulting in a longer operating cycle as shown in Fig. 7.3.

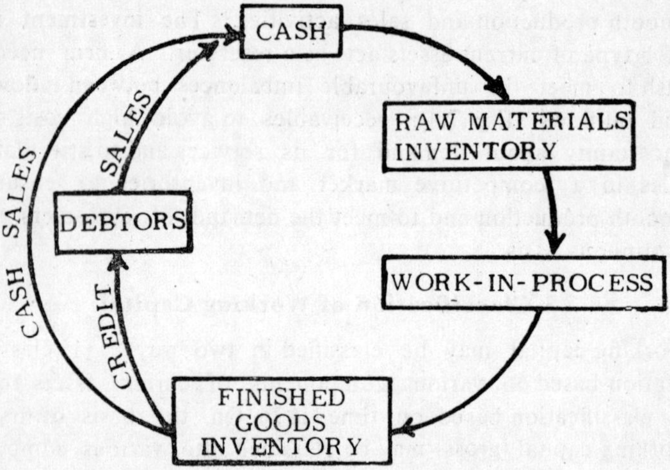

Fig. 7.3 **Operating cycle of a manufacturing unit**

Since the production and sales flows are not instantaneous and the perfect matching between cash inflows and outflows is not feasible (Fig. 7.4), it becomes necessary for a firm to

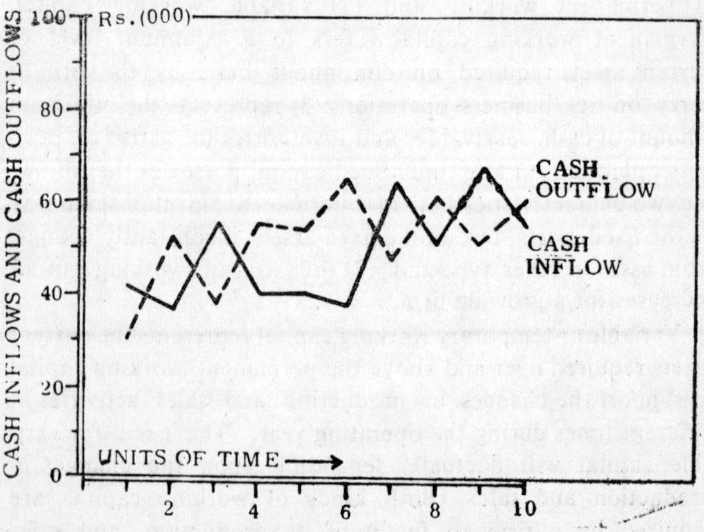

Fig, 7.4 **Cash infiows and cash outflows**

invest an adequate amount of funds in current assets for smooth production and sales activities. The investment in each type of current assets acts as a reservoir. A firm needs cash to meet the unfavourable imbalances between inflows and outflows (Fig. 7.4); receivables to avoid high costs of uncertainty about demand for its services and to stimulate sales in a competitive market and inventories to ensure smooth production and to meet the demand of customers on continuous basis.

7.3 Classification of Working Capital

Working capital may be classified in two ways: (1) classification based on various components of current assets and (2) classification based on time [107]. On the basis of first, working capital (gross) may be classified into various components of current assets such as cash, marketable securities, receivables and inventories. This classification is important for a financial manager because a careful planning and control of cash, receivables and inventories is required to ensure the firm's liquidity and profitability.

Using time as a basis, working capital may be classified as (1) permanent working and (2) variable working capital. Permanent working capital refers to a minimum level of current assets required on continuous basis by the firm to carry on its business operations. It represents the minimum amount of cash, receivables and inventories to carry on business operations at any time. Such capital possesses the following two characteristics: (1) it is permanent in the same way as the fixed assets, but unlike fixed assets, it constantly changes from asset to other type and (2) the size of working capital increases for a growing firm.

Variable or temporary working capital represents the current assets required over and above the permanent working capital to support the changes in production and sales activities at different times during the operating year. The need for variable capital will fluctuate depending upon the changes in production and sales. Both kinds of working capital are required by a firm to facilitate its production and sales

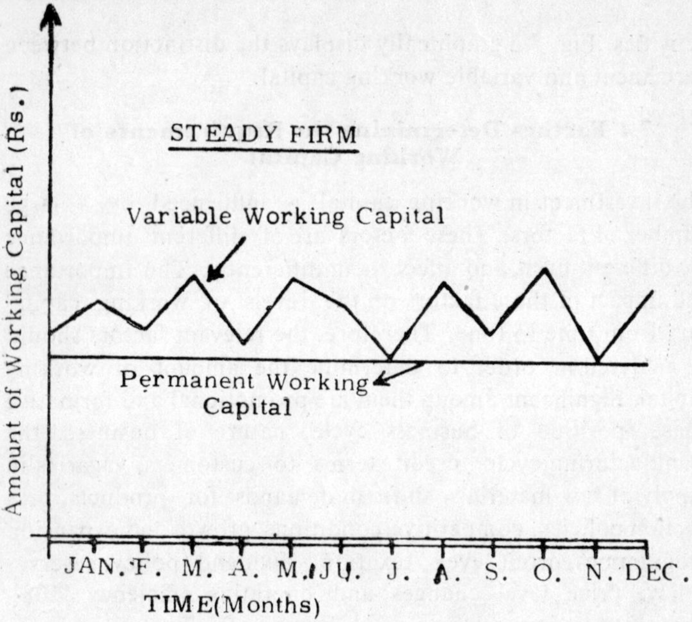

Fig. 7.5 **(a) : Permanent and variable working capital**

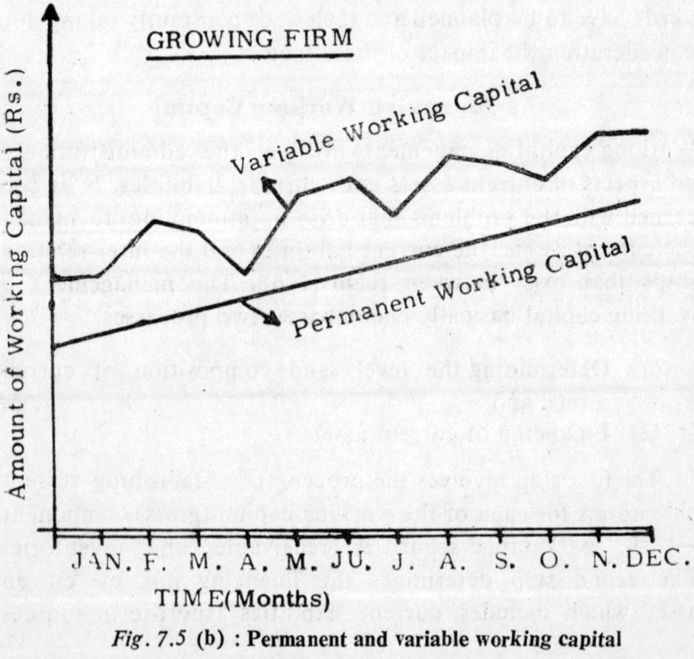

Fig. 7.5 **(b) : Permanent and variable working capital**

activities. Fig. 7.5 graphically displays the distinction between permanent and variable working capital.

7.4 Factors Determining the Requirements of Working Capital

The investment in working capital is influenced by a large number of factors. These factors are of different importance for different firms and affect them differently. The importance and impact of these factors on the levels of working capital vary from time to time. Therefore, the relevant factors should be analysed in order to determine the amount of working capital. Significant among them are promotional and formative phase, position of business cycle, nature of business, the manufacturing cycle, credit terms to customers, vagaries in supply of raw materials, shifts in demands for products, production policies, competitive conditions, growth and expansion programmes, profit levels, taxation, dividend policy, reserves policy, price level changes and operating efficiency [108]. These factors exert their varied degrees of influence on working capital requirements over time. Thus, the working capital needs have to be planned and reviewed constantly taking into consideration the impact of these factors.

7.5 Managing Working Capital

Working capital management involves the administration of all aspects of current assets and current liabilities. It is concerned with the problems that arise in attempting to manage the current assets, the current liabilities and the inter-relationships that exist between them [106]. The management of working capital basically encompasses two processes:

(1) Determining the levels and composition of current assets; and
(2) Financing of current assets.

The first step involves the process of establishing acceptable norms for each of the working capital (gross) components —cash, marketable securities, receivables and inventories. The second step determines the financing mix of current assets which includes current liabilities (short-term sources)

and long-term sources. The basic purpose of working capital management is to develop the effective policies for each of the components of current assets and their financing so that a satisfactory level of working capital is maintained and its twin objectives—liquidity and profitability—is ensured.

Working capital management has many aspects which make it an important function of the financial manager [109]. First, it is related to the day-to-day operations of the firm and hence consumes much of the financial manager's time and involves personnel from several management areas. For example, inventory management involves the managers of purchasing, production and sales areas of management. Secondly, over one-half of a firm's total investment in assets is usually tied up by the investment in current assets. In India, current assets constituted 62 per cent of total net assets in 1975-76 in a sample of 1650 companies [110]. Hence, it required a special attention of the financial manager on a continuing basis. Third, the current assets are very sensitive to the sales of the firm. The increase in sales requires more investment in inventories and receivables. The increased demand for investment in current assets creates a need for financing the working capital.

The acceptable norms of investment for each of the components of working capital should be determined. For this purpose, the management of various components of working capital—cash, receivables and inventories—is discussed separately, though effective management of one component is not possible without simultaneous of others.

7.6 Cash Management

The term cash refers to coins, currency, generally acceptable equivalent of cash such as cheques, drafts and demand deposits in banks, and near cash assets such as marketable securities and time deposits in banks. The main characteristics of near cash assets is that they are readily converted into cash.

Cash is the basic input for keeping the business running on continous basis and also the ultimate output of the firm's operations. Therefore, a satisfactory level of cash should be kept on a continuing basis, as the paucity of cash will disrupt the

business and excessive cash will remain idle contributing nothing towards firm's profitability, because cash as an asset has no earning power. The objectives of cash management should be to maintain adequate cash position to meet the cash disbursement needs and to invest the excess cash in profitability.

7.6.1 Motives for holding cash

Keynes (111) has identified three motives for holding cash: (*a*) the transactions motive, (*b*) the precautionary motive, and (*c*) the speculative motive. The transactions motive for holding cash is to enable the firm to meet the normal cash needs of the business such as payments for purchases, wages, operating expenses, taxes and dividends. The precautionary motive for holding cash is the desire to keep cash to meet any unexpected contingencies. The size of cash held under precautionary motive will depend upon the predictability of cash inflows and outflows. The cash for speculations is held in order to take advantage of profitable opportunities that may arise due to changes in security prices and interest rates. This is not a common feature of corporate financial management and hence the companies except investment and finance companies, normally do not engage in speculations. Generally, the cash is held only for transactions and precautionary motives.

7.6.2 Planning and control of cash

The quantum of cash held for transaction and precautionary motives depends upon a variety of factors. Some of the significant factors are the credit position of the firm, status of firm's receivables and inventory accounts, nature of the business, the amount of sales in relation to assets, the expected net cash flows, the maturity schedules of firm's liabilities and management's attitude towards risk. All these factors should be analysed simultaneously in determining the level of cash to be held by the firm.

The process of cash control involves four steps:

(*a*) Projecting cash flows—inflows and outflows—for a particular period such as a day, week, month, quarter or

year. This is known as cash planning.

(*b*) Managing the cash inflows and outflows.

(*c*) Determining the appropriate level of cash balances.

(*d*) Investing the excess cash in marketable securities.

(*a*) **Cash planning**: Cash planning refers to a projected cash statement from a forecast of expected cash inflows and outflows for a given period. It is a technique to plan for and control the use of cash. It helps in projecting the cash flows and hence cash surplus which reduces firm's profitability and cash deficits which can cause the firm's sickness.

Cash Budget may be used to plan for and control the cash inflows and outflows. A cash budget is a summary statement of the expected cash inflows and outflows of the firm over a period of time. Cash budget may be prepared for any period of time say daily, weekly, or monthly. It provides information to the financial manager about the timing and amount of cash flows over the given period that assists him to determine the future cash needs of the firm, plan for financing these needs, and exercise control over the cash of the firm [112].

There are two methods of preparing cash budgets. These are (1) the receipts and disbursements methods and (2) the adjusted net income method. The first method involves the forecasting for each item of receipts and payment for a given period. The adjusted net income method involves the process of projecting the working capital flows.

(*b*) **Managing cash inflows and outflows**: Once the expected cash inflows and outflows are established, a comparison should be made between the projected cash flows and actual cash flows in order to identify the deviations and to take necessary follow up action. The effectiveness of such corrective measures will depend upon a good reporting system that highlights such deviations in time. Periodic cash reports—daily, weekly, monthly—may be used to have a running comparison between the projected and actual cash flows. This will help to decide whether, when and to what extent financial plans are to be adjusted in the light of deviations between projected and actual cash flows.

The financial manager should make every effort to speed up the cash collections and to delay the cash disbursements without impairing the credit standing of the firm. To accelerate cash collections, the time gap at following stages of cash flow stream should be minimised:

(1) The time gap between the receipt of the customer's order and the invoicing of the supply to the customers;
(2) The time gap between billing and collection of dues;
(3) The time lag between the collection of cheques and Their conversion into spendable cash.

Various techniques may be used to speed up the cash collections. Some of the important ones are—(*a*) the lock-box system and (*b*) concentration banking system or decentralised collection procedure. In a lock-box system, a number of collection centres are established depending upon the volume of remittances. At each centre, a post office box is hired and customers are instructed to remit payment to the post office box. The local bank is authorised to collect the remittances from the lock-box. The local bank picks up the cheques daily or even more at regular times and deposits in the firm's account. The bank prepares a detailed statement of such collections and sends it to the firm. The lock-box system reduces the time lag between the receipt of cheques and their deposit in the bank.

In a concentration banking system, the collection of cheque is made through a number of collection centres established by the firm. The collection centres deposit the collected cheques in their local bank accounts. Funds above a pre-determined minimum level are transferred to the concentration bank each day. A concentration bank is one with which the firm has a major account—usually a disbursement account [112]. This system reduces the time lag between the mailing of cheques and collecting the cash for the firm's use.

(*c*) **Determining the appropriate level of cash**: The firm should keep cash at optimum level. The optimum level should be determined by a trade-off between the transactions cost of keeping a too small cash balance and

opportunity costs of the excess cash balance as shown in Fig. 7.6.

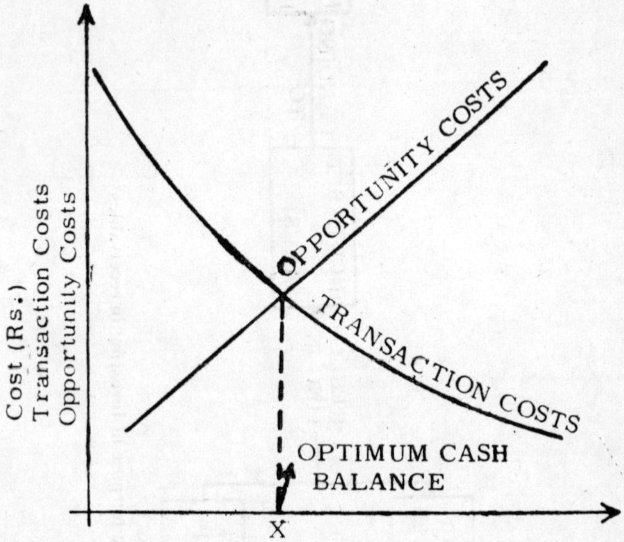

Fig. 7.6 **Optimum cash balance**

(*d*) **Investing the excess cash in marketable securities**: The firm should have the excess cash in various types of marketable securities. The selection of securities should be made on the basis of the three basic features of security: risk of default, marketability and maturity.

In brief, the designing and implementation of overall cash control system calls for the effective cash reporting and information system which has to be constantly reviewed and modified to meet the new and changing requirements.

7.7 Receivables Management

The term receivables represents the amount of debt owed to the firm as a result of the sale of goods or services. Firms make sales of goods or services to the customers on credit and collect the bills in near future. This type of credit is called trade credit and results only from credit sales of goods or

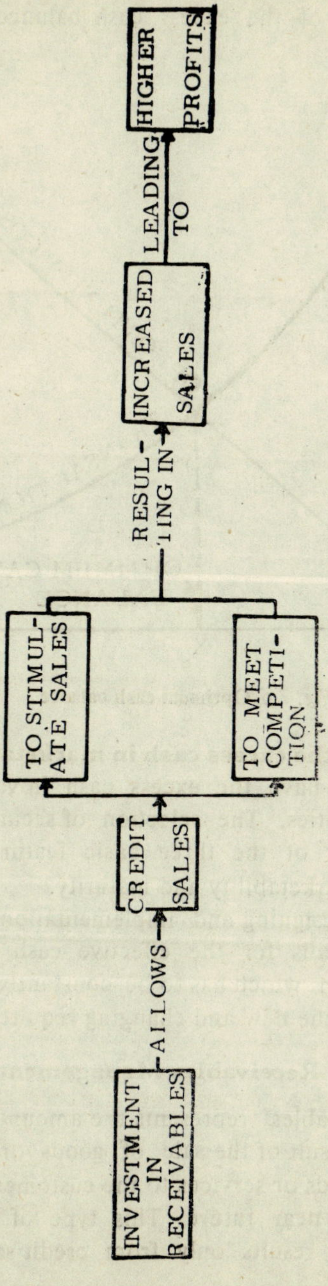

Fig. 7.7 **Flowc hart showing the purpose of investing in receivables**

services. The trade credit creates receivables to be collected in the near future by the firm. Firms invest in receivables (grant credit sales) in order to stimulate sales in a competitive market and hence to generate higher profit. The purpose of maintaining receivables is illustrated in Fig. 7.7. The level of investment in receivables is determined by the volume of credit sales and the average collection period. Increase in receivables increases sales and profits, but it involves risk and cost also. Therefore, receivables should be managed effectively. The objective of receivables management should be 'to promote sales and profits until that point is reached where the return on investment in further funding of receivables is less than the cost of funds raised to finance that additional credit' [113]. The firm should maintain an optimum investment in receivables (Fig. 7.8) which is determined by a trade off between costs

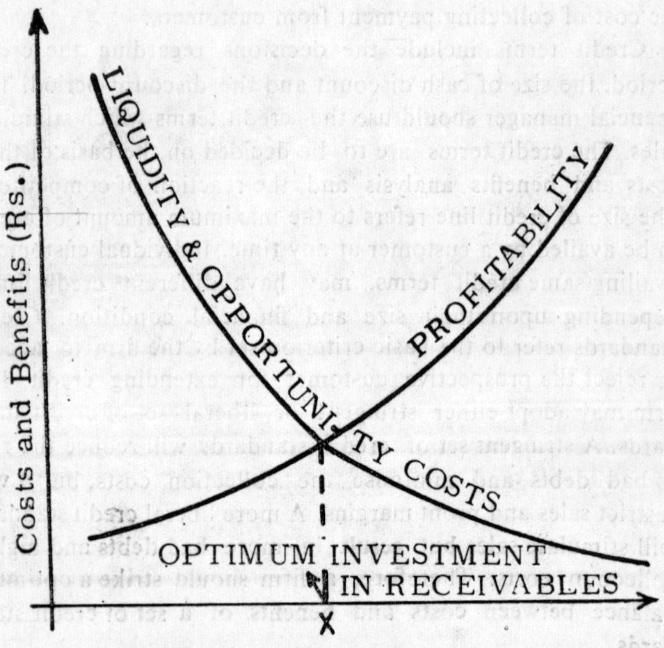

Fig. 7.8 **Optimum Investment in Receivables**

and benefits of granting sales. The costs include bad debt losses, collection costs, cash discounts and opportunity costs.

7.7.1 Aspects of receivables management

Effective planning and control of receivables requires the determination of credit policies regarding (*i*) extension of credit (*ii*) collection of receivables from customers and (*iii*) monitoring and controlling the level of receivables.

(*i*) **Credit extension policies**: Credit extension policies guide the financial manager to decide the customers to be granted credit, the terms of payment on such credit and the amount of credit. Credit extension policies require decision concerning (*a*) credit terms, (*b*) the size of the credit line, and (*c*) the credit standards. These decisions much depend upon the firm's level of sales and receivables, the resulting cost of financing the investment in receivables, bad debt losses and the cost of collecting payment from customers.

Credit terms include the decisions regarding the credit period, the size of cash discount and the discount period. The financial manager should use the credit terms which stimulate sales. The credit terms are to be decided on the basis of their costs and benefits analysis and the reaction of competitors. The size of credit line refers to the maximum amount of credit to be availed by a customer at any time. Individual customers, availing same credit terms, may have different credit limits depending upon their size and financial condition. Credit standards refer to the basic criterion set by the firm to accept or reject the prospective customer for extending credit. The firm may adopt either stringent or liberal set of credit standards. A stringent set of credit standards will reduce the risk of bad debts and minimise the collection costs, but it will restrict sales and profit margins. A more liberal credit standard will stimulate sales but result in more bad debts and higher collection costs. Therefore, a firm should strike a optimum balance between costs and benefits of a set of credit standards.

The objective as well as subjective information relating to customers should be used in extending credit to them. The objective information relating to a customer is:

(*i*) Customer's record of adhering to credit terms of other suppliers and commercial banks.
(*ii*) Experience of key personnel.
(*iii*) Growth rate of the business.
(*iv*) Time length of the business.
(*v*) Financial ratios measuring liquidity, degree of financial leverage and profitability.

Apart from the above, some subjective information, though difficult to measure, should also be used by the firm while extending credit. The subjective information is the applicant's capacity to pay, the willingness to pay and general economic conditions. The above information may be collected from the various sources such as financial statements, trade references, bank references and credit bureau reports.

(*ii*) **Credit collection policies**: Credit collection policies refer to the procedures used to encourage customers to pay their bills in time. The collection policies should accelerate the collections especially from slow payers and minimise the bad debt losses. The collection process includes several steps such as polite letters, strong worded letters, telephone, telegrams, personal visit by the firm's representative and finally legal action if necessary. But the firm should be very cautious in taking the above steps, because a stringent collection policy may result in loss of permanent business, while a lenient collection policy will increase receivables and bad debt losses. Hence the collection policies should be tailored in the light of needs and activities of individual customer.

(*iii*) **Monitoring and controlling the level of receivables**: The credit monitoring and control process attempts to detect the deviations between the actual and optimum level of receivables and to take corrective measures in time. It involves the process of appraising the effectiveness of credit granting and credit collection policies. Various measures may be used to monitor the level of receivables. These are (*i*) the average collection period (*ii*) the ageing schedule to accounts receivables and (*iii*) the delinquency ratio. Once the deviations are detected, the cause or causes of devia-

tions are to be identified in order to take corrective actions depending upon the individual case.

7.8 Inventory Management

The term inventory refers to the goods held for eventual resale by the firm. It refers to the stocks of the product manufactured by a company for sale and the components that make up the product. Inventories of a manufacturing company are comprised of raw materials, work-in-process, and finished goods. Raw materials are those basic input goods that have not yet been committed to production. Work-in-process includes those materials that have been committed to the production process but have not been completed. Finished goods are completed products ready for sale. The stocks of raw materials and work-in-process are maintained to facilitate efficient and smooth production and stock of finished goods is required to ensure smooth marketing operations.

7.8.1 Benefits and costs of holding inventories

Holding inventories—raw materials, work-in-process and finished goods—enable the firm to separate the activities of purchasing, producing and selling (Fig. 7.9). The separation of these functions results in a number of benefits to the firm such as avoiding losses of sales, gaining quantity discounts, reducing order costs and achieving efficient production runs.

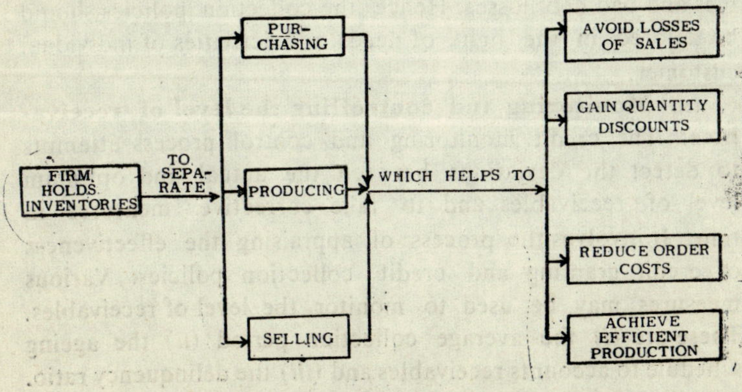

Fig. 7.9 **Benefits of holding inventoreis**

But, on the other hand, holding inventory exposes the firm to a number of risks and costs. The costs associated with inventories are (*a*) materials costs e.g. cost of purchasing the goods plus transportation and handling; (*b*) ordering costs e.g. cost of purchase order forms, the clerical and order processing cost in the purchase department, the postage and stationery costs, the costs of receiving and inspection of goods; (*c*) carrying costs e.g. storage costs, insurance, damage and theft, obsolescence and spoilage; (*d*) cost of funds tied up in inventory; and (*e*) stock out costs. The objective of inventory management should be to minimise the total inventory cost. The advantages of carrying inventories must be weighted against its costs in order to determine the optimum level of inventory.

7.8.2 **Techniques of inventory management**

The objective of inventory management is to achieve maximum efficiency in production and sales operations with the least investment in inventory. To achieve this, there are various techniques which may be applied for effective inventory control. The techniques applied for effective inventory control are:

(*i*) ABC Analysis or Control by Importance and Exception.
(*ii*) Economic Order Quantity (EOQ) System.
(*iii*) Stock Level System i.e. determining the levels of Safety Stock, Re-order point and maximum inventory.
(*iv*) Perpetual Inventory System which includes quantitative perpetual inventory, quantitative cum valued perpetual inventory and physical perpetual inventory system.
(*v*) Establishment of system of budgets.
(*vi*) Review of slow and non-moving items.
(*vii*) Use of inventory control ratios e.g. Inventory turnover ratio (Average cost of goods sold/Average total inventories at cost), raw materials turnover ratio (cost of raw materials consumed/Average raw materials inventory at cost), Work-in-process turnover ratio

(cost of manufacture/Average work-in-process inventory at cost), Finished goods turnover ratio (cost of goods sold/Average finished goods inventory at cost), Slow moving stores/Total inventory.

The above mentioned techniques of inventory management are very useful in determining the right balance between over investment and under investment in inventories and thus achieving maximum efficiency in production and sales with minimum investment in inventories. Many sophisticated techniques are also available to handle inventory management problems more efficiently and effectively and the improvement is still continuing [114].

7.9 Determinants of Effective Working Capital Management

The management of working capital is one of the most important factors that influence decisions taken by the commercial banks, financial institutions, suppliers of commodities, Government agencies, shareholders and investors in dealing with the firm. They look into the effectiveness of working capital management by using several financial ratios based on published annual reports of firms and on the basis of their individual perceptions.

7.9.1 Ratios used in practice

Some of the most commonly used financial ratios are given in Table 7.1 [115]. Such analysis is generally based on certain norms established in general or in relation to a specific industry. For example, a current ratio exceeding 2 : 1 is considered an indicative of effective working capital management. The Tandon Committee [116] has also suggested certain norms for fifteen industries relating to inventories and receivables which are to be followed by commercial banks in granting working capital credit to the borrowing companies. Although the committee has suggested norms for fifteen industries only, yet it was emphasised that industries not covered should also follow the suggested norms and the commercial banks should

TABLE 7.1: **Financial ratios used by twelve large banks and two financial institutions**

Ratio	Number of banks and financial institutions using a ratio
Current Assets/Current Liabilities	14
Debt/Equity	14
Finished Goods Inventory/Sales	9
Receivables/Sales	9
Raw Materials Inventory/Raw Materials Consumption	9
Total Inventory/Sales	6
Retained Profit/Profit after tax	5
Borrowings/Total Liabilities	5
Sundry Creditors/Purchases	5
Profit after tax/Net worth	4
Profit after tax/Sale	4
Sales/Total Assets	4
Raw Materials Inventory/Sales	2
Debt/Sales	1

keep in view the purpose and spirit behind these norms in extending working capital credit facilities. However, the validity of such norms has been questioned from time to time because these norms may be substantially different for different firms on account of various factors affecting working capital requirements and differences in accounting practices relating to the valuation of assets and measurement of profits e.g. depreciation practices, valuation of inventories etc. A more substantive problem relates to the difficulty in interpreting multiple indicators providing contradictory signals and directions (refer Chapter 5).

7.9.2 Judgemental approach

Appraising the effectiveness of working capital management purely based on judgemental approach or perceptious is also likely to have lesser validity as there is evidence to believe that the perceptions of individuals are influenced by their biases. Bhattacharyya [115] conducted a study to test the consistency between the perceptions of individuals at two

different points of time. The study was based on a sample of ten companies and five external financial analysis. Financial analysts were asked to classify each company into either effective or not effective in working capital management on the basis of published annual reports. A few days later, the annual reports of the same companies were given to the same financial analysts, without disclosing the identity of the companies, to classify them into either effective or not effective in the management of working capital. The results of the study are shown in Table 7.2 which clearly reveals that the perceptions of financial analysts at two stages vary quite considerably. It is clear from Table 7.2 that decisions relating to effectiveness in the management of working capital based on perceptions cannot be reliable on account of lack of consistency between the perceptions of individuals at two different points of time.

7.9.3 Development of MDA model

Keeping the above in view, it has been realised to design a model based on quantitative methods to determine the effectiveness of working capital management so that the current operational practices in formulating the policies of working capital management and appraising the credit worthiness in granting capital loans may be improved. The objective of the study was to determine the determinants of effective working management. A sample of 78 companies—39 sick companies and 39 non-sick companies—was taken (refer Chapter 5) and the statistical techniques known as Factor Analysis and Multiple Discriminant Analysis (MDA) were applied (refer Chapter 5) using financial ratios as variables, to classify the companies in terms of their effective or ineffective working capital management. The study is based on the assumption that the working capital management of sick companies is not effective, as there is an empirical evidence (refer Chapter 2) that the shortage of working capital funds is one of the most important factors causing sickness in companies.

A discriminant function consisting of four variables has been arrived at as the best profile of ratios (for detail refer

TABLE 7.2: **Perceptions of five financial analysts about the effectiveness of working capital management in ten companies**

Companies	External Financial Analysts					No. of Analysts identifying the company as effective/not effective			
	1	2	3	4	5	State I		State II	
						effective	Not effective	effective	Not effective
A	(1, 0)	(1, 1)	(1, 1)	(1, 0)	(0, 0)	4	1	2	3
B	(1, 1)	(1, 1)	(1, 1)	(0, 1)	(0, 0)	3	2	4	1
C	(1, 0)	(1, 0)	(1, 0)	(0, 1)	(0, 0)	3	2	1	4
D	(1, 1)	(0, 0)	(1, 1)	(1, 1)	(0, 1)	3	2	4	1
E	(1, 1)	(0, 1)	(0, 1)	(1, 0)	(1, 1)	3	2	4	1
F	(1, 0)	(0, 0)	(0, 0)	(0, 0)	(1, 1)	2	3	1	4
G	(1, 1)	(1, 0)	(1, 1)	(1, 1)	(0, 1)	4	1	4	1
H	(1, 0)	(0, 0)	(0, 1)	(1, 1)	(0, 1)	2	3	3	2
I	(0, 1)	(1, 0)	(0, 0)	(0, 0)	(1, 1)	2	3	2	3
J	(0, 0)	(0, 1)	(0, 0)	(1, 0)	(0, 1)	1	4	2	3
Total number of times out of ten the perceptions differ in two stages	5	5	3	5	4				

Note: '1' indicates 'effective' and '0' indicates 'not effective'. **(1, 0)** would thus indicate that company under consideration was classified as 'effective' during the first stage when name of the company was disclosed and 'not effective' during the second stage when the name of the company was not disclosed.

Chapter 6) in determining the effectiveness of working capital management. The final best discriminant function is as under:

$$Y = 14.5166V_2 + .0015V_{25} + .8715V_{31} + .7914V_{35}$$

where

Y = Overall discriminant score
V_2 = Cash Flow/Total Tangible Assets
V_{25} = Current Assets/Current Liabilities
V_{31} = Net Sales/Total Tangible Assets
V_{35} = Defensive Assets/Total Operating Expenditure

Cash flow is computed by adding back depreciation to the figure of net profit after tax. The other above mentioned ratios have been explained in detail in Chapter 6.

The variables in the above discriminant function are least correlated with each other in both the groups, namely, Not effective and Effective companies in the management of working capital and thus each variable provides additional information about the effectiveness of working capital management. The correlation matrix given in Table 7.3 indicates the intercorrelations between the variables in the discriminant function.

TABLE 7.3: **Correlation matrix of variables in the discriminant function**

	V_2	V_{25}	V_{31}	V_{35}
Variables	(CF/TTA)	(CA/CL)	(NS/TTA)	(DA/TOE)
V_2	1.00	.202	—.308	.232
(CF/TTA)		(.376)	(.414)	(—.181)
V_{25}	.202	1.00	—.176	—.016
(CA/CL)	(.376)		(.443)	(.196)
V_{31}	—.308	—.176	1.00	—.254
(NS/TTA)	(.414)	(.443)		(—.421)
V_{35}	.232	—.016	—.254	1.00
(DA/TOE)	(—.181)	(.196)	(—.421)	

Note: Top row of numbers indicates the intercorrelations between variables of 'not effective' (sick) group of companies, the bottom row of numbers, enclosed in parenthesis, represents the intercorrelations between variables of 'effective' (non-sick) companies.

The *F*-ratio was also computed to test the overall discriminating power of the discriminant function. The *F*-ratio is significant at 1 per cent level of significance [i.e. $F=19.83887 > F_{1,\,76}(.01)=6.98$] and hence, leaves no doubt about the overall discriminating power of the discriminant function.

The computations were carried out on IBM 360/44 computer available at Computer Centre, University of Delhi.

The cut off point of the discriminant function is 1.7068. If the value of the company's discriminant score is below the cut off point, the company would be classified as ineffective in working capital management, otherwise as effective in working capital management.

7.9.4 **Empirical results**

(1) **Initial sample**: The discriminant function was tested on a sample of 78 companies consisting of 39 Not effective (sick) and 39 Effective in working capital management. The discriminant scores of each company are computed by using the parameters of the discriminant function as given in Table 7.4.

The companies are classified either as 'Not Effective' (sick) or 'Effective' (healthy) in working capital management on the basis of their individual discriminant function scores and the cut off point of the discriminant function (i.e. cut off point =1.7068). If the company's discriminant score is below the cut off point, the company is classified as 'Not effective' (sick) in working capital management or vice versa. The results given in Table 7.5 clearly indicate that 94.87 per cent of the companies in the sample are correctly classified by the discriminant function.

(2) **Test sample**: The discriminant function was applied to a test sample of 40 textile companies, since the real effectiveness of the model lies in classifying those companies which are not used to develop the parameters of the discriminant function. A sample of 40 textile companies—20 Not effective (sick) and 20 Effective (healthy) in working capital management—was taken and their discriminant scores were computed by using the parameters of the discriminant function. The companies 'Not effective' in working capital management were

TABLE 7.4: **Discriminant score values of 78 companies**

Not Effective (sick) in working capital management		Effective (healthy) in working capital management	
Company number	*Y*-Score	Company number	*Y*-Score
1	0.2503	1	5.3251
2	0.1319	2	11.5909
3	—5.3600	3	5.6881
4	3.5974*	4	2.3834
5	−0.7071	5	2.5981
6	−2.4233	6	2.1885
7	1.3871	7	9.9748
8	0.6942	8	3.5372
9	−0.0887	9	3.0623
10	−0.0641	10	4.0046
11	−0.6514	11	3.0422
12	1.3260	12	2.8990
13	—1.5890	13	3.6219
14	−1.8855	14	2.2803
15	0.6499	15	2.2712
16	0.5679	16	3 1674
17	0.5785	17	2.6807
18	0.1620	18	3.3123
19	0.0602	19	2.9563
20	0.0734	20	3.6739
21	—2.0967	21	2.3334
22	1.4877	22	3.6503
23	2.8735*	23	3.2045
24	3.8542*	24	3.8137
25	0.6073	25	3.9152
26	—5.1288	26	2.8898
27	—0.4008	27	3.2461
28	−1.6646	28	4.1067
29	−0.6083	29	2.7624
30	0.3693	30	3.3917
31	—1.8575	31	3.9960
32	−1.2531	32	4.1881
33	—2.8188	33	2.9626
34	−4.0588	34	3.4283
35	—0.4641	35	2.8063
36	−1.5162	36	1.9265
37	—1.5891	37	3.1376
38	−0.7012	38	2.2739
39	0.4929	39	1.3922*

Note: The misclassified companies are marked with (*).

TABLE 7.5: **Membership classification matrix**

Actual membership	Predicted membership: Not Effective (sick cos)	Predicted membership: Effective (healthy cos)	Total number	Number misclassified	% of correct classification
Not Effective (Sick Cos)	36	03	39	03	92.31
Effective (Healthy Cos)	01	38	39	01	97.44
Total	37	41	78	04	94.87

TABLE 7.6: **Discriminant score values of 40 textile companies**

Not Effective (sick) in working capital management: Company number	Y-Score	Effective (healthy) in working capital management: Company number	Y-Score
1	—.04707	1	4.4689
2	0.5383	2	2.5597
3	—3.3135	3	2.6291
4	0.4531	4	2.8420
5	—0.1031	5	3.2346
6	—2.8476	6	3.2012
7	—0.3484	7	3.2082
8	—0.8614	8	2.8525
9	—2.8081	9	2.8668
10	—2.7622	10	3.1497
11	—1.9787	11	3.6676
12	—0.2195	12	2.6581
13	—0.9843	13	2.3109
14	—1.6287	14	2.5310
15	—5.5191	15	2.0096
16	—2.8250	16	1.6101*
17	—0.4012	17	3.3962
18	2.0543*	18	2.7872
19	—3.3106	19	4.9752
20	—3.2369	20	3.0364

Note: The companies marked with (*) are misclassified.

selected from the list of sick textile companies taken over by the Government. The discriminant score values of 40 companies are given in Table 7.6.

Using the cut off point (i.e. 1.7058) of the discriminant function as the criteria of classification, the companies in the sample are classified either into ineffective or effective in working capital management. The results given in Table 7.7 clearly indicate that the discriminant model is very effective in classifying the companies in the sample as 'Not effective' (sick) or 'Effective' (healthy) in working capital management. The model correctly classified 95 per cent of the companies in the sample.

TABLE 7.7: **Membership classification matrix**

Actual membership	Predicted membership		Total number	Number mis-classified	% correctly classified
	Not Effective (sick cos)	Effective (healthy cos)			
Not Effective (Sick Cos)	19	01	20	01	95
Effective (Healthy Cos)	01	19	20	01	95
Total	20	20	40	02	95

7.9.5 **Ranking of variables**

The relative importance of each variable to the total discriminating power of the function is also determined on the basis of scaled vector of each variable. The scaled vector of each variable is computed by multiplying corresponding elements to the square roots of the diagonal elements of the variance-covariance matrix. The ranking of four variables in classifying the companies either as 'Not Effective' (sick) or 'Effective' (healthy) in the management of working capital is given in Table 7.8.

TABLE 7.8: **Relative importance of discriminant function variables**

Variable	Scaled vector	Ranking
CF/TTA	1.7116	1
CA/CL	0.0106	4
NS/TTA	1.0812	2
DA/TOE	0.4846	3

Table 7.8 clearly indicates that the cash flow to total tangible assets ratio is the most significant variable followed by net sales to total tangible assets in classifying the companies into two groups—'Not Effective' (sick) and 'Effective' (healthy) in working capital management.

7.9.6 **Conclusions**

Our analysis brings out three such variables which are to be given more weightage in appraising the effectiveness of working capital management than have been assigned to them in the past both by corporate managers and managers of banks and financial institutions. These variables are cash flow to total tangible assets, net sales to total tangible assets and defensive assets to total operating expenditures. These variables are to be incorporated along with the traditional ratio-current assets/current liabilities in a format of appraising the effectiveness of working capital management. The company's performance measured in terms of these four variables can be effectively monitored graphically on a continuing basis. The cut off point of discriminant function would be of considerable use to the individual companies in appraising the effectiveness of working capital management and locating the areas in which they are ineffective compared to the mean scores of effective companies. It would be of great help to the managers of banks and financial institutions in identifying the credit seeking companies as effective or ineffective in the management of working capital and hence, in taking credit granting decisions.

Apart from the above four determinants of effective working capital management, there are certain managerial

attributes, based on empirical evidence, which also help in achieving relative effectiveness in the management of working capital [115]. These are

(*i*) ability to manage the levels of liquidity and financial mobility compared to other companies in the same industry;

(*ii*) ability to establish effective information system between the areas of finance and marketing; and

(*iii*) ability to determine the level of assets to be held in marketable securities compared to other companies in the same industry.

In conclusion it is brought out that banks and other credit granting institutions can effectively use the important and sensitive variables for monitoring the performance of working capital management. These variables can be graphically plotted to see the trends. The use of discriminant model can enhance the quality of the appraisal system in the management of working capital. The corporate managers should concentrate on the firm's performance relating to the discriminant function variables and the above mentioned managerial attributes in order to achieve the effectiveness in the management of working capital.

8

MIS FOR MONITORING INDUSTRIAL SICKNESS

8.0 Information and Reporting System

One of the basic causes of growing sickness in industry is the lack of adequate information and reporting system. In discussing the cause-wise breakdown of sickness in industry, it has been identified that over 22 per cent of industrial sickness can be attributed to lack of good management. When some key personnel are missing in an industrial unit and the reporting system is inadequate, the ability of the management to respond to malfunctioning in the industry considerably decreases with the result corrective measures are not taken in time. The industrial sickness keeps on increasing from incipient state to grave situation. While examining a large number of sick units, it has also been observed that information and reporting system in the organisation is usually poor. There is considerable variation even where there is some form of reporting between companies in the same industrial group and between different industrial groups also. The reports are not submitted to the management in time and are seldom carefully scanned for variance analysis.

8.1 Reporting System

The reporting system has to be designed to meet the requirements of industries during implementation phase for new industries which are being set up and for production phase when they are in operation. The reporting system can be in two parts: (*a*) Reporting for implementation phase and (*b*) Information system for production phase.

8.1.1 Reporting for implementation

It has been discussed in Chapter 2 that poor implementation is one of the main factors leading to cost and time overshoots in industries when they are being set up and resulting in sickness to a very large extent. Very often no effort is made in developing a reporting system and the extent of slippages in different activities of the projects is not brought to the notice of the management resultin g in poor response and correcting measures. The poor implementation results from the following reasons:

(*a*) Inadequate planning of various phases of projects
(*b*) Poor anticipation of the bottlenecks in projects
(*c*) Lack of contingency planning to overcome bottlenecks

8.1.2 Planning of project phases

A project plan can be presented through a network of activities or through a bar chart. The bar chart method is simple and convenient, an example for the manufacture of brakes by the bar chart method is given in Fig. 8.1. It is important to keep watch on various phases in the implementation and to anticipate bottlenecks and plan for alternative actions well in time so that completion of project phase is not delayed. A network of activities in a project is, however, a better approach for planning. It considerably helps in arresting the time and cost overshoots as illustrated in Fig. 8.2 (*a*) and (*b*) where the activities and project milestone have been related with financial expenditures on project. Such plans and periodic review are very useful in the follow up of the implementation phase.

8.1.3 Contingency planning

The contingency planning aims at providing alternative approach when an activity or a group of activities in a project gets delayed; for instance if one of the vendors defaults in providing components and sub-systems or the contractor fails in construction, alternative solutions are thought of and action initiated. If a careful watch is kept on different activities, bottlenecks can be anticipated in different areas.

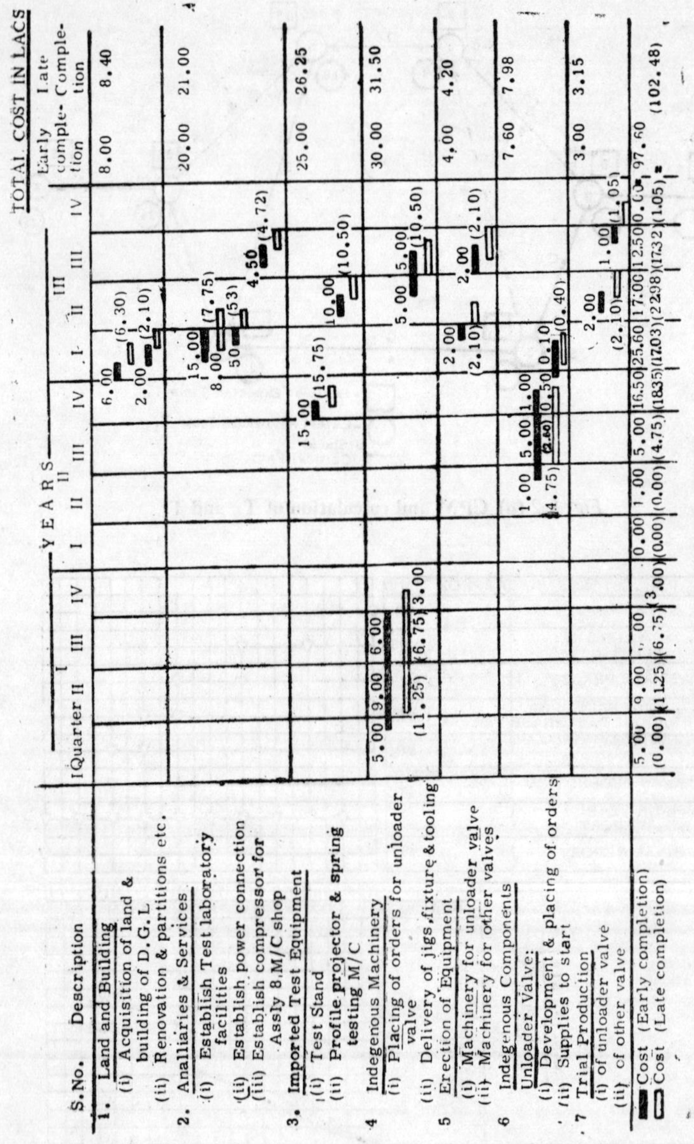

Fig. 8.1 **Bar chart for grau brakes**

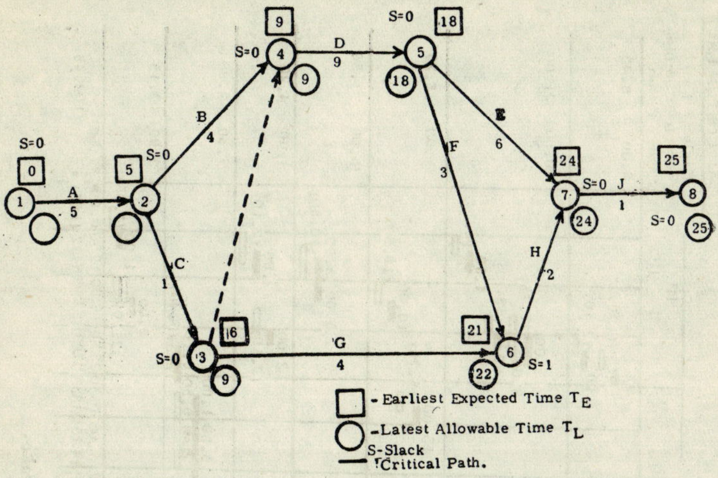

Fig. 8.2 (a) **CPM and calculation of T_E and T_L**

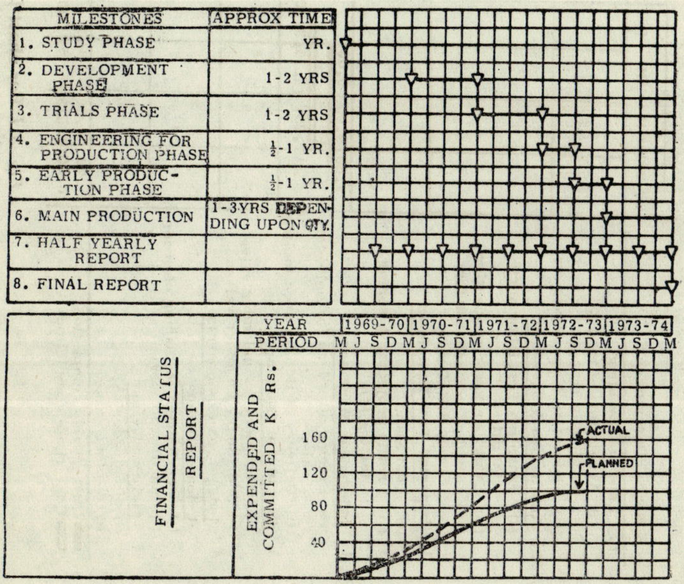

Fig. 8.2 (b) **Project milestones and financial expenditures**

Splitting orders or parallel activity planning are well known steps which can be attempted. In a shortage economy of our country, bottlenecks are normal. To overcome these and to plan alternative actions is the task of management. It has been noticed that industries which have been successfully implemented in time, have made good use of contingency planning. Periodic reviews [Fig. 8.2 (*b*)] and a good reporting system during implementation phase is very useful in preventing time and cost overshoots.

Network planning or bar chart approach has proved very useful in estimating delays leading to timely corrective measures.

8.2 Information System for Production Phase

The requirement of information system during the production phase is such as to provide a quick check on the health of a unit in the periodic review. It should make use of key parameters of information which can be broadly grouped into:

(*a*) **Basic data**: This is about the project, its promoters, management, capital structure etc. This can be organised initially and any changes in it can be supplemented. It will be better to maintain it in a folder, which can be converted into a computer file.

(*b*) **Operational data**: This is the performance of the company. This should be organised into (*i*) activity (*ii*) profitability (*iii*) cash management and liquidity position. This data is collected on quarterly or half-yearly basis.

8.2.1 Basic data

The basic data about an industry should be organised in several groups. It is then easier to create a computer file for each of these groups when computerisation of MIS is undertaken. Even in manual maintenance of this data, it is convenient to make changes when required in the appropriate

CONCERN

INDUSTRY: MAJOR HEAD SUB-HEAD

SECTOR: Private/Co-op./Pub. Ltd./Joint/Public/Private Ltd.

PROJECT: New Expansion Diversification Modernisation

REGD. OFFICE

Telex: ....

Gram: ....

Phone: ....

ADMN. OFFICE

Telex: ....

Gram: ....

Phone: ....

FACILITIES APPLIED FOR (if jointly specify)

A. Rupee Loan ....

B. FCL ....

C. Underwriting ....

REF. NO. & DATE OF RECEIPT OF APPLICATION

LOCATION TOWN: ....

District: ....

State : ....

WHETHER LOCATED IN NOTIFIED LESS DEVELOPED AREA: | YES | NO |

WHETHER ELIGIBLE FOR:

Institutional concession

Central subsidy

State subsidy

Fig. 8.3 (a) **Basic data of a company**

ESTIMATED PROJECT COST (Rs. in lacs)	ORIGINAL	REVISED	FINAL

CHECK OF ANTECEDENTS:

A. Branch enquiry ....
B. Banker's report..........
C. Collaboration (IIC/Missions)..........
D. Consultants ....

FINANCING PROPOSAL	Estimated	(Rs. in lacs) Approved
A. SHARE CAPITAL		
Equity-prom.		
Public		
Preference		
B. LOANS FROM INSTNS.		
C. DPG/FLG		
D. INTERNAL ACCRUALS		
E. CENTRAL SUBSIDY		
TOTAL:		

EQUITY/DEBT RATIO:

PROMOTER'S CONTRIBUTION

PROMOTERS	ESTIMATED AMT (lacs)	ESTIMATED Percentage	APPROVED AMT (lacs)	APPROVED Percentage

IIM'S DECISION REGARDING SHARING OF ASSISTANCE (Rs. in lacs)

INSTN.	RL	FCL	U/WTG E.	U/WTG P.

APPRAISING OFFICERS

A. TECH..........
B. FIN..........
C. COORD..........
D. OTHER INSTITUTIONS PARTICIPATING ....

Fig. *8.3* (*b*) **Basic data of a company**

PROMOTERS: Whether large industrial house/New entrepreneur/ Technocrat or Non-resident

A. ....

B. ....

C. ....

D. ....

DIRECTORS	Functions	Interest Represented
A.	....	....
B.	....	....
C.	....	....
D.	....	....
E.	....	....
F.	....	....

BRIEF PARTICULARS OF THE PROJECT

....

....

....

....

....

PROJECT REPORT BY ....

....

MARKET SURVEY BY ....

TECH. COLLABORATORS: Give name of consultant and financial participation (if any)

GOVT. APPROVAL	REFERENCE	VALID UP TO
A. Letter of intent		
B. Industrial licence		
C. C.G. clearance		
D. Important licence		
E. Foreign collaboration		
F. M.R.T.P. clearance		

Fig. 8.3 (c) **Basic data of a company**

PROGRESS RECORD	DATE DUE	DATE COMPLETED	REMARKS
a. Receipt of application			
b. Despatch of application to H.O./other institution			
c. Flash Report			
d. Date of treating application as complete			
e. Reference to SEM			
f. Site Inspection			
g. Despatch of Appraisal Report			
h. AC Meeting or sanction by lead institution			
i. IIM Reference			
j. Board Meeting			
k. Letter of intent			
l.			
m.			
n.			
o.			
p.			

Fig. 8.3 (d) **Basic data of a company**

group. The following groups are suggested for keeping the basic data:

(*a*) Project location, classification and promoter's details. (*b*) Financial assistance sought or obtained from financial institutions, state level corporation and banks. (*c*) Particulars of project, collaborators and their details. (*d*) Cost of project. (*e*) Capital structure. (*f*) Details of shareholders and equity base. (*g*) Securities. (*h*) Schedule of repayments to lenders.

An illustration of a format design regarding the basic data of a company at the level of a financial institution is given in Fig. 8.3 (*a*) to (*d*).

8.2.2 **Operational data**

The operational data from the companies should be reported preferably every quarter or may be even half yearly depending upon the nature of the activity and the requirement of the reporting system. This should consist of details relating to the activity concerned with the items and quantities produced during the quarter, the details of profitability and cash management during the same period. It is possible to lay out an information format to report on these three aspects of the operational data. However, the contents will have to be listed depending upon the nature of the operations in a unit. The operational data should be meaningful for critical appraisal and assessment. It should have the key elements of information. A format design is given in Fig. 8.4 (*a*) to (*c*). Eventually a data base has to be built and a computerised file created for each one of these elements of information and kept updated. This should be done for each industrial group. The operational data has to be adequate to meet the requirements of appraisal in respect of financial, operational and technical working of the industrial unit. The information should be adequate to plot graphically the trends of growth in respective areas over several quarters.

Position as on

Product Group	Orders on hand at the beginning of the quarter A		Orders received during the quarter B		Despatches during the quarter C		Orders on hand at the end of the quarter (A+B−C)	
	Quantity	Value	Quantity	Value	Quantity	Value	Quantity	Value
1.								
2.								
3.								
4.								
Total								

N.B. : The data on capacity utilisation and plant utilisation in the quarter should also be given separately.

Fig. 8.4 (a) **Activity level**

Position as on

	Last quarter ending Estimated Actual	Present quarter Estimated Actual
1. Sales		
2. Less excise duty		
3. Net sales (Item 1—Item 2)		
4. Cost of sales		
(a) Raw materials consumption		
(b) Power and fuel		
(c) Salaries and wages		
(d) Consumable stores		
(e) Repairs and maintenance		
(f) Other manufacturing expenses		
(g) Depreciation		
Sub-Total		
Add opening stock in process and finished goods		
Total cost of sales		
5. Gross profit (Item 3—Item 4)		
6. Other overheads		
(a) Interest		
(b) Selling, general and administrative expenses		
7. Operating profit (Item 5—Item 6)		
8. Other income/expenses Net (±)		
9. Profit before tax (Item 7+Item 8)		

Fig. 8.4 (b) **Profitability**

	Position for the period		
	End of period value in Rs.	Last financial year	Remarks Stage of sickness if any
Current assets			
1. Cash			
2. Sundry debtors			
3. Total inventory			
i) Raw materials			
ii) Stock in process			
iii) Finished goods			
4. Other current assets (loans, advances etc.)			
5. Total current assets 1 + 2 + 4			
Current liabilities			
6. Sundry creditors			
7. Bank borrowings (for working capital only)			
8. Other current liabilities (statutory liabilities, advance received etc.)			
9. Total current liabilities (6 + 7 + 8)			
10. Net working capital (5–9)			
11. Appropriate financial ratios			
12. Trends in ratios			

Fig. 8.4 (c) **Cash management and liquidity**

8.3 Indicators of Sickness

The information reporting system should be used to appraise the health of the unit. The following indicators based on the use of operational data are used to assess the incidence of sickness in the industrial units:

(*a*) Physical indicators as reflected by the key elements of information, signals, and symptoms in the company's performance in the quarterly reports;
(*b*) Graphical indicators plotted taking total production, profitability, capacity utilisation etc. and their trends during several quarters;
(*c*) Data from commercial banks on transactions in the quarter; and
(*d*) Use of MDA score.

8.3.1 Physical indicators

The physical indicators include selected data on the plant performance, capacity utilisation, important financial ratios and their changes, if any. In the early stages of sickness the physical indicators appear in the form of signals and an example of this is shown in Fig. 8.5. The decline in stock market share, inefficient management practices in the areas of finance, production, marketing and labour relations do provide indications of growing mismanagement. However, occasional plant breakdowns are not of much consequence but when they start recurring the malfunctioning has to be recognised. An example of the plant breakdown and the hours lost in production called as operational and technological parameter in case of a sugar industry is shown in Fig. 8.6. The plant and equipment starts getting aged and needs replacement. Because of the breakdowns plant utilisation starts decreasing and the hours lost become very significant physical indicators of sickness. Consequently, capacity utilisation decreases. Plant breakdowns are quite normal in old textile, jute and engineering industries where technology is becoming obsolete and operational costs are constantly increasing. Replacement programme of the old equipment is not systematically worked out in spite of the

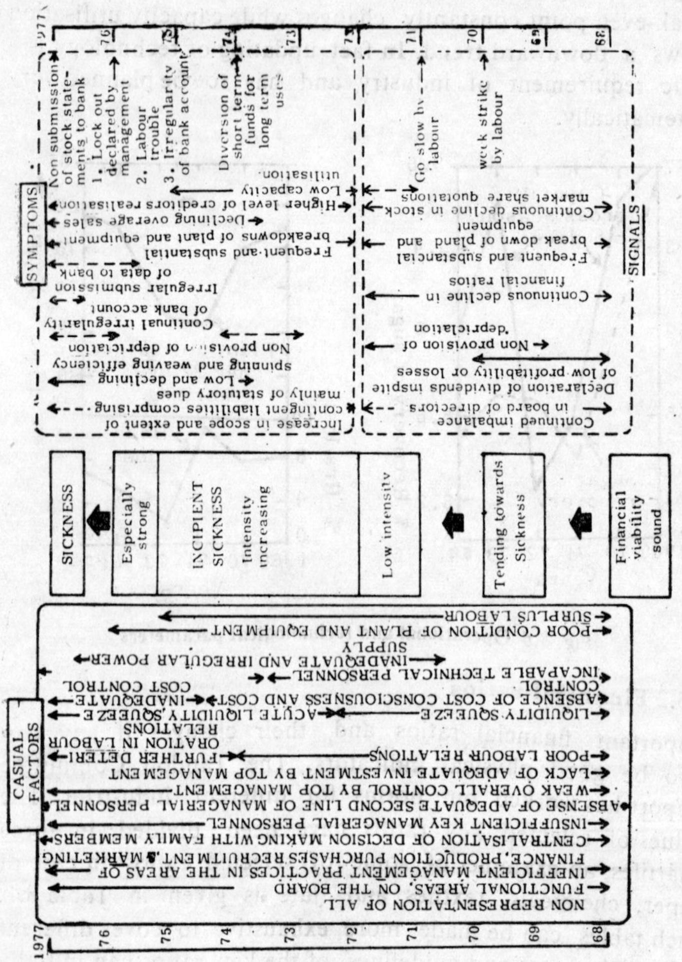

Fig. 8.5 **Signals and symptoms of sickness**

fact that depreciation is worked out each year by companies. Replacement of obsolete technology is also necessary as the break-even point constantly changes while capacity utilisation shows a downward trend. In fact updating of technology is a basic requirement of industry and has to be planned very systematically.

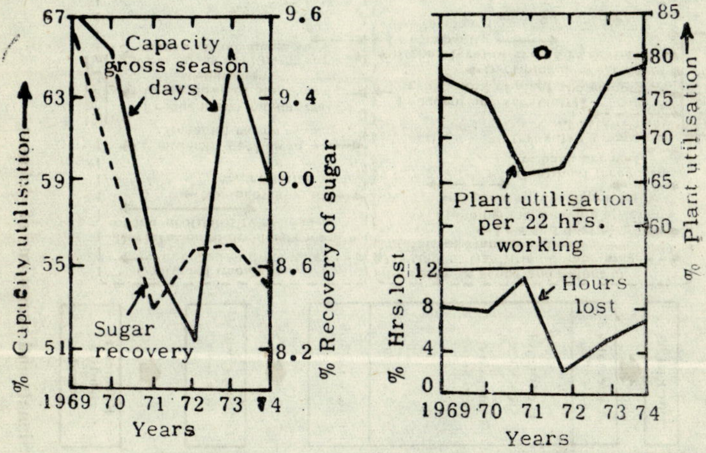

Fig. 8.6 **Operational and technological parameters**

8.3.2 Financial ratios

Important financial ratios and their changes if any can also be good physical indicators. The Tandon Committee Report has worked out norms for different industries. The values of selected key ratios have been divided in three quartiles, an example of some of selected ratios in case of paper, chemicals, textiles and jute is given in Table 8.1. Such tables can be made more exhaustive to cover different industrial groups and guidelines of the key ratios can initially be laid down as measure of performance.

8.3.3 Proneness to sickness

A combination of several factors can be a good guide towards estimating the proneness to sickness. An example of this in respect of profitability and liquidity is shown in Table 8.2. A combination of technical factors like plant and equipment

TABLE 8.1: **Selected financial ratios**

Ratio		Industry: Paper	Chemicals	Textiles	Jute
Current assets/ Current liabilities	Q_1	1.45	1.98	1.40	1.28
	M	0.93	1.38	1.16	1.11
	Q_3	0.69	1.07	0.91	0.99
Long term debt/ Net worth	Q_1	0.13		0.15	0.07
	M	0.39	0.19	0.34	0.21
	Q_3	0.70	0.72	0.67	0.34
Total outside Liabilities/Net worth	Q_1	0.89	0.62	1.44	1.89
	M	1.57	1.12	2.15	2.46
	Q_3	3.01	1.79	3.26	3.02
Net sales/Net fixed assets	Q_1	2.06	3.85	6.56	8.81
	M	1.58	1.86	4.47	6.13
	Q_3	0.95	1.01	2.81	5.15
Net sales/Current assets	Q_1	2.45	2.16	3.02	3.28
	M	2.08	1.72	2.33	2.73
	Q_3	1.50	1.25	1.96	2.31

Q_1=First quartile
M=Median
Q_3=Third quartile

utilisation and operational factors like availability of critical raw materials and skills is shown in Table 8.3. The shaded region (in dark line) indicates the combination of factors which lead to onset of sickness and need to be carefully watched.

TABLE 8.2: **Profitability and liquidity**

Profitability	Liquidity		
	High	Medium	Low/Lack
High	Poised for growth Healthy	Healthy	Expanding (Needs watch)
Medium	Idle cash (Needs watch)	Unstable Operations	Overtrading (Needs watch)
Low/Lack	Liquidation (Needs watch)	Contracting Business (Needs watch)	Sick

TABLE 8.3: **Availability of critical raw materials skills**

Technical factors (plant and equipment utilisation)	Operational factors (raw materials availability)		
	Excellent	Medium	Poor
Excellant	Healthy	Needs watch	Sick
Medium	Healthy	Sick	Very Sick
Poor	Needs watch	Sick	Very Sick

8.3.4 **Graphical indicators**

The graphical indicators are really the trends which can be plotted over a period of time extending from one to two years where data is noted in every quarter and put on a graph. The trends in financial, operational and technical parameters during 2 or 3 quarters preceding the quarter for appraisal can give sensitive indication regarding the health of the unit. The parameters can be selected in the field of capacity utilisation, profitability, production and sales turnover. These are good graphical indicators. An example of the selected graphical indicators including variation in solvency and liquidity ratios is given in Fig. 8.7. It is not surprising to find that sickness when it starts seeping in an industrial concern is indicated in

the trends. If, however, there are comparative values available of a healthy unit of the same industrial group, the variations in sick units can be easily appreciated. For this reason study of healthy and sick units in the same group of industry is very helpful.

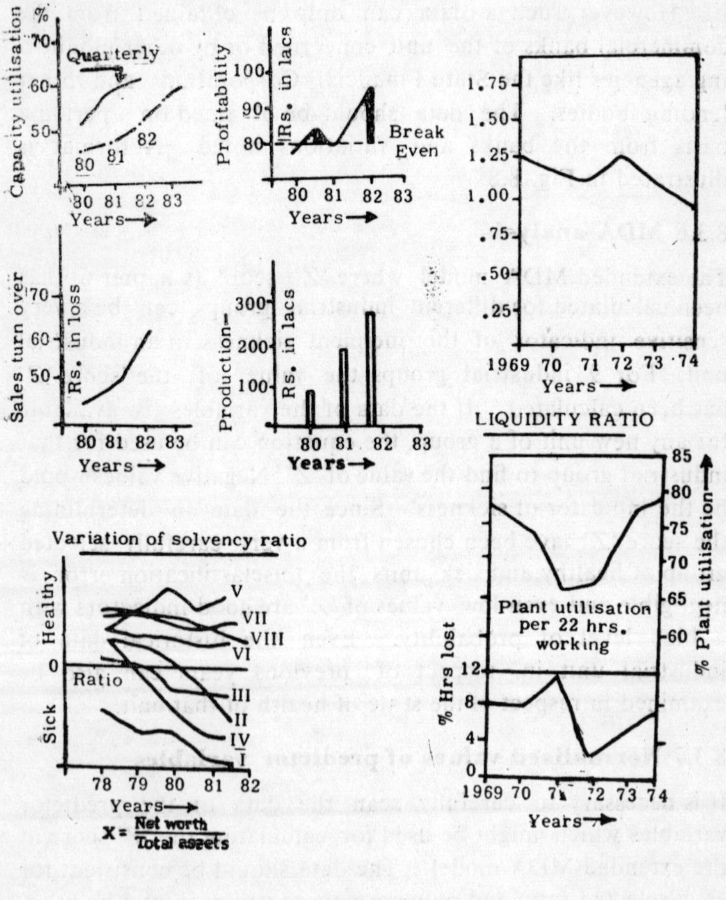

Fig. 8.7 **Graphical indicators**

8.3.5 Commercial bank data

The variation in the working capital management and the imbalances in the bank borrowing are also very useful indicators. The working capital management has been exclusively discussed in Chapter 7. The uncontrolled swings can provide first vital information to the banker and also to the management if they monitor it well and are keen to find reasons for it. However, such a data can only be obtained from the commercial banks of the unit concerned or by other monitoring agencies like the State Financial Corporations and other lending bodies. The data should be obtained on a periodic basis from the banks and variations noted. A format is illustrated in Fig. 8.8.

8.3.6 MDA analysis

The extended MDA model where '*Z*' score (Chapter 6) has been calculated for different industrial groups can be a very sensitive indicator of the incipient sickness in an industrial unit. For 9 industrial groups the value of the score '*Z*' has been calculated. If the data of the variables is available for any new unit of a group, the equation can be used for that industrial group to find the value of '*Z*'. Negative values would be the indicator of sickness. Since the data in determining the score '*Z*' have been chosen from a very carefully selected group of healthy and sick units the misclassification error is negligible and even low values of '*Z*' are good indicators with a high level of probability. Even the historical data of industrial unit in respect of previous years can also be examined in respect of the state of health of that unit.

8.3.7 Normalised values of predictor variables

It is necessary to carefully scan the data of the predictor variables which might be used for calculating the '*Z*' score in the extended MDA model. The data should be consistent for each selected ratio and only normalised values should be used. The method to normalise the values of a ratio is to use the following equation:

Name of the bank	Nature of facility	Description and value of security	Margin %	Drawing power	Amount outstanding	No. of over-trading
1	2	3	4	5	6	7

Remarks: Indicate irregular accounts, if any, and reasons therefor.

Fig. 8.8: Monthly data from commercial banks on borrowings

$$\text{Normalised } X = \frac{X - \bar{X}}{\mu}$$

where $\bar{X}$ is the mean of the value of the variable over several periods

μ is its standard deviation and X is the observed value of the variable in the appraisal period.

The use of the normalised values of variables keeps the variability within control.

8.3.8 New industrial units

The 'Z' score equations have been given for 9 groups of industries. However, any new group of industries can also be analysed and 'Z' score equation determined if the data of the ratios is available over a period of time both in respect of healthy and sick units. It is also possible to use new predictor variables drawn from operational and technical areas which are likely to significantly contribute to the health of the unit relevant to the industry. However, consistency of data, sensitivity of variables and the 'T' test have to be performed before using the MDA model.

8.4 Monitoring of Health

The early stages of sickness can be detected if the signals which originate in the areas of financial, technical and operational environment of an industrial unit are carefully noted and catalogued. The reporting system has to be organised to take note of these events. Fig. 8.9 illustrates the stages where sick signals and symptoms can be noted and the state of health of the unit put under observations. It is in these early stages of incipient sickness that remedial measures can quickly restore the normal working of the unit and prevent further deterioration. Inspection procedures need to be tightened and periodic reviews enforced to improve performance. Experience has shown that rehabilitation of a sick unit is time consuming and results in loss of industrial production and finance. In fact the dictum "Prevention is better than cure" can be applied effectively if an information system based on key indicators is organised.

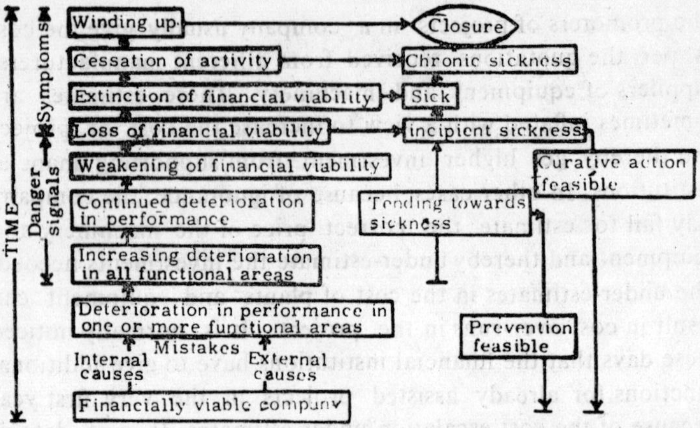

Fig. 8.9 **Stages of sickness**

8.5 Data Bank

The information and reporting system can be developed effectively if there is a data bank in the industrial unit. It is necessary to build a data bank for different industrial groups in financial institutions, state level finance corporations, and other financing and corporate bodies. Such a data bank would greatly help in the process of project appraisals and in monitoring of implementation of projects and in keeping a watch on the time and costs which keep on escalating year after year. The data bank must also have data on the cost of plant and equipment, suppliers and types of technology available in the appropriate areas.

8.5.1 Cost of plant and equipment

In every project depending upon the industry it is located that the machinery, plant and equipment constitute a major part of the total cost of project. The bigger the project, the larger is the investment in this area. While estimating the total outlay required and also the escalation factor and the margin money, a data bank is very useful in the respective industrial areas if it has the data on plant and equipment costs. It helps even in estimating the likely cost over-runs and the need for rehabilitation resources if and when needed.

8.5.2 Invoicing

The promoters of projects in a company usually give the cost as per the quotations received from different manufacturers/ suppliers of equipment and machinery. These estimates are sometimes inflated with a view to increase the cost of project and thereby get higher investment from supporting financial institutions. In other cases, because of ignorance, the company may fail to estimate the correct price of the machinery and equipment and thereby under-estimate the investments needed. The under-estimates in the cost of plants and equipment can result in cost over-runs in the project. It is normally noticed these days that the financial institutions have to give additional sanctions for already assisted projects in the very first year because of the cost escalation/under-estimates. If cost data is available in the data bank and is kept updated in major fields of industries it will be of a great assistance to the project appraisal authorities at various levels. The keeping of data for important industrial groups can be shared between different financial institutions of state and centre and also by the Government if and when required.

8.5.3 Standard suppliers

Data banks can also be useful in the identification of proper plants and equipment for specific industries, spare parts, and standard suppliers. At the time of project appraisal, this reference can be of great help. Data bank can also be helpful in the analysis of time estimates and delivery period for different types of equipment and machinery from standard suppliers in different industrial groups like sugar, paper, textile, cement, steel and chemicals. These industries can be chosen as priority areas for building the data bank between different financial institutions and state level corporations.

8.5.4 Selection of technology

In selected fields, the data bank may also contain information on the developments in technology, infra-structure facilities necessary and available in the country and even a list of technologists for consultation where needed. These can be of

great use in the appraisal of the selection of technology in projects. It is an area seldom investigated and appraised while considering the project loans. A technology assessment cell has to be set up in the financial institutions like IFCI as shown in Fig. 8.10 if this type of appraisal is to be undertaken.

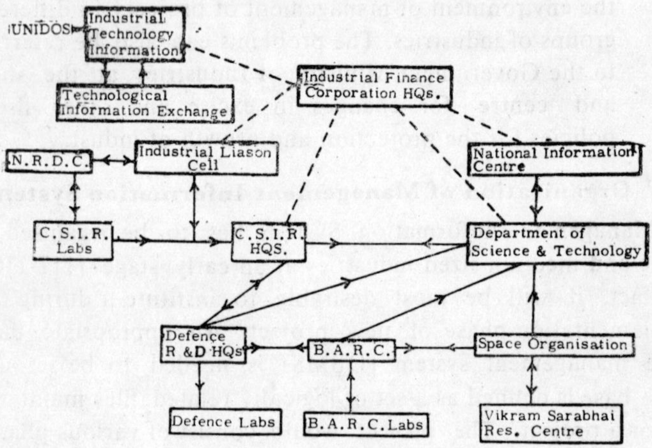

Fig. 8.10 **Technology assessment**

8.5.5 Break-even point

There is a general escalation in the prices of raw materials and other inputs needed in industry. The break-even point of capacity utilisation in many industries has to be periodically reviewed. Alternatively, in a new project the economic size of it in various areas has to be estimated. This is particularly true for high cost industries. A data bank can prove useful in this assessment.

8.6 Need for Data Bank at Institutional Levels

Some of the important reasons for setting up of a data bank at institutional levels are as follows:

(*a*) To provide for project appraisal groups a tool for cost appraisal and on over-invoicing, under-invoicing and comparative assessment of plant equipment and machinery costs;

(*b*) To determine the escalation factor in the project cost in different sectors of industry from time to time;

(*c*) To appreciate the changes taking place in the various sectors of industry and thereby to determine the guidelines for investment in projects; and

(*d*) To appreciate the type of problems being generated in the environment of management of projects in different groups of industries. The problems can also be referred to the Government/Ministry of Industries at the state and centre for changes in excise and other fiscal policies for the protection and growth of industry.

8.7 Organisation of Management Information System

A Management Information System has to be organised in large and medium sized industries at an early stage [117-118]. In fact, it will be most desirable to institute it during the implementation phase of new project. An appropriate data base management system (DBMS) is needed to be set up. Data base is defined as a set of logically related files maintained for a project. The project would consist of various phases involving construction of building, purchase, procurement of plant and equipment, sources and vendors of materials, installation and pre-production runs. Each one of these phases would have a number of activities and would generate data in respect of cost and time schedules. Each of these phases is required to be continuously monitored with a view to see that their progress is in accordance with the plans. Computer reports are required to be generated periodically for assessment and in all critical areas of decision making to prevent cost and time over-shoots. Accordingly, appropriate software has to be developed which will be the part of DBMS. Contingency planning has to be organised to keep implementation within control.

8.8 Organisation for Computerisation of Information System

The outline of an organisation of Management Information System [119] is given in Fig. 8.11. The input data has to be coded in the form of numbers, or in alpha numeric characters.

This data is required to be processed with a view to convert it into information relevant for decision-making. The reliability and quality of this information would depend upon how data collection has been organised. If the data is collected at the source where it is generated, the accuracy would be the highest; if on the other hand the same is derived from secondary sources, accuracy may be compromised. Special emphasis has, therefore, to be put on the data capture for which necessary formats have to be designed depending upon the need. The processing of data would have to be through an appropriate computer system.

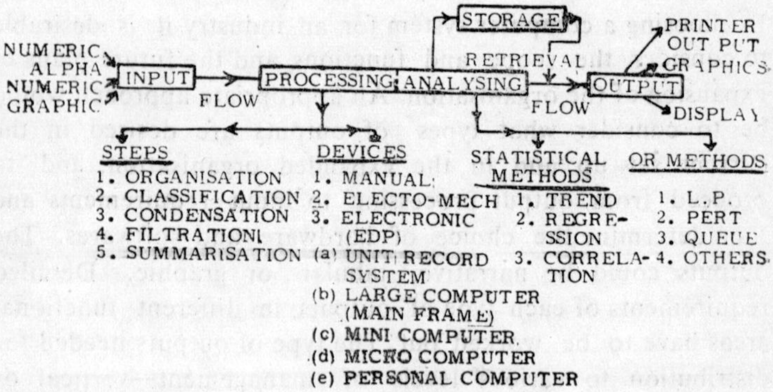

Fig. 8.11 **Organisation of MIS**

8.9 Choice of Computer System

The choice of a computer system includes the selection of four basic components. The Central Processing Unit is the heart of the computer. The second is the choice of the size of the memory. This has to be considered depending upon the area of application in the CPU. Data to be processed and instructions contained in the programme are stored in the primary memory. The CPU accesses the memory directly to retrieve and store instructions or data.

A choice about the secondary storage has also to be made. These include magnetic disks and tapes. The contents of the secondary storage cannot be accessed directly by the computer.

A data channel controls interchanges between the central processing and the secondary storage.

Input/output devices are the fourth important components. These are needed to communicate with the computer. These devices include terminals, card readers, punchers and printers. Usually, a data channel handles communication between input/output devices and the CPU. Control units are required to interface the data channel with each physically different secondary storage and input/output device. An example of the structural configuration of main frame, mini and micro computer is given in Appendices I and II.

8.10 From Output to Input

In choosing a computer system for an industry it is desirable to consider the scope and functions and the future plans of expansion of the organisation. An appropriate approach would be to consider what types of outputs are desired in the current set up and in the expanded organisation, and to proceed from output processing to input requirements and then determine the choice of hardware and softwares. The outputs could be narrative, tabular or graphic. Detailed requirements of each type of outputs in different functional areas have to be worked out. The type of outputs needed for distribution to various levels of management—vertical or horizontal levels—have also to be considered. If there are areas of "Exception Reporting" they have also to be outlined. Once the choice of different types of outputs has been determined, the next step is to consider the processing techniques needed for converting the data into the right type of information. The processing technique could determine the type of programmes or software needed for processing. If there are areas of using standard packages they can be considered. The choice of language could be determined by the type of applications required. For instance, for scientific application Fortran-4 could be useful while for business applications Cobol or Basic would be desirable.

The factors on which the choice of a computer system—whether hiring or outright purchase—would depend upon the total requirement of the computerisation in the current and

expanded organisation. The size of memory, CPU, secondary storages and input/output devices have to be considered in the light of total requirements. The plan or the implementation of the computer system has to be worked out. Lastly, the cost of system whether indigenous or imported has to be seen in the light of the available resources. The need for systems analysts, skilled technical and maintenance personnel would also have to be considered for the satisfactory operation of the system.

8.11 Cost and Benefit Analysis of Computerised MIS

The total cost involved in a computer based information system may be broadly classified into three components:

(*i*) **Development cost**: This is a one time cost involved in analysing the existing system, determining the needs of the new system, designing the new system, and programming, debugging etc.

(*ii*) **Implementation cost**: This is also a one time cost in carrying out the test run, parallel run etc. before actual switch over to the new system is done. The implementation of the system also involves training of personnel of the user departments responsible for supplying the input data and those making use of the computer generated reports. Training of personnel of the system department regarding the operation is also necessary.

(*iii*) **Operating cost**: This is a recurring cost and is spent during the actual operations of the system after implementation. Operating costs involve cost of computer time and other data preparation equipment, personnel operating the system, infrastructure and stationery.

8.11.1 Benefits

It is often difficult to exactly quantify the benefits of a computer based information system. The benefits may be enumerated in terms of speed, accuracy, reduction in manpower etc. but mere statement of these benefits without attaching any value to them does not take us very far. Some of the benefits like reduction in manpower may be easily

quantified while others like the quality of decisions, accuracy etc. may be difficult to quantify.

The benefits can be in the following form:

(*i*) Direct reduction of cost due to reduced manpower requirement in the organisation, of space and furniture, of the saved employees, stationery etc.

(*ii*) Avoiding duplication of effort in collection and manipulating of information by having an organised integrated flow and processing of information.

(*iii*) Faster reaction time—The time between the occurrence of an event in the organisation and the corresponding corrective action taken by the management is called the reaction time. This reaction time can be considerably reduced by organising the flow of information on an exception basis and processing it at a fast speed on the computer. Faster reaction time enhances the efficiency of the organisation and leads to better utilisation of the resources of the organisation.

(*iv*) Improved accuracy—Computer systems are designed to collect data from the basic source documents. All subsequent transfers of data from one file to another takes place mechanically on the computer. The transfer of data and all other arithmetic operations within the computer are quite fast and contribute to the improved accuracy and speed of processing.

8.12 **Management Information and Decision Analysis System**

Monitoring of project progress during production phase can be made continuous. It is then possible to detect early signs of sickness if and when they appear. A data base in respect of selected ratios from financial, technical and operational areas will be needed for each industrial group and a multiple discriminant analysis carried out to determine '*Z*' score in respect of the industry to be investigated. In case the '*Z*' score equation is available, the values can be fitted to examine the state of health. Using trend analysis and making use of other indicators it should be possible to continuously monitor the health of the industrial unit with a high degree of reliability. A flow chart for this decision analysis system is given in Fig. 8.12. The appraisal reports can be brought out

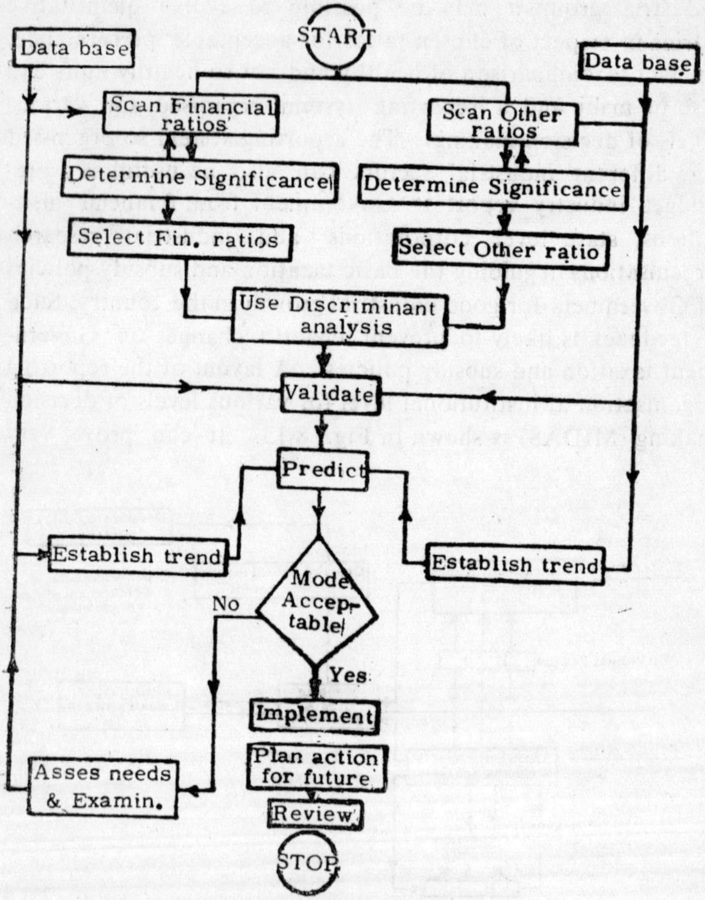

Fig. 8.12 **Decision analysis system**

periodically from this computerised management information and decision analysis system (MIDAS). In each industrial group it may be possible to evolve quantitative norms in respect of chosen ratios for acceptable performance. In fact a comparison of healthy and not so healthy units can also be made and a reporting system organised for various levels of decision making. The reporting system so organised for different industrial sectors can also be useful as a pre-budget industry report to Government from financial institutions, state level corporations and industrial research organisations in guiding the basic taxation and subsidy policies of Government for good industrial growth in the country. Such a feedback is likely to prevent chaotic changes in Government taxation and subsidy policies. A layout of the reporting organisation at institutional level for various levels of decision making (MIDAS) is shown in Fig. 8.13. It can prove very

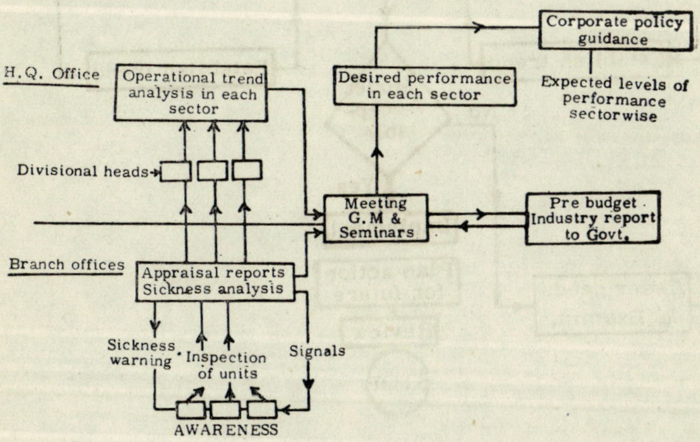

Fig. 8.13 **Management information and decision analysis system (MIDAS)**

useful in monitoring the performance of industrial units and in helping the corporate institutions in the country in keeping a good watch on the industrial growth in various sectors of Indian economy.

8.13 MIS in Management Process

Once the information system is organised, it is possible to provide reviews for important operational functions of the industrial unit like production, marketing, research, development and planning etc. and link them up with resource requirements for the purpose of long term or strategic planning or short term like tactical planning. A block representation of MIS in management process is shown in Fig. 8.14. Such computer outputs periodically are needed for the purposes of improving the productivity of the organisation and to consider malfunctioning if any because of organisational overlook in different areas.

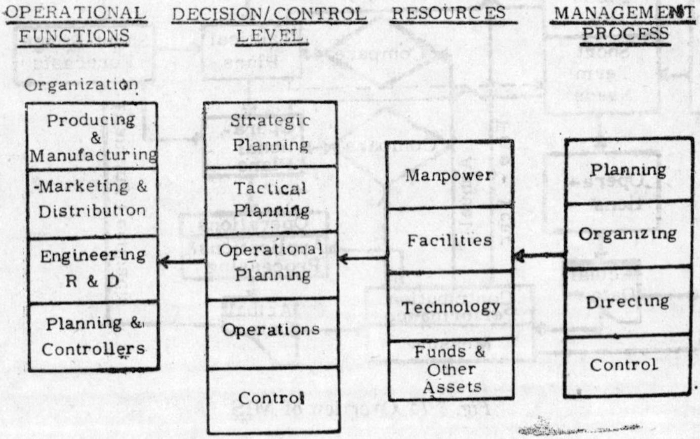

Fig. 8.14 **MIS in management process**

8.14 Overview of MIS

It has been said, "IF YOU WANT TO MANAGE BUSINESS *WELL*, MANAGE ITS *FUTURE*, AND TO MANAGE *FUTURE*, YOU HAVE TO MANAGE *INFORMATION*".

There is an explosion of knowledge. New materials are being developed and better technology is becoming available as science progresses. It is possible to examine various alternatives from cost-effectiveness point of view if new technology or materials/machines become available and compare the

strategic and tactical plans in the light of the objectives of the organisation. A computerised output can help this process as shown in Fig. 8.15, and enable the management to plan better future and thus ensure GROWTH. Computerised MIS in large organisations can thus help and improve the decision making in strategic, tactical and operational planning in industries.

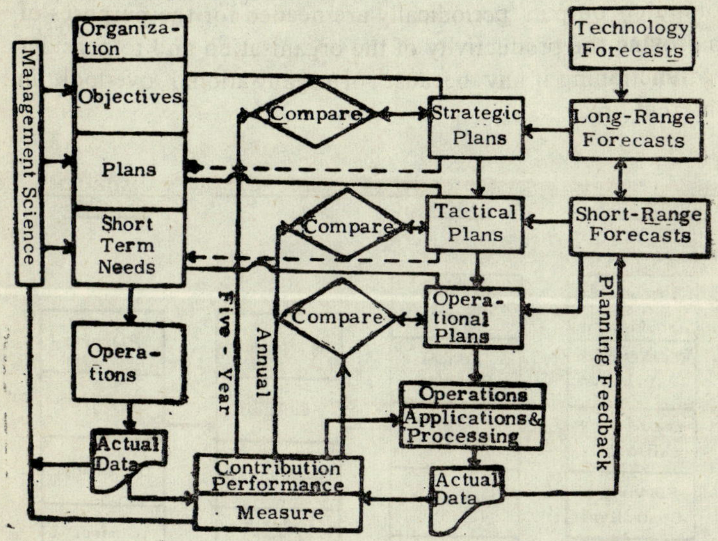

Fig. 8.15 **Overview of MIS**

9

PREVENTION OF SICKNESS

9.0 Categorisation of Sickness

Industrial projects which fall in the sick category have been extensively studied and analysed. In Chapter 2, over 200 projects have been analysed to find the areas of deficiencies. The sick industries can be grouped in three areas. These are—

(*a*) Born Sick
(*b*) Made Sick
(*c*) Sickness is Thrust on Them

Poor appraisal, second-hand plant and equipment, inadequate market survey, poor implementation, one customer—one product type situations result into born sick industries. Poor management, diversion of funds contribute to the second category of industries. Changes in governmental policies, strategic shortage of raw materials, sudden withdrawal of Government subsidies due to political reasons, lead to sickness in industries which is beyond their control and can be attributed to environmental factors. In preventing the sickness, therefore, the role of the following agencies has been identified:

I. Term Lending Institutions
II. Commercial Banks
III. Entrepreneur
IV. Government

These agencies can effectively stem the sickness if they make use of signals and symptoms (Chapter 3) that are generated by the industrial unit in its working and by using an information

and reporting system (Chapter 8) of important key parameters of the industrial enterprise.

9.1 Role of Term Lending Institutions

The term lending institutions have to carry out appraisal of important key areas in the project plan. Many projects are 'born sick' because appraisal has not been carried out satisfactorily. The task of the term lender to avert sickness commences with the appraisal of the project.

9.1.1 Appraisal of management

The term lender can forestal more than fifty per cent chances of sickness if he evaluates properly the management of the project. A competent and vigilant management can be expected not only to find solutions to the day-to-day problems of the unit, but also to anticipate the problems-to-be and take timely steps to avoid them. Management evaluation is a difficult task but with experience, a term lender would develop the sixth sense to differentiate between a desirable and undesirable entrepreneur. The term lender can always obtain reports on the prospective borrower from bankers and other known sources, particularly regarding his antecedents and business reputation.

9.1.2 Market survey

Market potential for a new product is often uncertain and if a project is supported by the term lender without ascertaining that the end-products would have a reasonable market, he may soon have a sick unit on his hands. Whenever an entrepreneur markets only one product for a specific customer, the unit runs into problems because customers are known to change their demand midstream. Either the need changes or the quantity required is reduced making the industrial unit sick.

9.1.3 Machinery and equipment

At times, the project is based on second-hand machinery. Such a project can easily become sick if the reconditioning of the second-hand equipment is not satisfactorily done or the technicians to instal the equipment are not available in good

time. Extra care has, therefore, to be exercised by the financing institutions to ensure that the second-hand equipment would have a reasonably long life after reconditioning, and in case of any deficiency in the equipment, ready assistance from the sellers would be available. There are cases when an entrepreneur decides to patronise a new process. Not only the term lender should insist that a new process should be proved on sufficiently large pilot plant, but performance guarantee should also be insisted upon from the party providing the process.

9.1.4 Satisfactory implementation

Time element is all important in the implementation of a project and the term lender has to ensure that all avoidable delays at the appraisal stage and during the disbursement of the sanctioned assistance are eschewed scrupulously. Prompt action during these stages would not only result in the implementation of the project without overruns and on schedule, but would also establish proper rapport between the term lender and the entrepreneur so essential for the term lender while monitoring the project later. It must be emphasised that promptness is not to be achieved at the cost of proper appraisal of the project, or by making disbursements without observing the usual precautions. In fact, a good appraisal is the other important step that a term lender has to take to forestal sickness in the unit. Normally, the appraisal is handled by the financial and technical officers of the term lending institutions, who have the necessary background and the experience for the job. Nevertheless, there would be cases where outside experts would have to be consulted. In a few cases, it may also become necessary to visit foreign countries to observe the working of similar plants or understand an unknown process/ knowhow. When the above consultations/visits are dictated by the exigencies of the situation, there should be no hesitancy in the lending institution because of the substantial expenditure involved, which may not be recoverable from the entrepreneur, and may invite criticism from one or the other quarter.

9.1.5 Role of nominee directors

Adequate monitoring of the assisted project is equally imperative to detect incipient sickness. Before disbursement of the sanctioned assistance is completed, the unit should be inspected by a team of technical and financial officers of the term lender. The reports received from the unit regarding progress of construction should be carefully scrutinised to find any deviation in cost estimates and/or time schedule and major variation should be immediately enquired into. The nominee director is an important monitoring person in the hands of the term lenders provided the appointee is competent. His task is rather difficult since while serving as watch dog for the institution appointing him, to be really useful, he has also to get himself accepted by the other members of the Board. If the nominee has the necessary tact and the requisite experience, he can easily be an instrument to detect sickness in the unit before it starts developing roots.

9.2 Role of Commercial Banks

It will be readily agreed that a commercial bank is of vital importance to an industrial unit in as much as it provides to the unit the liquid resources needed to keep the unit going. The position enables the commercial bank to come into close contact with the operations of the unit. It is the commercial banker, therefore, who should be able to discern the first warning signals of impending sickness in the unit.

9.2.1 Feedback from commercial banks

It may go a long way in detection/prevention of incipient sickness if the term lender and the commercial banker realise that they are the two wheels on which the project has to proceed to success and that success can be achieved only if both of them function in unison. If one of them tries to strengthen its position at the cost of the other, or keeps away any information about adverse developments in the unit, eventually both will suffer as also the unit itself. There is a dire need for cooperation between the two lenders from the very inception

of the project, and it has to be continued throughout the life of the project.

9.2.2 **Warning signals**

For instance, if the drawings in the account exceed the permissible drawing power continuously over a period, the banker can safely conclude that the customer is short of funds. If the account runs consistently in excess of the sanctioned limit, the customer might be indulging in over-trading. If the bills drawn by the seller on his buyers are returned unpaid, it may be a pointer to the unacceptability of the end-products of the unit in the market. It can as well be said that a good look at the ledger account of a customer (bank's) by an experienced banker can throw a flood of light on the state of the business of the customer—at least, reveal enough for the banker to knit his eye-brows.

9.2.3 **Market intelligence**

The apprehensions raised by the scrutiny of the ledger account can be counter-checked by the banker with market intelligence, which he has perforce to build in his system of working. Only when and if the market reports corroborate the banker's earlier apprehensions raised by the ledger account, the banker need commence action to arrest impending sickness. An innocuous visit to the unit by the banker might help in crystallising the picture further.

9.2.4 **Stemming sickness**

Discussions with the entrepreneur could be the first step in the desired direction provided the intention is to help the entrepreneur to come out of the difficulties. Any undue pressure at this stage to recover even a part of the bankers' dues and/or to strengthen the security is bound to complicate the existing unsatisfactory situation and also prompt the customer to keep back the information regarding adverse developments. Normally, provision of additional finance/credit, reduction in the prescribed margin and some latitude in repayment of the overdues would help in remedying incipient sickness. In more difficult cases, reduction in the rate

of interest for a temporary period, or funding/writing off overdue interest might take care of the problem. And where the above concessions/reliefs do not produce the desired result, the banker would be right in concluding that incipient sickness is fast becoming chronic and he should bring the term lender into the picture for concerted further action.

9.3 The Role of the Entrepreneur

In a way, it should be the sole responsibility of the entrepreneur who conceives, implements and manages the project, to avert sickness in the unit set up by him. This can normally be done if the entrepreneur does his home work properly while drawing up the project, if he pays adequate attention to the deficiencies pointed out by the appraising officers of the financial institutions, if he selects the suppliers of machinery and process carefully, if he appoints the financial and other staff in time, if he affects economy to keep the project cost within the original estimates and implements the same according to the time schedule.

9.3.1 Management board

The industry should have a Board with competent persons from all disciplines needed to run the unit successfully, appoint a dynamic chief executive to implement the policies formulated by the Board and ensure a proper second line of defence by appointing professional go-getters. And above all, at the first sign of any adverse development in the unit, he should take his banker and term lender into confidence. Fortunately, the old thinking of the bankers to "put on the heat" when the borrower is in difficulties, is being gradually replaced by a desire to understand the problems of the entrepreneur when he faces crisis and to find solutions so that the unit functions smoothly.

9.3.2 Partners in enterprise

The term lenders consider themselves as partners in the enterprise (Fig. 9.1) being managed by the entrepreneur and are fully conscious that the recovery of their lent funds depends on the capability of the unit to generate surpluses.

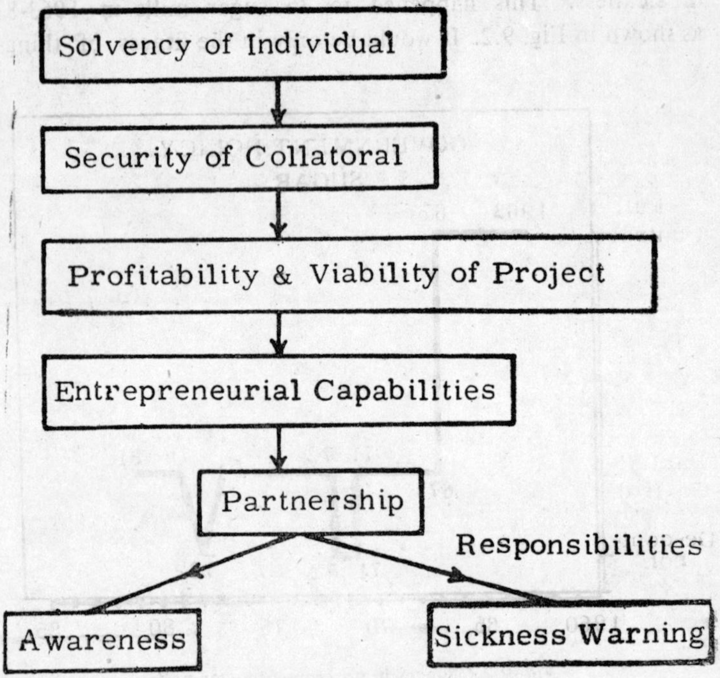

Fig. 9.1 **Changing role of development banks**

In the circumstances, the entrepreneur can freely confine his problems to the lenders and make use of their expert advice in averting sickness before it is too late.

9.4 The Role of the Government

The Government can help in controlling sickness by not making sudden and frequent changes in the industrial policies. It has to be appreciated that setting up of an industrial unit is an investment decision, which has to take into account future returns.

9.4.1 Sudden changes in industrial policy

When several changes are made successively in the industrial policy by the Government, it not only discourages new investment but also upsets future plans causing sickness in the established units. Withdrawal of subsidies can also result

in sickness. This happened to 36 sugar mills in 1963-81 as shown in Fig. 9.2. It would be only in the fitness of things

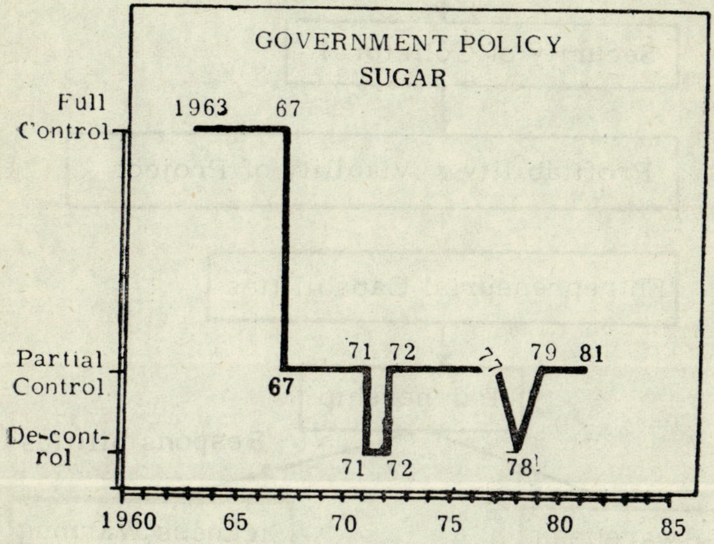

Fig. 9.2 **Changes in government sugar policy**

if the term lenders, who are expected to know the pulse of each industry financed by them, are taken into confidence by the Government, before effecting any major modifications in the industrial policy. The financial institutions and the representatives of industry can also be prompted to come together occasionally with or without Government participation with a view to discussing the problems of the industry in general or of any particular industry and evolving solutions including recommendations to the Government to modify its existing policies.

9.4.2 Resistance to change

The law as it stands today does not empower the term lenders to make changes in the management of an assisted unit even when they are convinced that incipient sickness in the unit is entirely due to the incompetence and/or dishonesty of the existing management and it is apparent to them that

without a change in management, the unit would soon become chronically sick. Strangely enough, when the management is efficient and honest, any changes suggested in the management by the lenders are readily accepted but a management which is not above board, usually resists management changes.

9.4.3 Power to change

It would be a great help if the apex term lenders are vested by the Government with powers to make management changes in units assisted by the public financial institution when it is proved to its satisfaction that sickness in a unit has set in and the same can be attributed entirely/mainly to deficient management. In particular, term lenders may be authorised to appoint in units suffering from incipient sickness whole-time financial, technical and marketing directors. Such directors, of course, would have to be empowered to report to the financial institution and also given immunity from penalties for acts done in good faith. Term lenders can be required to prepare a panel of experienced persons, who could take up such challenging assignments, while retired officers from the public and private sectors with adequate background could be one source for building up such a panel.

9.5 Trouble Shooters

Term lenders should also have a team of trouble shooters out of its own staff and staff of other term lenders. These trouble shooters can be imparted on-floor training in well-managed industrial units and in case of need, can be rushed to trouble spots at short notice to hold the fort till better or long term arrangements can be made. The persons to be deputed to sick units will, of course, have to be selected very carefully. They must be made to realise, before deputation, that their appointments in the industrial units under an institutional umbrella are not to be regarded as seats of power to show-off or bully the existing managements, and that the assignments are to be accepted as challenges in the service of community by improving, through hard work and

dedication, the working of the units in the interests of the financial institutions, the shareholders and the economy in general. And further, that the appointees would be expected to establish proper rapport with the erring management through tact and forbearance. The financial institutions may thus be able to provide to the industry a set of dynamic professionals who can be relied upon to deliver the goods. Once the confidence is established in the institutions and their professionals, maybe, the units in trouble would voluntarily ask for professionals on short or long term basis. If this happens, we may be able to put real breaks to sickness in industry.

10

REHABILITATION

10.0 Introduction

The incidence of industrial sickness both in large and small scale industry, has continued to rise. The number of large sick industrial units availing of bank credit of Rs. 1 crore and above increased to 463 at the end of June 1983 from 435 as at the end of June 1982. The bank credit outstanding against these units amounted to Rs. 1913.10 crores at end June 1983 as compared to Rs. 1728.95 crores as at the end of June 1982, showing an increase of Rs. 184.15 crores. Small scale units are also reported to have been gripped by the sickness. According to the information furnished by scheduled commercial banks for the quarter ended June 1983, the number of sick industrial units identified by bank in the small scale sector more than doubled, rising to 64,388 units at the end of June 1983 from 26,973 units at the end of June 1982. Bank credit outstanding against these units rose to Rs. 626.52 crores at the end of June 1983 from Rs. 393.67 crores a year ago. As regards the overall incidence of sickness in industrial units, both small and big, financed by the banking system, there were 66062 sick units involving an amount of Rs. 2792.63 crores which constituted 7.9% of banks' total advances [120].

The progressive increase in sickness in industry is shown in Fig. 1.1 (Chapter 1). Keeping in view the growing incidence of industrial sickness and the resources blocked in sick units, it is realised that solutions are to be found to rehabilitate sick units and hence to overcome the problem of widespread sickness in Indian industry.

Rehabilitation is a remedy considered for industrial units which have already become sick and are on the verge of virtual collapse. Some viable policy measures are required to revive the sick units. Ad-hoc remedies and commitments to keep the unit running would not help to overcome the problem of industrial sickness in the long run.

Rehabilitation has been discussed under two heads:

(*i*) What has been done at the various levels—the Union Government, the Reserve Bank of India and the Financial Institutions—to rehabilitate sick units?

(*ii*) What should be done to revive sick units?

The measures evolved to rehabilitate sick units at various levels are discussed as follows:

10.1 Policy Measures by the Government

The Government has made certain policy pronouncements on sick units from time to time. The various policy measures taken by the Government to revive sick industrial units are as under:

(*i*) Soft Loan Scheme, 1976
(*ii*) Merger Policy, 1977
(*iii*) Policy guidelines on sick units, 1978
(*iv*) New Strategy, 1981
(*v*) Industrial Reconstruction Bank of India Bill, 1984
(*vi*) Policy guidelines on sick units in the Union Budget 1985-86.

10.1.1 Soft loan scheme

The soft loan scheme was introduced in November 1976 for modernising the five selected industries, namely, cotton textiles, jute, cement, sugar and specified engineering industries. The main objective of the scheme is to provide financial assistance on concessional terms to the weaker units in these five groups for modernisation, replacement and renovation of their old plant and machinery.

The scheme is being operated by the IDBI with participation of IFCI and ICICI. The IFCI is the lead institution for

jute and sugar industries, IDBI for cotton and cement industries and ICICI for engineering industries. However, the overall responsibility of operating the scheme is vested in IDBI. Loans, under the soft loan scheme, are provided on concessional terms not only in regard to the rate of interest, but also in regard to other provisions such as the promoter's contribution, debt equity ratio, initial moratorium and repayment period. In pursuance of the decision taken by the Union Government in November 1977, loans under this scheme are exempted from the convertibility clause.

Under the soft loan scheme, the units have been classified into three groups—weak, not so weak and better off units. 'Weak' units are those in respect of which erosion in paid-up capital and reserves is above 50 per cent, 'not so weak' units are those in respect of which such erosion is up to 50 per cent and 'better off' units as those without such erosion. The entire financial assistance to 'weak units' is given at concessional rate of 7.5 per cent, while the concessional part is reduced in the case of 'not so weak' and 'better off' units on a grading scale depending upon the financial position of the units.

The industrial unit should have been in operation for at least 10 years to be eligible for assistance under the soft loan scheme. The plant and equipment proposed to be replaced should have also been in use for more than 10 years. The 10 years' criterion is relaxable, if the project aims at increase in exports, import substitution, energy saving and anti-pollution measures.

The operations of soft loan scheme are given in Table 10.1 [121]. Since the introduction of scheme in November 1976 to end-June 1983, cumulative sanctions of IDBI, IFCI and ICICI under the soft loan scheme amounted to Rs. 1024.5 crores for 592 proposals and disbursements amounted Rs. 574 crores. Of the total amount of actual disbursement under the soft loan scheme, textile industry received the highest amount of Rs. 325.8 crores followed by engineering industry Rs. 115.5 crores, cement industry Rs. 69.9 crores, sugar industry Rs. 48.4 crores and jute industry Rs. 14.5 crores. As at the end-June 1983, 32 applications were pending for Rs. 151.8

crores as against 19 applications for Rs. 43 crores as at the end-June 1982.

TABLE 10.1: **Operations of soft loan scheme (IDBI, IFCI and ICICI)**

(Position as at the end of June 1983)

(*Amount in Rs. crores*)

Industry	Sanctions		Disbursement amount	Pending applications	
	No. of units	Amount		No. of units	Amount
Cotton Textile	364	516.9	325.8	25	78.7
Cement	23	144.2	69.9	01	3.0
Sugar	37	62.7	48.4	—	—
Jute	26	51.4	14.5	03	57.9
Engineering	142	249.3	115.5	03	12.2
Total	592	1024.5	574.1	32	151.8

A modified scheme known as soft loan scheme for modernisation was introduced to cover all industries effective from January 1, 1984. With effect from March 1984, the rate of interest on loans up to Rs. 4 crores was reduced from 12.5 per cent to 11.5 per cent which may further be reduced to 10 per cent for weak units. The assistance under the soft loan scheme in excess of Rs. 4 crores carries the normal lending rate of interest of the Financial Institutions. The entire assistance sanctioned under the scheme, whether on the concessional rate of interest or at normal lending rate of interest, is exempt from the applicability of 'convertibility clause'.

10.1.2 Merger policy 1977

In 1977, the Union Government evolved a scheme of merger of sick units with healthy ones with a view to revive sick industrial units. In the Finance Act, 1977, the Government introduced certain fiscal concessions under section 72-A of the Income-tax Act whereby a healthy unit taking over a sick unit was allowed to carry forward and set off the accumulated losses and unabsorbed depreciation of the latter against

its own tax incidence. However, it was stipulated that the merger should be in the public interest. In respect of the amalgamations mooted by MRTP companies, the requirement was an overwhelming public interest. Three conditions were laid down for overwhelming public interest:

(*a*) The amalgamated companies should have experience of manufacturing the same products as produced by the sick unit proposed to be taken over by it.

(*b*) The sick unit considered for merger with a healthy unit should belong to an industry suffering from widespread and chronic sickness.

(*c*) There must be a demonstrable gain to public interest through the proposed merger.

It was further required that (1) the sick unit to be taken over should have employed staff numbering more than 100 and (2) it should have assets of more than Rs. 50 lakhs. These two conditions were applicable to both MRTP and non-MRTP companies.

In September 1980, the Union Government decided to withdraw all the above conditions on account of tardy progress of company takeover under the scheme. The liberalisation led to more expeditious clearance of merger proposals which is clear from the data that between 1978 and September 1980, only 16 schemes had been approved, while between September 1980 and June 1981 the number of approvals was 25.

Until August 1979, the Government did not allow amalgamations of inter-connected companies or subsidiaries with their principal units taking the view that such mergers were against the basic objectives of the policy relaxation under Section 72-A of the Income Tax Act. But in August 1979, in a bid to make the scheme more attractive, it was decided to throw open the tax concession also to companies mergering with their subsidiaries or inter-connected units.

10.1.3 **Policy guidelines on sick units 1978**

The policy 1978 on sick industries recognised that the revival of a sick unit cannot be the responsibility of any single agency and that it can be achieved effectively only by a sharing of the responsibility by Central Government, State Governments,

Financial Institutions, Reserve Bank of India and the management itself. The policy stated that closer and more vigilant involvement of financial institutions in units with management of doubtful competence or integrity would be essential. For this purpose the policy statement announced that a group of professional directors would be set up jointly by financial institutions. This group would report to the financial institutions on measures that should be taken to prevent industrial sickness. In the case of industrial units which were already sick, the policy advocated rehabilitation through joint efforts of State Government and financial institutions who were provided financial and managerial support with suitable restructuring of the management. It also announced that proposals for the merger of sick units with healthy ones would be examined by special authority under the Income Tax Act of 1961. The steps under the Industries (Development and Regulation) Act would be considered only when the above courses of actions failed.

In order to examine all the alternative courses of actions and to decide on the most suitable measures the policy statement proposed to set up a screening committee under chairmanship of Secretary, Industrial Development with representatives of the Finance Ministry, Reserve Bank of India and financial institutions. A major decision that the 1978 policy statement announced was not to return to the same management which had been taken under Industries (Development and Regulation) Act.

10.1.4 New strategy 1981

A new strategy for sick units was announced by the Union Industry Ministry in last week of June 1981. The strategy aimed at preventing sickness in industry, quick rehabilitation of sick units and an early decision on the future of sick units. The new strategy stated that four factors would be weighed properly while reviving sick units:

(*a*) There may be denotification of management followed by the liquidation of the unit;

(*b*) The unit may be sold as an on-going concern;

(*c*) The liabilities of sick units may be restructured with the permission from high court;

(*d*) The sick units may be nationalised through the acquisition of assets or shares.

The major plank of this new strategy was the provision that units employing over 1000 persons or having an investment of Rs. 9 crores or more in fixed assets should be nationalised, if the RBI, the financial institutions and the State Governments were unable to prevent the growing sickness in sick units. This would, however, be subject to three further considerations. A sick unit would be nationalised provided that (*a*) the line of production is critical to the economy, (*b*) the unit has been functioning as another unit with large ancillary linkages and (*c*) its closure would cause substantial dislocation and throw out of employment, such a large number of persons that it would not be possible to provide alternative jobs to them.

It was also mentioned in the new strategy that it would not be desirable to nationalise a unit which was inherently non-viable. The new strategy had, therefore, emphasised the need for the concerned administrative ministry to satisfy itself regarding the viability of the unit before a decision was taken to nationalise it.

An examination of these broad features of the new strategy aimed at curing the industrial sickness revealed that it completely left out small sector units from its scope even though the incidence of sickness among these units was by no means insignificant.

In December 1983, the Government of India decided to set up a Guidance Committee to examine cases of problem projects and to suggest the various alternative measures for resolving the problems of revival of sick units. The committee will examine cases referred to by the Reserve Bank, public financial institutions, commercial banks and administrative Ministries/Departments of the Central Government. It will not, however, consider cases of units taken over by the Government under the provisions of the Industries (Development and Regulation) Act, 1951 and cases of nationalised units.

10.1.5 Industrial Reconstruction Bank of India (IRBI) Bill, 1984

Parliament passed a Bill on August 7, 1984 to convert the Industrial Reconstruction Corporation of India Ltd. (IRCI), which is a company registered under the Companies Act, into a statutory corporation to be called the Industrial Reconstruction Bank of India (IRBI) with a view to overcoming the inherent difficulties which had been faced by the IRCI in its efforts to rehabilitate and reconstruct sick industrial units and to make it the principal credit agency for revival of sick units.

The IRBI will function as the principal credit and reconstruction agency for the revival of sick industrial units and will coordinate the work of other institutions engaged in the revival of industries. It will assist and promote the rehabilitation of industrial concerns. The IRBI's functions would cover not only reconstruction assistance to sick units but also developmental assistance combined with merchant banking.

The authorised capital of the IRBI will be Rs. 200 crores and paid up capital will be Rs. 50 crores comprising of Rs. 20 crores of the IRCI's paid-up capital, conversion of Central Government loans to IRCI into capital to the extent of Rs. 20 crores and Rs. 10 crores direct subscription by the Central Government. The IRBI could receive interest free loans from Central Government ranging from Rs. 40 crores to Rs. 80 crores every year depending upon the magnitude of its operations [122]. It could also raise foreign loans with guarantees from the Government of India. In addition to its normal funds, a special fund would be set up for the purpose of financing any loan or advance or entering into any arrangements which are not supported by the RBI, the scheduled commercial banks and the financial institutions.

The IRBI would be empowered to take over the sick industrial units under its assistance for the purpose of managing and running them, lease them out or sell them as running concerns or prepare schemes for reconstruction by scaling down the liabilities with the approval of the Central Government. The new institution would be empowered to take certain decisions in conformity with MRTP and FERA rules so as to permit

large multi-national houses to participate in reconstructions plans for sick units. It would also be empowered to expedite cases of amalgamation. The legislation of converting IRCI into IRBI as a statutory organisation is a welcome step.

10.1.6 **Policy guidelines on sick units in the union budget 1985-86**

The Government is contemplating legislation to deal with sick units [123]. Under the proposed legislation, managements which are held responsible for making units sick would be blacklisted. Such managements would not be given Government assistance or assistance from financial institutions or banks for existing units and for new ventures. It was also proposed to set up a Board for Financial and Industrial Reconstruction, which would provide a speedy mechanism for amalgamation, mergers and devise such other solutions as might be necessary to deal with the problem of sick units in the large and medium sector.

Under the proposed legislation, managements of sick units, whose net worth had been eroded by 50 per cent, would be required to seek a fresh mandate from their shareholders and report to a Government body. If 100 per cent net worth had been lost, the management would be deemed to be responsible for mismanagements and would not have further role to play in running the affairs of the unit and also would not receive any further financial assistance from anywhere for new ventures.

10.2 **Role of the Reserve Bank of India**

The Reserve Bank of India through its Sick Industrial Undertaking Cell, which was created in 1976 in its Department of Operations and Development (DBOD), monitors the performance of commercial banks in identifying the sick units and initiates appropriate remedial measures whenever necessary and coordinates the efforts of Government, banks and financial institutions in rehabilitation of potential viable sick units. This cell also attends to processing of applications received from banks for credit authorisation in respect of sick units and disposal of proposal from banks for supportive measures, viz.

charging concessional rate of interest, reduction in margin, funding of interest etc. for rehabilitation of potentially viable sick units. The Reserve Bank has directed each bank to create a sick industrial undertaking cell at the central office and regional offices to identify and monitor the potentially viable sick units and determining the various steps necessary for their rehabilitation. In 1979, it undertook studies of the organisational set up in banks for monitoring sick units.

With a view to ascertaining the magnitude of and the reasons for industrial sickness, as also monitoring the performance of banks in rehabilitation of such units, the Reserve Bank has prescribed submission of quarterly returns on sick units by banks. The Reserve Bank has asked banks to furnish a quarterly statement of all sick units enjoying aggregate credit limit of Rs. 1 crore and above from the banking system. According to the quarterly review note on sick units prepared by the Reserve Bank [120] based on the data furnished by the commercial banks, there were 463 large sick industrial units (each with credit limit of Rs. 1 crore and above from the banking system) and 64388 sick small scale industrial units as at the end of June 1983. Out of the 463 large sick units identified by banks, viability studies in respect of 409 were completed; of these, 345 units were considered as potentially viable and 248 units were put under nursing programme as at the end-June 1983. Out of 64388 sick small scale units, 5983 units were considered by banks as potentially viable and 50384 units as non-viable. Banks had put 2257 (out of 5983) potentially viable units under nursing programme. Banks have yet to assess the viability of the remaining 8021 units with outstanding credit of Rs. 77.39 crores.

A committee was appointed by the Reserve Bank of India under the Chairmanship of Shri T. Tiwari (Chairman, IRCI Ltd.) to look into legal and other difficulties faced by banks and other financial institutions in rehabilitation of sick industrial undertakings and to suggest remedial measures including changes in law. The committee submitted its final report in July 1983, which is under consideration of the Government of India.

In order to curtail sickness among small scale units, a

number of remedial measures were taken by the Reserve Bank of India. Under the Margin Money Scheme for revival of sick units, a sum of Rs. 54 lakhs was sanctioned to five State Governments for 1983-84. The All India Small Scale Industries Board constituted a Standing Committee on industrial sickness to suggest remedial measures for rehabilitation of sick units.

The Standing Coordination Committee, which was appointed in January 1979 following the recommendations of the Inter-Institutional Group (Bhucher Committee) to consider issues pertaining to coordination between banks and term lending institutions, was reconstituted under the chairmanship of Shri A. Ghosh, Deputy Governor of the Reserve Bank of India in August 1983. The committee will provide a standing forum for sorting out inter-institutional problems relating to term lending in the light of experience gained in the past and review the involvement of banks and term lending institutions in extending term credit, besides dealing with compilation and sharing of information on term credit and any other issues that may be referred to it. The revival of the Standing Coordination Committee would help in speedier and effective implementation of schemes for revival of potentially viable sick units.

In April 1983, at the instance of the Central Government, the Reserve Bank asked banks to evolve methods and mechanisms to diagnose sickness in industrial units at the incipient stage itself and bring it to the notice of the concerned administrative ministries immediately. If there is no proper response from the concerned ministry, the matter should be brought to the notice of the Finance Ministry. Banks were also advised not to nominate the same officer on Boards of too many assisted units.

10.3 **Role of the Financial Institutions—IDBI, IRCI and IFCI**

The role played by the term lending institutions—Industrial Development Bank of India (IDBI), Industrial Reconstruction Corporation of India (IRCI) and Industrial Finance Corporation of India (IFCI)—in rehabilitation of sick industrial units is discussed as follows:

10.3.1 Industrial Development Bank of India

Industrial Development Bank of India was established in July 1964. The main objective was to bring into existence an apex institution to coordinate the activities of other financial institutions and banks providing term finance to industry and also to provide direct financial assistance to industrial units to bridge the gap between the supply of and demand for medium and long-term finance.

To deal with the problems of sick industrial units, a Rehabilitation Finance Division (RFD) was created by IDBI in February 1976. The Rehabilitation Finance Division has been playing an important role in the matters of rehabilitation of sick industrial units and surveillance of their performance. The measures adopted for rehabilitating sick industrial units include identification of causes of sickness, assessment of rehabilitation needs, formulation of appropriate measures in consultation with participating institutions and banks, close monitoring of sick units and periodical evaluation of the impact of rehabilitation measures.

The Industrial Development Bank of India had given-rehabilitation assistance to 202 sick units involving outstanding loan of Rs. 280.6 crores by the end of June 1984. The industrywise break-up of assisted sick units and the out standing credit to these units is given in Table 10.2 [124]. As at the end of June 1984, four industries—cotton textiles, sugar, paper, metal and engineering—together accounted for 65 per cent of 202 sick units and over 70 per cent of the total amount of credit outstanding to the sick units.

TABLE 10.2: **Industrywise assistance to sick units by IDBI—position as at the end June 1984**

(*Amount in Rs. crores*)

Industry	No. of sick units	Loan outstanding at the end June 1984
Food Manufacturing		
(*a*) Sugar	23	26.5
(*b*) Others	—	—
Textiles	49	62.5
Jute	3	3.1
Paper and Paper Products	15	49.7
Rubber Products	5	19.8
Basic Industrial Chemicals (excluding Fertilisers)	14	25.0
Fertilisers	2	0.4
Misc. Chemicals	1	0.7
Cement	3	5.5
Basic Metal Industry	15	23.6
Metal Products	2	0.8
Machinery (other than Electricals)	31	38.5
Electrical Machinery	11	5.9
Transport Equipment	3	2.6
Services	3	1.5
Others	22	14.5
Total	202	280.6

Statewise break-up of assisted sick units and the credit outstanding to these units as at the end of June 1984 is given in Table 10.3 [124]. Statewise, four States namely Maharashtra, West Bengal, Karnataka and Tamil Nadu accounted for over 50 per cent of the total amount outstanding against sick units. Other States with substantial amount locked up in sick units were Assam, Uttar Pradesh, Andhra Pradesh and Kerala.

TABLE 10.3: **Statewise assistance to sick units by IDBI (position as at the end June 1984)**

(*Amount in Rs. crores*)

State	No. of sick units	Loan outstanding as at the end June 1984
Andhra Pradesh	16	20.6
Assam	4	21.5
Bihar	4	8.0
Gujarat	20	13.2
Goa	1	3.4
Haryana	7	12.2
Himachal Pradesh	2	0.9
Jammu & Kashmir	1	0.4
Karnataka	9	24.5
Kerala	12	14.0
Maharashtra	42	59.1
Madhya Pradesh	7	5.9
Meghalaya	1	2.7
Delhi	4	2.7
Orissa	3	2.7
Punjab	8	7.5
Rajasthan	5	2.9
Tamil Nadu	9	24.3
Uttar Pradesh	20	21.1
West Bengal	27	33.0
Total	202	280.6

During the year 1984, rehabilitation assistance of Rs. 23 crores was sanctioned to 27 units (including units where rehabilitation measures involved expansion/diversification schemes) as against Rs. 4 crores sanctioned to 4 units during the preceding year. IDBI has been closely associated with the work of a Working Group (Textile Commissioner as Convenor) appointed by the Union Government to deal with the growing incidence of sickness in textile industry. Viability studies were undertaken in respect of a number of closed and sick mills and packages of assistance were worked out for revival of viable units. In case of Basic Metal and Engineering Industry, IDBI jointly with other institutions undertook viability studies

of mills which were considered *prima facie* potentially viable by a study team appointed by the RBI.

A Special Rehabilitation Cell in RFD attends to the problems of sick units referred to IDBI by the commercial banks, other financial institutions, State Governments and Central Government. Of the 19 references (10 from banks and 9 from State Governments and other agencies) received by the Cell, viability studies were prepared in respect of five cases and need based assistance is being sanctioned. Necessary action was initiated in respect of the remaining cases and the concerned banks/State Governments/other agencies were suitably advised.

Since the introduction of soft loan scheme in November 1976 to end June 1984, IDBI sanctioned loan assistance of Rs. 490.8 crores and disbursed Rs. 374.7 crores to six industries viz. textiles, jute, sugar, cement, enginnering and basic industrial chemicals (Table 10.4).

TABLE 10.4: **Soft loan assistance sanctioned and disbursed by IDBI up to June 30, 1984**

(*Amount in Rs. crores*)

Industry	Sanctions	Disbursements
Cotton Textiles	307.6	236.4
Jute	16.6	8.3
Sugar	28.0	24.9
Cement	55.6	46.4
Engineering	82.1	58.7
Basic Industrial Chemicals	0.9	—
Total	490.8	374.7

Following the recommendations of the Study Group constituted by RBI, IDBI has indicated its broad agreement to set up Soft Loan Assistance Fund (SLAF) for providing quasi-equity assistance carrying nominal service charge of 1 per cent and reference against loans granted by institutions to sick small scale industrial units at concessional rates. Operational details are being worked in consultation with the Government and Reserve Bank of India.

10.3.2 Industrial Reconstruction Corporation of India Ltd. (IRCI)

The Industrial Reconstruction Corporation of India Ltd. was established in April 1971 as a specialised financial institution to promote and operate schemes for industrial development and in particular to provide financial assistance for the reconstruction and rehabilitation of sick industrial units. To achieve the task of reconstruction and rehabilitation of sick industrial units, the IRCI adopted a two-pronged strategy: to introduce professional management on modern lines in the units concerned and to create a proper management outlook having regard to the social climate in which managements have to function.

The Industrial Reconstruction Corporation of India Ltd. assisted 102 industrial units during the year ending March 1984 compared with 88 units in the preceding year. The financial assistance sanctioned during 1983-84 amounted to Rs. 64.9 crores, 12.1 per cent higher than in the previous year while disbursements increased by 5.8 per cent to Rs. 38.2 crores. The cumulative sanctions and disbursements up to end-March 1984 were Rs. 266.00 crores and Rs. 184.9 crores respectively. The financial assistance sanctioned and disbursed up to the end of March 1984 is shown in Table 10.5 [125].

TABLE 10.5: **Financial assistance sanctioned and disbursed by Industrial Reconstruction Corporation of India Ltd.**

(Amount in Rs. crores)

Year (April-March)	No. of units	Sanctions	Disbursements
1982-83	88	57.9	36.1
1983-84	102	64.9	38.2
Cumulative position as at the end of March 1984	242	266.0	184.9

The IRCI provided credit facilities to various state level institutions/Union Territories agencies like SFCs and SIDCs to help rehabilitation of sick small scale units. Till the end of March 1984, the IRCI sanctioned such facilities to 17 state

level/Union Territories agencies for a total amount of Rs. 8.5 crores and disbursed Rs. 1.5 crores.

The IRCI diversified its activities into ancillary lines incidental and allied to its task of rehabilitation such as consultancy, services, merchant banking and equipment leasing and till the end of March 1984, it sanctioned Rs. 3.7 crores and disbursed Rs. 3 crores under the scheme. The IRCI consultancy service was intended to help banks and financial institutions to assess intrinsic worth of sick units which seek assistance for revival. The merchant banking services of IRCI were provided to units for amalgamation, merger and reconstruction while the equipment leasing was an extension of the IRCI's hire-purchase scheme.

Now, the Industrial Reconstruction Corporation of India Ltd. has been converted into a statutory corporation known as Industrial Reconstruction Bank of India (IRBI) by passing a Bill in Parliament on August 7, 1984.

10.3.3 **Industrial Finance Corporation of India (IFCI)**

Industrial Finance Corporation of India is a national level development bank, set up in 1948 by an Act of Parliament with the objective of providing medium and long term finance to industrial concerns in India. IFCI's role extends to the entire industrial spectrum of the country encompassing principally project financing operations and promotional activities.

Industrial Finance Corporation of India through its Problem Cases Department (PCD) processes and monitors the cases of sick industrial units and undertakes the remedial measures to revive the sick units. As soon as a sick case is transferred to PCD, it is thoroughly reviewed in order to draw a rehabilitation scheme to restore the unit back to normal health. The Problem Cases Department closely monitors the implementation of rehabilitation scheme drawn for a sick industrial unit. An attempt is also made to see that the weak unit merges with a healthy unit with requisite managerial and financial resources.

The Problem Cases Department in IFCI, in consonance with the Government's policy towards revival of sick units, evolved rehabilitation schemes in respect of eight cases, strengthened the management set up in one case, brought about changes in management/controlling interest in five cases, leased out and/or agreed to support in holding on operations in three cases, approved schemes of merger in three cases and reached arrangements for settlement of dues in two cases [126]. Reports about the inherently non-viable units are made to the Central Government from time to time and liaison is maintained with the concerned State Governments involved in such cases.

IFCI has been providing concessional assistance for modernisation under the 'Soft Loan Scheme' to jute and sugar industries being a lead institution for them since November 1976. As on March 31, 1984, IFCI had assisted 333 projects, to the extent of Rs. 189.6 crores both under the earlier 'Soft Loan Scheme' and the modified 'Soft Loan Scheme' for modernisation

It is apparent from a review of measures to revive sick industrial units that the Central Government, Reserve Bank of India, commercial banks and financial institutions have been striving hard and spending a sizeable amount of resources for the rehabilitation of sick industrial units. However, the results have not been very satisfactory. The number of sick industrial units, both in large and small scale units, is increasing at alarming rate. Therefore, there is a need to develop more effective rehabilitation programme so that sickness can be stemmed earlier and units made productive.

10.4 **Revival of Sick Units—What Should be Done?**

The reasons for sickness in industrial units have been brought out in the second chapter while analysing 200 cases of sick industrial units over a decade of their existence. The deficiencies have been identified. However, it is important to evolve measures for the orderly revival of these sick units so that they can become productive again. Before considering various aspects of rehabilitation, it is important to assess whether a sick unit can attain viability in a reasonable time

and put back in production. A viability study therefore has to be undertaken. While potentially non-viable units should be closed or merged and the affected people found suitable re-employment, only such units which can be revived should be considered for further assistance, subsidies and rehabilitation. A lot of literature has appeared on the rehabilitation programmes of sick units. Some of the authors like Ashoke Dutt [127]. Chakravarty [128], Desai [129], K.N. Pillai [130] and Iyer [131] have given a list of steps that need be taken to rehabilitate the sick units and their management problem.

10.5 Viability Study

The general principles involved in viability studies are indicated by the factors affecting viability in a sick unit. These normally vary among companies, industrial groups and institutions. However, the approach to viability study has to be based on the analysis of post operations of the unit with a view to determine its strength and weaknesses with regard to the various functional areas i.e. marketing, production, personnel and finance. The viability study should be carried out under three major heads: (*a*) Market Analysis, (*b*) Technical Analysis and (*c*) Financial Analysis.

10.5.1 Market analysis

A market analysis should contain a brief description of the market, methods of transportation, existing rates of transportation, channels of distribution and general trade practices. The analysis should include past and present demand including determination of quantity and value of consumption as well as the category of products being manufactured by the unit which are likely to be needed by the consumers. The competitive position of the products such as selling price, quality and market practice of competitors should be indicated. An estimate of future demand of product or products and product share of the market considering the demand, supply, competitivee position etc. should be projected.

10.5.2 Technical analysis

The technical analysis has to throw light on the technical feasibility regarding the manufacturing of the product or products in the light of the future demand. It should estimate the cost and capital structure needed to support it. The technical analysis should contain a review of techniques or processes to be applied and other infrastructure support needed in the rehabilitation programme. The technical study in effect should be able to project the production costs in the light of the future demand and market situation.

The performance of the machinery and equipment and the capacity utilisation should be reviewed in the light of the future demand and if there are any modifications/extensions of the plant needed should be brought out. The technical analysis should also consider the availability of raw materials in the light of the future demand and the location of sources of supply, terms of payment and continuity of supply. The study should also estimate labour requirements and the breakdown of direct and indirect labour and supervision costs required for the manufacture of the products. If there are any waste products and other ecological factor, and methods of disposal of waste should be brought out.

10.5.3 Financial analysis

From market analysis, the gross income is evolved at a selling price. From technical analysis, the manufacturing cost is computed. To this, the cost of selling, administrative expenses, depreciation, interest on short-term and long-term borrowings and other recurring expenses are added. It should be possible then to estimate the net profit and the net return after the deduction of taxes.

An estimate of the working capital required to finance current assets, and inventory must be brought out. The inventory comprises raw materials, spares and stores, sem-finished and finished products. It is to be noted that larger production and sales result in increased accounts receivable due to credit being given to customers (60 to 90 days) and this in turn leads to liquidity problem or absence of adequate cash. It

would, therfore, be necessary to prepare a cash flow analysis, to project balance sheet, profit and loss account for a few years. Mode of repayment of loan with interest can then be planned and indicated as part of the viability study.

10.5.4 Government policy

In a recent policy statement of the Government on sick industry, it has also been pointed out that the following options should also be considered in the viability studies:

(*a*) Rehabilitation of the sick unit through State Government and financial institutions who would provide both financial and managerial support with suitable restructuring of management wherever necessary.

(*b*) Proposal, if any, for the merger of the sick unit with a healthy unit in the private sector. This is to be examined in consultation with the specified authority under the Income-tax Act, 1961.

It is only where neither of the above two alternative courses of actions is feasible or desirable, that the sick unit would be taken over under the Industries (Development and Regulation I&D) Act, 1951, Section 18B. The Central Government has also set up a Screening Committee under the chairmanship of Secretary, Industrial Development with representatives of the Finance Ministry and Reserve Bank of India who will examine all alternative courses of action open and decide on the suitable measures which could be taken before they recommend for initial takeover of management

When a sick unit is taken over under the Industries (D&R) Act, the following major changes in management take place:

(*a*) The existing directors and managers vacate their office.

(*b*) The shareholders become dormant.

(*c*) The government appointed persons acquire the powers of the directors.

(*d*) As annual general meeting is not required to be held, accountability is completely altered. The authorised person is only required to report to the Central Government.

10.6 Rehabilitation Programme

The rehabilitation programme will involve the following major issues which have to be sorted out after it has been decided that the sick unit is viable and should be rehabilitated:

(*a*) Change of management.
(*b*) Development of a suitable management information system.
(*c*) A settlement with the creditors for payment of their dues in a phased manner taking into account the expected cash generation as per viability study.
(*d*) Determination of the sources of additional funds needed to refinance. This may involve an analysis of the disposal of excess stocks or assets, if any, and rapid collection of outstanding bills etc.
(*e*) Modernisation of plant and equipment or expansion of an existing programme or even diversification of the products being manufactured.
(*f*) Concession or reliefs or assistance to be allowed by the state level corporation, financial institutions and Central Government.

10.6.1 Change of management

The finding of a suitable manager is perhaps the most difficult problem of sick units particularly where it is found that sickness has been attributed to bad management or the management's integrity and honesty has been doubtful. However, the choice of a good manager can make a big difference in the working of the unit as has been experienced by a public sector unit—Hindustan Latex [132]. Before 1981 the unit was gravely sick. A newly appointed Chairman introduced a new style of management in which workers'

suggestions were invited, considered and implemented. The result of this style of management was better capacity utilisation and within two years the organisation not only became solvent but earned several crores in profit. The strikes which were endemic in 1980-81 virtually disappeared through workers' participation and placement of better personnel in key areas. The workers were also given a fair share of increase in productivity and profit. They also got a good performance award. The plant was expanded and modernised and improved the quality of its product.

In India, there appears to be shortage of top level management personnel. The sick unit which requires better management becomes a victim of this acute shortage. Managers of proven ability are usually absorbed by the healthy units. The sick units usually get a superannuated person with practical no stake for his career. A good manager is hard to find and very difficult to be loaned or deputed from a working industrial unit. The government and the financial institutions are now agreed that a pool of experienced managers should be constituted but it is as yet not in existence. Needless to say that the greatest need of a sick unit is an appropriate top manager who can put the unit back on rails again.

It has to be recognised that the chronic ailment from which management of a sick unit suffers is the lack of objective and corporate planning. The failure of the management is in setting up practical targets and finding co-ordination between different segments of the undertaking. In order to be economically successful, production and sales must go hand in hand and financial resources should be adequate to meet plan requirements. Sometimes the management fails to view the total requirements and as a consequence either production goes up without increase of sales or money is not available at the right time to purchase the needed raw materials. The manager of a sick unit has to strike a proper balance between liquidity and profitability. The working capital has to be adequate and to constantly monitor these activities a management information and reporting system should be thoroughly organised to constantly monitor these activities and sense deficiencies in key areas.

10.6.2 Management information system

Next to finding a proper manager, there is a need to build a proper management information system (Chapter 8). This system should help in the collection of information about the various aspects of the working of rehabilitation programme in accordance with the plan already worked out in the viable study. A periodic review of all activities would show up shortcomings and need for contingency planning at various stages to overcome shortfalls. The commercial banks should be made to cooperate and provide quarterly operating statements which show both actual and projected figures, statement of current assets and liabilities and quarterly fund flow. A good MIS should help in improving the response of the management in taking corrective actions in time. It should also provide an inbuilt check to ensure reliability on the data and particulars furnished by the unit.

10.6.3 Settlement with creditors

Settlement with creditors, deposit holders and Government bodies for payment of their dues is very important in a rehabilitation scheme. There should be an understanding to prevent any legal proceedings against the sick unit for recovery of their dues which can otherwise force the unit to stop operations and functioning. The creditors should be provided a plan for recovery of their dues in a phased manner, otherwise in the event of closure of the unit and forced sale of security, those agencies whose dues are not secured against block assets or movable items may not recover anything.

10.6.4 Additional working capital

There is a need for additional working capital in sick unit, the estimate for which should come out from the viable study. The commercial banks will have to be consulted to consider the following aspects:

(*a*) To provide fresh working capital facilities in the light of the rehabilitation programme in the form of new cash credit account.

(*b*) The shortfalls in the existing account may be transferred to working capital term loan account, the repayable account of which would be provided on the basis of the cash generation capacity of the unit.

(*c*) Banks may be requested not to stipulate any margin or to fix up some nominal margin on such advances until the unit turns the corner and starts cash generation.

(*d*) The old dues to the bank may be transferred to defer term loan account to be repaid over a period of 5 or 6 years after moratorium of one or two years depending on the cash generation by the unit.

(*e*) The loan should be given on a very low rate of interest.

Financial return showing the anticipated expenditure and accruals should be prepared for each month and the bank should release funds accordingly. The MIS should particularly include data on monthly profit and loss account, monthly fund flow statement, monthly hypothecated stock statement etc. The object is to maintain a strict financial discipline so that the sick unit continues to improve on a pre-chartered course of action.

10.6.5 Modernisation of plant and equipment

The sickness in several industrial units arises because of the outdated plant and equipment and also because of obsolete technology. For revival, therefore, it becomes necessary that a modernisation programme is also undertaken so that there could be an increase in productivity and the cost of products may also be brought at par with other competitive items in the market. The object of modernisation is to ensure optimum utilisation of the existing plant and machinery. Unutilisable machines, equipment and tools should be disposed of. Any extension or expansion of the existing plant if considered essential in the viability study as a pre-requisite for rehabilitation should be undertaken. If, however, diversification of products become necessary that may also be

considered. Such capital which may be required for purchase of new equipment or for modernisation should be included in the rehabilitation grant from the financial institutions or state financial corporations as part of the rehabilitation package.

10.6.6 **Concessions by financial institutions**

The financial institutions are IFCI, IDBI, ICICI and IRBI and state level financial corporations which provide term loans. These institutions also undertake assistance for rehabilitation in case of sick units and who normally initiate viability studies if they have already given term loans earlier. The institutions can be approached to grant the reliefs as a package deal for rehabilitation. The deal has to include (*a*) rescheduling for payment of old term loan, (*b*) funding of interest on old principal amount, (*c*) waivement of penal interest, if any, on old dues and (*d*) charging of lower rate of interest on fresh term loan as applicable on soft loans.

10.6.7 **Government assistance**

The type of Government assistance needed in respect of sick industrial units will have to be explored on a case to case basis. Very often, the commercial banks giving aid also ask for Government guarantee covering the commitment of the banks in respect of additional loans. It can also happen that the banks may ask the Government to finance partly cash losses on sick units. In case of sick units in the core sector of the economy, the Government also may consider grant of some reliefs in shape of excise rebate, concession in power tariffs, sales tax, supply of critical raw materials, etc. This and other aspects have to be explored and requisite Government assistance asked for in each case. It goes without saying that the Government has a definite role to play in the rehabilitation of sick units as the Government is interested in providing welfare measures and protection to people already employed in the sick units.

10.6.8 **Cost reduction**

The sick units should be given special attention to cost reduc-

tion in the normal operations of the unit. The cost reduction can be carried out in all the departments by carefully scrutinising the working and the necessity of incurring expenditures in these areas. Some of the important areas of cost reduction are listed below:

(*i*) **Organisational structure**

(*a*) Reduction in management posts.
(*b*) Reduction in emoluments of posts.
(*c*) Tight approval procedures for recruitment.
(*d*) Elimination of some depots and service departments.

(*ii*) **In marketing and sales organisation**

(*a*) Review of policy for travel and entertainment and reduction of expenditure.
(*b*) Freeze on advertisements.
(*c*) Modification of commission structure.
(*d*) Possibility of reduction in sales promotion staff by appoinment of agents, dealers or traders.
(*e*) Reconsideration of sales discount or trade discount or cash discount.
(*f*) Distribution policy by owned trucks instead of hired trucks.
(*g*) Examining the location of godowns and warehouses.
(*h*) Examining the inventory held in these godowns and reducing it where necessary.

(*iii*) **In finance and accounting department**

(*a*) Elimination of unnecessary and voluminous reporting system.
(*b*) Centralisation of cash management for effective deployment of funds to needy departments.
(*c*) Tight control on capital expenditure.

(*iv*) **In manufacturing department**

(*a*) By simplifying purchase procedure and reducing personnel employed therein.
(*b*) By providing production incentive schemes or rationalising them if already in existence.

(*c*) By introducing various insurance covers on plants and machinery.
(*d*) By exploring energy saving devices and reducing power consumption.
(*e*) By using better material handling equipment and facilities.
(*f*) By carrying out work study and better job allocation to the people already employed and retraining of those found surplus.

10.6.9 Contingency planning and personal goals

Very often the corporate plans do not include contingency planning to overcome shortfalls and delays. Every key manager ought to know what contingeney planning he should undertake in the event of delays and shortfalls in purchase, production and hold ups of all types. This could be possible if individual managers are given a goal to achieve. It is normally seen that executives become ineffective and allow roofs to cave in around them if they are not under some kind of pressure. If personal goals are set up, and these are constantly reviewed, an internal pressure can be generated.

10.6.10 Trust and confidence in employees

There is a need to develop trust and confidence with the people working in the establishment. Occasional meetings, bereavements, new year festivals provide a congenial setting to get to know each other. Welfare measures to look after sickness in workers' families and visits of key personnel can create a good environment of trust and confidence which is very necessary for the working of the company.

10.6.11 Workers' participation

Very often key executives of enterprises feel that they can never be wrong and they are intolerant of any adverse criticism. They forget to listen to the people. It has been observed in all good successful undertakings that employees' suggestions if listened to and implemented generally improve the working and productivity of industrial units. It is the listening and helping that go a long way to create a sense of loyalty. If

workers' participation is made a part of the normal working of the units one can bank on their help during crisis. It is possible to call upon them to work for long durations and at reduced pay when sickness sets in the units and is identified in early stages.

10.7 **Euthanasia (Mercy Killing)**

If the viable studies indicate that it is not possible to rehabilitate a sick unit, it should be allowed to die. In fact, Euthanasia is the answer. Industrial units do not have a claim to eternal life, any more than human beings. Attempts to keep terminally sick mills alive through expensive subsidies and credit have only served to spread the virus. The Government has been unwisely taking over sick textile, jute and other mills which have continuously shown losses. The tax payers money pumped in these units has not done any good. It is also a known fact that because of Government policy, the sick units remain sick while the industrialists become richer. Where gross mismanagement has led to sickness, there should be an appropriate punishment for the management. Government decision in black-listing such managers and denying them further assistance is a move in the right direction. Units which are chronically sick, uneconomic in size or have obsolete technology should not be supported. Thus, Euthanasia should be applied liberally to create a sense of fear and survival only by competition.

11

SICK INDUSTRIAL COMPANIES (SPECIAL PROVISIONS) BILL, 1985

11.0 **Summary**

A Bill to make a special provision to secure timely detection of sick and potentially sick companies and for setting up of a board of experts for speedy determination of the preventive, ameliorative, remedial and other measures was introduced in the Lok Sabha on 29th August 1985.

The Sick Industrial Companies (Special Provisions) Bill, 1985, lays the onus of reporting sickness and impending sickness at the stage of erosion of fifty per cent or more of the net worth of an industrial company on the board of directors.

The bill piloted by minister of state for finance, Janardhana Poojary, seeks to set up a "board for industrial and financial reconstruction" as also an "appellate authority for industrial and financial reconstruction".

The Bill provides for report to the board and hold a general meeting of the shareholders of the company if the accumulated losses of the industrial company as at the end of any financial year have resulted in erosion of fifty per cent or more of its peak net worth during the immediately preceding five financial years. The fact of the loss will have to be reported to the board within 60 days from the date of the finalisation of the audited accounts of the company for the financial year.

The board of directors will, at least 21 days before the date on which the meeting of shareholders is held, forward, to every member of the company, a report as to such erosion and the causes for such erosion.

Default in complying with the provision is sought to be made punishable with imprisonment which shall not be less than six months but which may extend to two years and with fine.

A "sick industrial company" has been defined as an "industrial company (being a company registered for not less than seven years) which has at the end of any financial year accumulated losses equal to or exceeding its entire net worth and has also suffered cash losses in such financial year and the financial year immediately preceding such financial year".

The chairman and members of the proposed board will be persons who are or have been or are qualified to be High Court judges or "persons of ability, integrity and standing who have special knowledge of, and professional experience of not less than 20 years in science, technology, economics, banking, industry, law, labour matters, industrial finance. . . ."

The chairman of the appellate authority will be a person who is or has been a judge of the Supreme Court or who is or has been a judge of a High Court for not less than five years. A member of the authority will be a person who is or has been a judge of a High Court or who is or has been an officer not below the rank of a secretary to the Government of India.

The salaries and allowances of the members and the administrative expenses of the board and the appellate authority will be defrayed out of the consolidated fund of India.

The statement of objects and reasons of the Bill said the ill-effects of sickness in industrial companies such as loss of production, loss of employment, loss of revenue to the Union and State governments and locking up of investible funds of banks and financial institutions are of serious concern to the government and the society at large.

The concern of the government is accentuated by the alarming increase in the incidence of sickness in industrial companies. In order to fully utilise the productive industrial assets, and afford maximum protection of employment and optimise the use of the funds of the banks and financial institutions, it would be imperative to revive and rehabilitate the

potentially viable sick industrial companies as quickly as possible.

The statement said the experience has been that the existing institutional arrangements and procedures for revival and rehabilitation of potentially viable sick industrial companies are both inadequate and time-consuming. A multiplicity of laws and agencies makes the adoption of a co-ordinated approach for dealing with sick industrial companies difficult. The need for enacting in the public interest, a legislation to provide for timely detection of sickness in industrial companies and for expeditious determination by a body of experts of the preventive, ameliorative, remedial and other measures that would need to be adopted with respect to such companies and for enforcement of the measures considered appropriate with "utmost practical despatch".

The Bill provides for enabling the board on receipt of a reference to make an inquiry for the purpose of determining whether the industrial company has become a sick industrial company. The board can allow time to a sick industrial company to make its net worth positive within a specified period. If the board decides that it is not practicable for it to make its net worth positive within a reasonable time, it may direct any public financial institution, designated as the operating agency, to prepare a scheme for rehabilitation of the company.

If the board inquiry shows that it would be just and equitable to wind up the sick industrial company, it would forward its opinion to the concerned High Court for winding up of the company. The board may, however, sell the assets of the company and forward the sale proceeds to the High Court for distribution in accordance with the provisions of the Companies Act, 1956.

11.1 Sick Companies Bill, 1985

To make, in the public interest, special provisions with a view to securing the timely detection of sick and potentially sick companies owning industrial undertakings, the speedy determination by a board of experts of the preventive

ameliorative, remedial and other measures which need to be taken with respect to such companies and the expeditious enforcement of the measures so determined and for matters connected therewith or incidental thereto.

Be it enacted by Parliament in the thirty-sixth year of the Republic of India as follows:

11.1.1 **Chapter I**

Preliminary: (1) This Act may be called the Sick Industrial Companies (Special Provisions) Act, 1985. (2) It extends to the whole of India. (3) It shall come into force on such date as the Central Government may by notification in the Official Gazette, appoint and different dates may be appointed for different provisions of this Act and any reference in any provision of this Act to the commencement of this Act shall be construed as a reference to the commencement of that provision. (4) It shall apply, in the first instance, to all the scheduled industries other than the scheduled industry relating to ships and other vessels drawn by power. (5) The Central Government may, in consultation with the Reserve Bank of India, by notification, apply the provisions of of this Act, on and from such date as may be specified in the notification, to the scheduled industry relating to ships and other vessels drawn by power.

2. It is hereby declared that this Act is for giving effect to the policy of the State towards securing the principles specified in clauses (*b*) and (*c*) of article 39 of the Constitution.

3. (1) In this Act, unless the context otherwise requires: (a) "Appellate Authority" means the Appellate Authority for Industrial and Financial Reconstruction constituted under section 5; (*b*) "Board" means the Board for Industrial and Financial Re-construction established under section 4; (*c*) "Chairman" means the Chairman of the Board or, as the case may be, the Appellate Authority; (*d*) "company" means a company as defined in section 3 of the Companies Act, 1956, but does not include a Government company as defined in section 617 of that Act; (*e*) "industrial company" means a company which owns one or more industrial undertakings;

(*f*) "industrial undertaking" means any undertaking pertaining to a scheduled industry carried on in one or more factories by any company but does not include: (*i*) an ancillary industrial undertaking as defined in clause (*aa*) of section 3 of the Industries (Development and Regulation) Act, 1951; and (*ii*) a small scale industrial undertaking as defined in clause (*j*) of the aforesaid section 3; (*g*) "Member" means a Member of the Board or, as the case may be, the Appellate Authority and includes the Chairman thereof; (*h*) "notification" means a notification published in the Official Gazette; (*i*) "operating agency" means any public financial institution as may be specified by general or special order as its agency by the Board; (*j*) "prescribed" means prescribed by rules made under this Act; (*k*) "public financial institutions" means any of the following institutions, namely: (*i*) Industrial Credit and Investment Corporation of India Limited, a company formed and registered under the Companies Act, 1913; (*ii*) the Industrial Development Bank of India, established under section 3 of the Industrial Development Bank of India Act, 1964; (*iii*) the Industrial Reconstruction Bank of India established under section 3 of the Industrial Reconstruction Bank of India Act, 1984; (*iv*) such other institution as the Central Government may, by notification, specify: Provided that no institution shall be so specified unless it has been established or constituted by or under any Central Act, or not less than fifty-one per cent of the paid-up share capital of such institution is held or controlled by the Central Government or by any one or more of the institutions mentioned in sub-clauses (*i*) to (*ii*) or partly by the Central Government and partly by one or more of the institutions mentioned in sub-clauses (*i*) to (*iv*); (*l*) "Reserve Bank" means the Reserve Bank of India constituted under section 3 of the Reserve Bank of India Act, 1934; (*m*) "Scheduled Bank" means a bank for the time being included in the Second Schedule to the Reserve Bank of India Act, 1934; (*n*) "scheduled industry" means any of the industries specified for the time being in the First Schedule to the Industries (Development and Regulation) Act, 1951; (*o*) "sick industrial company" means an industrial company (being a company registered for not less

than seven years) which has at the end of any financial year accumulated losses equal to or exceeding its entire net worth and has also suffered cash losses in such financial year and the financial year immediately preceding such financial year. *Explanation*—For the purposes of this clause: (*i*) "cash loss" means loss as computed without providing for depreciation; (*ii*) "net worth" is the sum total of the paid-up capital and free reserves; (*iii*) "free reserves" means all reserves credited out of the profits and share premium account but does not include reserves credited out of re-evaluation of assets, write back of depreciation provisions and amalgamation; (*p*) "State level institution" means any of the following institutions, namely: (*i*) State Financial Corporations established under section 3A and institutions notified under section 46 of the State Financial Corporations Act, 1951; (*ii*) State Industrial Development Corporations registered under the Companies Act, 1956; (*iii*) such other institutions, being companies and not being public financial institutions, engaged in the development or financing of industrial undertakings, as the Central Government may, by notification, specify.

Provided that no institution shall be so specified unless not less than fifty-one per cent of the paid-up share capital thereof is held by any State Government or Governments or by any institution or institutions mentioned in sub-clauses (*i*) and (*ii*) or partly by one or more public financial institutions or institutions mentioned in sub-clauses (*i*) and (*ii*) and partly by one or more State Governments.

The following is the second part of the text of Sick Companies Bill, 1985:

(2) (*a*) Words and expressions used and not defined in this Act shall have the meanings, if any, respectively assigned to them in the Companies Act, 1956. (*b*) Words and expressions used but not defined either in this Act or in the Companies Act, 1956 shall have the meanings, if any, respectively assigned to them in the Industries (Development and Regulation) Act, 1951.

(3) Any reference in this Act to any other enactment or any provision thereof, shall, in relation to an area in which such enactment or such provision is not in force, be construed

as a reference to the corresponding law or the relevant provision of the corresponding law, if any, in force in that area.

11.1.2 Chapter II

Board and Appellate Authority for Industrial and Financial Reconstruction: 4. (1) With effect from such date as the Central Government may, by notification, appoint, there shall be established a Board to be known as the "Board for Industrial and Financial Reconstruction" to exercise the jurisdiction and powers and discharge the functions and duties conferred or imposed on the Board by or under this Act.

(2) The Board shall consist of a Chairman and not less than two and not more than fourteen other Members, to be appointed by the Central Government.

(3) The Chairman and other Members of the Board shall be persons who are or have been or are qualified to be High Court Judges, or persons of ability, integrity and standing who have special knowledge of, and professional experience of not less than twenty years in science, technology, economics, banking, industry, law, labour matters, industrial finance, industrial management, industrial reconstruction, administration, investment, accountancy, marketing or any other matter, the special knowledge of, or professional experience in which, would in the opinion of the Central Government be useful to the Board.

5. (1) The Central Government may, by notification, constitute, with effect from such date as may be specified therein, appellate authority to be called the "Appellate Authority for Industrial and Financial Reconstruction" consisting of a Chairman and not more than three other Members, to be appointed by that government, for hearing appeals against the orders of the Board under its Act. (2) The Chairman of the Appellate Authority shall be a person who is or has been a Judge of the Supreme Court or who is or has been a Judge of a High Court for not less than five years. (3) A member of the Appellate Authority shall be a person who is or has been a Judge of a High Court or who is or has been an officer not below the rank of a Secretary to the Government of India or who is or has been a Member of the Board for not less than three years.

6. (1) Before appointing any person as the Chairman or other Member, the Central Government shall satisfy itself that the person does not and will not have any such financial or other interest as is likely to affect prejudicially his functions as such member. (2) The Chairman and every other Member shall hold office for such period, not exceeding five years, as may be specified by the Central Government in the order of his appointment, but shall be eligible for reappointment: Provided that no person shall hold office as the Chairman or other Member after he has attained the age of sixty-five years. (3) Notwithstanding anything contained in sub-section (1), a Member may—(*a*) by writing under his hand and addressed to the Central Government resign his office at any time; (*b*) be removed from his office in accordance with the provisions of Section 7. (4) A vacancy caused by the resignation or removal of the Chairman or any other member under sub-section (3) or otherwise shall be filled by fresh appointment. (5) In the event of occurrence of a vacancy in the office of the Chairman by reason of his death, resignation or otherwise, such one of the Members as the Central Government may, by notification, authorise in this behalf shall act as the Chairman till the date on which a new Chairman, appointed in accordance with the provisions of this Act to fill such vacancy, enters upon his office. (6) When the Chairman is unable to discharge his functions owing to absence, illness or any other cause such one of the Members as the Chairman may authorise in writing in this behalf, shall discharge the functions of the Chairman, until the date on which the Chairman resumes his duties. (7) The salaries and allowances payable to and the other terms and conditions of service of the Chairman and other Members shall be such as may be prescribed: Provided that neither the salary and allowances nor the other terms and conditions of service of the Chairman or any other Member shall be varied to his disadvantage after his appointment. (8) The Chairman and every other Member shall before entering upon his office, make a declaration of fidelity and secrecy in the form set out in the Schedule to Act. (9) The Chairman

or any other Member ceasing to hold office as such shall not hold any appointment or be connected with the management or administration in any company in relation to which any matter has been the subject matter of consideration before the Board or, as the case may be, the Appellate Authority, for a period of five years from the date on which he ceases to hold such office.

7. (1) The Central Government may remove from office any Member who—(*a*) has been adjudged as insolvent, or (*b*) has been convicted of an offence which, in the opinion of the Central Government, involves moral turpitude, or (*c*) has become physically or mentally incapable of acting as a Member, or (*d*) has acquired such financial or other interest as is likely to affect prejudicially his functions as a Member, or (*e*) has so abused his position as to render his continuance in office prejudicial to the public interest. (2) Notwithstanding anything contained in sub-section (1) no Member shall be removed from his office on the ground specified in clause (*d*) or clause (*e*) of that sub-section unless the Supreme Court on a reference being made to it in this behalf by the Central Government, has on an inquiry held by it in accordance with such procedure as it may specify in this behalf, reported that the Member ought, on such grounds, to be removed.

8. (1) The Central Government shall appoint a Secretary to the Board and a Secretary (by whatever name called) to the Appellate Authority to exercise and perform, under the control of the Chairman, such powers and duties as may be prescribed or as may be specified by the Chairman. (2) Subject to such restrictions and conditions as may be prescribed, the Board or, as the case may be, the Appellate Authority may appoint such other officers and employees as may be necessary for the efficient performance of its functions. (3) The salaries and allowances payable to and the conditions of service of the Secretary and other officers and employees of the Board and the Appellate Authority shall be such as may be prescribed: Provided that such Secretary, officer or other employee shall, before entering upon his duties, make a declaration of fidelity and secrecy in the form set out in the Sehedule.

9. The salaries and allowances payable to the Members and the administrative expenses, including salaries, allowances and pension, payable to or in respect of the officers and other employees of the Board and the Appellate Authority shall be defrayed out of the Consolidated Fund of India.

10. No act or proceeding of the Board or, as the case may be, the Appellate Authority shall be questioned on the ground merely of the existence of any vacancy or defect in the constitution of the Board or the Appellate Authority or any defect in the appointment of a person acting as a Member of the Board or the Appellate Authority.

11. The Chairman and other Members and the officers and other employees of the Board and the Appellate Authority shall be deemed to be public servants within the meaning of section 21 of the Indian Penal Code.

12. (1) The jurisdiction, powers and authority of the Board or the Appellate Authority may be exercised by Benches thereof. (2) The Benches shall be constituted by the Chairman and each Bench shall consist of not less than two members. (3) If the Members of a Bench differ in opinion of any point, they shall state the point or points on which they differ and the case shall be referred by the Chairman of the Board or, as the case may be, the Appellate Authority for hearing on such point or points by one or more other Members and such point or points shall be decided according to the opinion of the majority of the Members who heard the case including those who first heard it.

13. (1) Subject to the provisions of the Act, the Board or, as the case may be, the Appellate Authority, shall have powers to regulate—(*a*) the procedure and conduct of the business; (*b*) the procedure of the Benches, including the places at which the sittings of the Benches shall be held; (*c*) the delegation to one or more members of such powers or functions as the Board or, as the case may be, the Appellate Authority may specify. (2) In particular and without prejudice to the generality of the foregoing provisions, the powers of the Board or, as the case may be, the Appellate Authority, shall include the power to determine the extent to which persons interested

or claiming to be interested in the subject matter of any proceeding before it may be allowed to be present or to be heard, either by themselves or by their representatives or to cross-examine witnesses or otherwise to take part in the proceedings. (3) The Board or the Appellate Authority shall, for the purposes of any inquiry or for any other purpose under this Act, have the same powers as are vested in a civil court under the Code of Civil Procedure, 1908 while trying suits in respect of the following matters, namely:

(*a*) the summoning and enforcing the attendance of any witness and examining him on oath;

(*b*) the discovery and production of document or other material object producible as evidence;

(*c*) the reception of evidence on affidavit;

(*d*) the requisitioning of any public record from any court or office;

(*e*) the issuing of any commission for the examination of witness; and

(*f*) any other matter which may be prescribed.

14. The Board or the Appellate Authority shall be deemed to be a civil court for the purposes of section 195 and Chapter XXVI of the Code of Criminal Procedure, 1973 and every proceeding before the Board or the Appellate Authority shall be deemed to a judicial proceeding within the meaning of sections 193 and 228 and for the purposes of section 196 of the Indian Penal Code.

11.1.3 **Chapter III**

References, inquiries and schemes: 15. (1) Where an industrial company has become a sick industrial company, the Board of Directors of the company shall, within sixty days from the date of finalisation of the duly audited accounts of the company for the financial year as at the end of which the company has become a sick industrial company, make a reference to the Board for determination of the measures which shall be adopted with respect to the company.

Provided that if the Board of Directors had sufficient reasons even before such finalisation to form the opinion that the company had become a sick industrial company, the Board of Directors shall within sixty days after it has formed such opinion, make a reference to the Board for the determination of the measures which shall be adopted with respect to the company.

(2) Without prejudice to the provisions of sub-section (1), the Central Government or the Reserve Bank or a State Government or a public financial institution or a state level institution or a scheduled bank may if it has sufficient reasons to believe that any industrial company has become, for the purposes of this Act, a sick industrial company, make a reference in respect of such company to the Board for determination of the measures which may be adopted with respect to such company.

Provided that a reference shall not be made under this sub-section in respect of any industrial company by:

(*a*) the government of any state unless all or any of the industrial undertakings belonging to such company are situated in such state; and

(*b*) a public financial institution or a State level institution or a scheduled bank unless it has, by reason of any financial assistance or obligation rendered by it or undertaken by it, with respect to such company, an interest in such company.

16. (1) The Board may make such inquiry as it may deem fit for determining whether any industrial company has become a sick industrial company:

(*a*) upon receipt of a reference with respect to such company under section 15; or

(b) upon information received with respect to such company or upon its own knowledge as to the financial condition of the company.

(2) The Board may, if it deems necessary or expedient so to do for the expeditious disposal of an inquiry under sub-section (1), require by order any operating agency to enquire into and make a report with respect to such matters as may be specified in the order.

(3) The Board or, as the case may be, the operating agency shall complete its inquiry as expeditiously as possible and endeavour shall be made to complete the inquiry within sixty days from the commencement of the inquiry.

(4) Where the Board deems it fit to make an inquiry or to cause an inquiry to be made into any industrial company under sub-section (1) or, as the case may be, under sub-section (2), it shall appoint one or more persons to be a special director or special directors of the company for safeguarding the financial and other interests of the company.

(5) The appointment of a special director referred to in sub-section (4) shall be valid and effective notwithstanding anything to the contrary contained in the Companies Act, 1956, or in any other law for the time being in force or in the memorandum and articles of association or any other instrument relating to the industrial company, and any provision regarding share qualification, age limit, number of directorships, removal from office of directors and such like conditions contained in any such law or instrument aforesaid, shall not apply to any director appointed by the Board.

(6) Any special director appointed under sub-section (4) shall:

(*a*) hold office during the pleasure of the Board and may be removed or substituted by any person by order in writing by the Board;

(*b*) not incur any obligation or liability by reason only of his being a director or for anything done or omitted to be done in good faith in the discharge of his duties as a director or anything in relation thereto; and

(*c*) not be liable to retirement by rotation and shall not be taken into account for computing the number of directors liable to such retirement.

17. (1) If after making an inquiry under section 16, the Board is satisfied that a company has become a sick industrial company, the Board shall after considering all the relevant facts and circumstances of the case, decide, as soon as may be by order in writing, whether it is practicable for the company to make its net worth positive within a reasonable time.

(2) If the Board decides under sub-section (1) that it is practicable for a sick industrial company to make its net worth positive within a reasonable time, the Board shall, by order in writing and subject to such restrictions or conditions as may be specified in the order, give such time to the company as it may deem fit to make its net worth positive.

(3) If the Board decides under sub-section (1) that it is not practicable for a sick industrial company to make its net worth positive within a reasonable time and that it is necessary or expedient in the public interest to adopt all or any of the measures specified in section 18 in relation to the said company it may, as soon as may be, by order in writing, direct any operating agency specified in the order to prepare, having regard to such guidelines as may be specified in the order, a scheme providing for such measures in relation to such company.

(4) The Board may—(*a*) if any of the restrictions or conditions specified in an order made under sub-section (2) are not complied with by the company concerned, review such order on a reference in that behalf from any agency referred to in sub-section (2) of section 15 or on its own motion and pass a fresh order in respect of such company under sub-section (3);

(*b*) if the operating agency specified in an order made under sub-section (3) makes a submission in that behalf, review such order and modify the order in such manner as it may deem appropriate.

18. (1) Where an order is made under sub-section (3) of section 17 in relation to any sick industrial company, the operating agency specified in the order shall prepare, as expeditiously as possible and ordinarily within a period of ninety days from the date of such order, a scheme with respect to such company providing for any one or more of the following measures, namely:

(*a*) the reconstruction, revival or rehabilitation of the sick industrial company;

(*b*) the proper management of the sick industrial company

by change in, or takeover of, management of the sick industrial company;

(*c*) the amalgamation of the sick industrial company with any other industrial company (referred to in this section as 'transferee industrial company');

(*d*) the sale or lease of a part or whole of any industrial undertaking of the sick industrial company;

(*e*) such other preventive, ameliorative and remedial measures as may be appropriate; and

(*f*) such incidental, consequential or supplemental measures as may be necessary or expedient in connection with or for the purposes of the measures specified in clauses (*a*) to (*e*).

(2) The scheme referred to in sub-section (1) may provide for any one or more of the following, namely:

(*a*) the constitution, name and registered office, the capital, assets, powers, rights, interests, authorities and privileges, duties and obligations of the sick industrial company or, as the case may be, of the transferee industrial company;

(*b*) the transfer to the transferee industrial company of the business, properties, assets and liabilities of the sick industrial company on such terms and conditions as may be specified in the scheme;

(c) any change in the Board of Directors, or the appointment of a new Board of Directors, of the sick industrial company and the authority by whom, the manner in which and the other terms and conditions on which, such change or appointment shall be made and in the case of appointment of a new Board of Directors or of any director, the period for which such appointment shall be made;

(*d*) the alteration of the memorandum or articles of association of the sick industrial company or, as the case may be, of the transferee industrial company for the purpose of altering the capital structure thereof or for such other purposes as may be necessary to give effect to the reconstruction or amalgamation;

(*e*) the continuation by, or against the sick industrial company or, as the case may be, the transferee industrial company

of any action or other legal proceeding pending against the sick industrial company immediately before the date of the order made under sub-section (3) of section 17;

(*f*) the reduction of the interest or rights which the shareholders have in the sick industrial company to such extent as the Board considers necessary in the interests of the reconstruction, revival or rehabilitation of the sick industrial company or for the maintenance of the business of the sick industrial company;

(*g*) the allotment to the shareholders of the sick industrial company, of shares in the sick industrial company or, as the case may be, in the transferee industrial company and where any shareholder claims payment in cash and not allotment of shares, or where it is not possible to allot shares to any shareholder the payment of cash to those shareholders in full satisfaction of their claims—(i) in respect of their interest in shares in the sick industrial company before its reconstruction or amalgamation; or (ii) where such interest has been reduced under clause (*f*) in respect of their interest in shares as so reduced;

(*h*) any other terms and conditions for the reconstruction or amalgamation of the sick industrial company;

(*i*) sale of the industrial undertaking of the sick industrial company free from all encumbrances and all liabilities of the company or other such encumbrances and liabilities as may be specified or to fix reserve price for such sale;

(*j*) method of sale of the assets of the industrial undertaking of the sick industrial company such as by public auction or by inviting tenders or in any other manner as may be specified and for the manner or publicity therefor;

(*k*) transfer or issue of the shares in the sick industrial company at the face value or at the intrinsic value which may be at discount value or such other value as may be specified to any industrial company or any person including the executives and employees of the sick industrial company; and

(*l*) such incidental, consequential and supplemental matters as may be necessary to secure that the reconstruction or amalgamation or other measures mentioned in the scheme are fully and effectively carried out.

(3) (*a*) A copy of the scheme prepared by the Board shall be sent, in draft, to the sick industrial company and the operating agency and in the case of amalgamation, also to the transferee industrial company and any other industrial company concerned in the amalgamation for suggestions and objections, if any, within such period as the Board may specify.

(b) The Board may make such modifications, if any, in the draft scheme as it may consider necessary in the light of the suggestions and objections received from the sick industrial company and the operating agency and also from the transferee industrial company and any other industrial company concerned in the amalgamation and from any shareholder or any creditors or employees of such industrial companies:

Provided that where the scheme relates to amalgamation of the sick industrial company the said scheme shall be laid before the transferee industrial company in the general meeting for the approval of the scheme by its shareholders and no such scheme shall be proceeded with unless it has been approved, with or without modification, by a special resolution passed by the shareholders of the transferee industrial company.

(4) The scheme shall thereafter be sanctioned, as soon as may be, by the Board (hereinafter referred to as the 'sanctioned scheme') and shall come into force on such date as the Board may specify in this behalf:

Provided that different dates may be specified for different provisions of the scheme.

(5) The Board may on the recommendations of the operating agency or otherwise, review any sanctioned scheme and make such modifications as it may deem fit or may by order in writing direct any operating agency specified in the order, having regard to such guidelines as may be specified in the order, to prepare a fresh scheme providing for such measures as the operating agency may consider necessary.

(6) When a fresh scheme is prepared under sub-section (4), the provisions of sub-sections (3) and (4) shall apply in relation thereto as they apply to in relation to a scheme prepared under sub-section (1).

(7) The sanction accorded by the Board under sub-section (4) shall be conclusive evidence that all the requirements of this scheme relating to the reconstruction or amalgamation, or any other measure specified therein have been complied with and a copy of the sanctioned scheme certified in writing by an officer of the Board to be a true copy thereof, shall, in all legal proceedings (whether in appeal or otherwise) be admitted as evidence.

(8) On and from the date of the coming into operation of the sanctioned scheme or any provision thereof, the scheme or such provision shall be binding on the sick industrial company, or as the case may be, on the transferee industrial company and also on the shareholders of both the companies.

(9) If any difficulty arises in giving effect to the provisions of the sanctioned scheme, the Board may, on the recommendation of the operating agency, by order do anything, not inconsistent with such provisions, which appears to it to be necessary or expedient for the purpose of removing the difficulty.

(10) The Board may, if it deems necessary or expedient so to do, by order in writing, direct any operating agency specified in the order to implement a sanctioned scheme with such terms and conditions and in relation to such sick industrial company as may be specified in the order.

(11) Where the whole of the undertaking of the sick industrial company is sold under a sanctioned scheme, the Board may distribute the sale proceeds to the parties entitled thereto in accordance with the provisions of section 529A and other provisions of the Companies Act, 1956.

19. (1) Where the scheme relates to preventive, ameliorative, remedial and other measures with respect to any sick industrial company, the scheme may provide for financial assistance by way of loans, advances or guarantees or reliefs or concessions or sacrifices from the Central Government, a State Government, any scheduled bank or other bank, a public financial institution or state level institution or any institution or other authority or creditors or concerned persons to the sick industrial company.

(2) Every scheme referred to in sub-section (1) shall be circulated to all concerned for their consent within a period of sixty days from the date of such circulation.

(3) Where the consent referred to in sub-section (2) is given by all concerned, the Board may, as soon as may be, sanction the scheme and on and from the date of such sanction the scheme shall be binding on the consenting authorities, institutions and persons.

(4) Where the consent is not given by any authority or institution or person under sub-section (2), the Board may adopt such other measures, including winding up of the sick industrial company, as it may deem fit.

20. (1) Where the Board, after making inquiry under section 16 and after consideration of all the relevant facts and circumstances and after giving an opportunity of being heard to all concerned parties, is of opinion that it is just and equitable that the sick industrial company should be wound up it may record and forward its opinion to the concerned High Court.

(2) The High Court shall, on the basis of the opinion of the Board order winding up of the sick industrial company and may proceed and cause to proceed with the winding up of the sick industrial company in accordance with the provisions of the Companies Act, 1956.

(3) For the purpose of winding up of the said industrial company, the High Court may appoint any officer of the operating agency, if the operating agency gives its consent, as the liquidator of the sick industrial company and the officer so appointed shall for the purposes of the winding up of the sick industrial company be deemed to be, and have all the powers of, the official liquidator under the Companies Act, 1956.

(4) Notwithstanding anything contained in sub-section (2) or sub-section (3), the Board may cause to be sold the assets of the sick industrial company in such manner as it may deem fit and forward the sale proceeds to the High Court for orders for distribution in accordance with the provisions of section 529A, and other provisions of the Companies Act, 1956.

21. Where, in relation to an inquiry or scheme, the circumstances so require, the Board may, through any operating agency, cause to be prepared:

(a) With respect to an industrial company, a complete inventory of:

(i) All assets and liabilities of whatever nature;

(ii) All books of account, registers, maps, plans, records, documents of title or ownership of property and all other documents of whatever nature relating thereto;

(b) A list of shareholders and a list of creditors showing separately in the list of creditors, the secured creditors and the unsecured creditors;

(c) A valuation report in respect of the shares and assets in order to arrive at the reserve price for the sale of a part or whole of the industrial undertaking of the company or for fixation of the lease rent or share exchange ratio;

(d) An estimate of reserve price, lease rent or share exchange ratio; and

(e) Proforma accounts, where no up-to-date audited accounts are available.

22. (1) Where an inquiry under section 16 is initiated or any scheme referred to in section 17 is under consideration of the Board or where a sanctioned scheme is under implementation, notwithstanding anything contained in the Companies Act, 1956 or any other law or the memorandum and articles of association of the sick industrial company or any other instrument having effect under the said Act or other law no proceedings for the winding up of such sick industrial company or for any proceedings for execution, distress, or the like against any of the properties of the sick industrial company or for the appointment of receiver in respect thereof, shall lie or be proceeded with further, except with the consent of the Board.

(2) Where the management of the sick industrial company is taken over or changed, notwithstanding anything contained in the Companies Act, 1956 or any other law or in the

memorandum and articles of association of such company or any instrument having effect under the said Act or other law:

(a) It shall not be lawful for the shareholders of such company or any other person to nominate or appoint any person to be a director of the company;

(b) No resolution passed at any meeting of the shareholders of such company shall be given effect to unless approved by the Board.

(3) During the period of consideration of any scheme under section 18 or where any such scheme is sanctioned thereunder, for due implementation of the scheme, the Board may by order declare with respect to the sick industrial company concerned that the operation of all or any of the contracts, assurances of property, agreements, settlements, awards, standing orders or other instruments in force, to which such sick industrial company is a party or which may be applicable to such sick industrial company immediately before the date of such order, shall remain suspended or that all or any of the rights, privileges, obligations and liabilities accruing or arising thereunder before the said date, shall remain suspended or shall be enforceable with such adaptations and in such manner as may be specified by the Board.

Provided that such declaration shall not be made for a period exceeding two years which may be extended by one year at a time so, however, that the total period shall not exceed seven years in the aggregate.

(4) Any declaration made under sub-section (3) with respect to a sick industrial company shall have effect notwithstanding anything contained in the Companies Act, 1956 or any other law the memorandum and articles of association of the company or any instrument having effect under the said Act or other law or any agreement or any degree or order of a court, tribunal, officer or other authority or of any submission, settlement or standing order and accordingly—

(a) Any remedy for the enforcement of any right, privilege, obligation and liability suspended or modified by such declaration, and all proceedings relating thereto pending

before any court, tribunal, officer or other authority shall remain stayed or be continued subject to such declaration; and

(b) On the declaration ceasing to have effect:

(i) Any right, privilege, obligation or liability so remaining suspended or modified, shall become revived and enforceable as if the declaration had never been made; and

(ii) Any proceeding so remaining stayed shall be proceeded with, subject to the provisions of any law which may then be in force, from the stage which had been reached when the proceedings became stayed.

(5) In computing the period of limitation for the enforcement of any right, privilege, obligation or liability, the period during which it or the remedy for the enforcement thereof remains suspended under this section shall be excluded.

11.1.4 **Chapter IV**

Proceedings in case of potentially sick industrial companies, misfeasance proceedings, appeals and miscellaneous:

23. (1) If the accumulated losses of an industrial company, as at the end of any financial year (hereinafter referred to as the relevant financial year) have resulted in erosion of fifty per cent, or more of its peak net worth during the immediately preceding five financial years:

(a) The company shall, within a period of sixty days from the date (hereinafter referred to as the relevant date) of finalisation of the duly audited accounts of the company for the relevant financial year:

(i) Report the fact of such erosion to the Board; and

(ii) Hold a general meeting of the shareholders of the company for considering such erosion;

(b) The Board of directors shall, at least twenty-one days before the date of which the meeting under sub-clause (ii) of clause (a) is held, forward to every member of the company a report as such erosion and the causes for such erosion;

(c) The company may, by ordinary resolution passed at the meeting held under clause (a), remove a director (being a

director appointed by the members of the company) and fill the vacancy created by such removal, so far as may be, in accordance with the procedure provided in sub-sections (2) to (6) of section 284 of the Companies Act, 1956.

(2) A director removed under sub-section (1) shall not be entitled to any compensation or damages for termination of his appointment as director or of any appointment terminating with that as director.

(3) If default is made in complying with the provisions of this section, every director or other officer of the company who is in default shall be punishable with imprisonment which shall not be less than six months but which may extend to two years and with fine.

24. (1) If, in the course of scrutiny or implementation of any scheme or proposal, it appears to the Board that any person who has taken part in the promotion, formation or management of the sick industrial company or its undertaking, including any past or present director, manager or officer or employee of the sick industrial company:

(a) Has misapplied or retained, or become liable or accountable for, any money or property of the sick industrial company; or

(b) Has been guilty of any misfeasance, malfeasance or non-feasance or breach of trust in relation to the sick industrial company, the Board may direct him to repay or restore the money or property or any part thereof, with or without interest, as it thinks just or to contribute such sum to the assets of the sick industrial company or the other person entitled thereto by way of compensation in respect of the misapplication retainer, misfeasance or breach of trust, as the Board thinks just, and also report the matter to the Central Government for any other action which that Government may deem fit.

(2) No directions shall be given by the Board under this section unless such person has been given an opportunity for making his submissions.

(3) This section shall apply notwithstanding that the matter is one for which the person may be criminally liable.

25. (1) Any person aggrieved by an order of the Board made under this Act may, within forty-five days from the date on which a copy of the order is issued to him, prefer an appeal to the Appellate Authority.

Provided that the Appellate Authority may entertain any appeal after the said period of forty-five days but not after sixty days from the date aforesaid if it is satisfied that the appellant was prevented by sufficient cause from filing the appeal in time.

(2) On receipt of an appeal under sub-section (1), the Appellate Authority may, after giving an opportunity to the appellant to be heard, if he so desires, and after making such further inquiry as it deems fit, confirm, modify or set aside the order appealed against.

26. No order passed or proposal made under this Act shall be appealable except as provided therein and no civil court shall have jurisdiction in respect of any matter with the Appellate Authority or the Board is empowered by, or under, this Act to determine and no injunction shall be granted by any court or other authority in respect of any action taken or to be taken in pursuance of any power conferred by or under this Act.

27. The Board may, by general or special order, delegate, subject to such conditions and limitation, if any, as may be specified in the order, to any Member or Secretary or other officer or employee of the Board or other persons authorised by the Board to manage any industrial company or industrial undertaking or any operating agency such powers and duties except the powers and duties under sub-sections (2) and (4) of section 16, section 17, sub-sections (3) and (4) of section 19, sub-section (1) and sub-section (4) of section 20, sub-section (3) of section 22 and section 24 under this Act as it may deem necessary.

28. (1) The Board shall furnish from time to time to the Central Government such returns as the Central Government may require.

(2) The Board may, for the purpose of efficient discharge of its functions under this Act, collect from, or furnish to:

(*a*) the Central Government, (*b*) the Reserve Bank, (*c*) the scheduled bank or any other bank, (*d*) the public financial institution, or (*e*) the State-level institution, such information as it may consider useful for the purpose in such manner and within such time as it may think fit.

29. (1) The Board or any operating agency, on being directed by the Board may, in order to take into custody or under its control all property, effects and actionable claims to which a sick industrial company is or appears to be entitled, request, in writing, the Chief Metropolitan Magistrate or the District Magistrate within jurisdiction any property, books of account or any other documents of such sick industrial company be situated or be found, to take possession thereof, and the Chief Metropolitan Magistrate or the District Magistrate, as the case may be, shall, on such request being made to him:

(*i*) take possession of such property, books of account or other documents; and

(*ii*) cause the same to be entrusted to the Board or the operating agency.

(2) For the purpose of securing compliance with the provisions of sub-section (1) the Chief Metropolitan Magistrate or the District Magistrate may take or cause to be taken such steps and use or cause to be used such force as may, in his opinion, be necessary.

(3) No act of the Chief Metropolitan Magistrate or the District Magistrate done in pursuance of this section shall be called in question in any court or before any authority on any ground whatsoever.

30. No suit or other legal proceeding shall be against the Board or the Appellate Authority or the Chairman or any other Member officer or other employee of the Board or the Appellate Authority, or operating agency or any other person authorised by the Board or the Appellate Authority to discharge any function under this Act for any loss or damage caused or likely to be caused by any action which is in good faith done or intended to be done in pursuance of this Act or any other law or provision having the force of law.

31. Where a receiver or an official liquidator has been appointed in any proceeding pending immediately before the commencement of this Act, in any High Court for winding up of an industrial company such proceeding shall not abate but continue in that High Court.

32. (1) The provisions of this Act and of any rules or schemes made thereunder shall have effect notwithstanding anything inconsistent therewith contained any other law except the provisions of the Foreign Exchange Regulation Act, 1973 and Urban Land (Ceiling and Regulation) Act, 1976 for the time being in force or in the Memorandum or Articles of Association of an industrial company or in any other instrument having effect by virtue of any law other than this Act.

(2) Where there has been under any scheme under this Act an amalgamation of a sick industrial company with another company, the provisions of section 72A of the Income-tax Act, 1961, shall subject to the modifications that the power of the Central Government under that section may be exercised by the Board without any recommendation by the specified authority referred amalgamation as they apply in relation to the amalgamation of a company owning an industrial undertaking with another company.

33. (1) Whoever violates the provisions of this Act or any sanctioned scheme, or any order of the Board, or the Appellate Authority and whoever makes a false statement or gives false evidence to the Board or the Appellate Authority, shall be punishable with simple imprisonment for a term which may extend to three years and shall also be liable to fine.

(2) No court shall take cognizance of any offence under sub-section (1) except on a complaint in writing of the Secretary or any such other officer of the Board or any such officer of an operating agency as may be authorised in this behalf by the Board.

34. (1) Where any offence, punishable under this Act, has been committed by a company, every person who, at the time the offence was committed was in charge of, and was responsible to the company for the conduct of the business of the company, as well as the company, shall be deemed to be guilty

of the offence and shall be liable to be proceeded against and punished accordingly:

Provided that nothing contained in this sub-section shall render any such person liable to any punishment, if he proves that the offence was committed without his knowledge or that he had exercised all due diligence to prevent the commission of such offence.

(2) Notwithstanding anything contained in sub-section (1), where any offence punishable under this Act has been committed by a company and it is proved that the offence has been committed with the consent or connivance of, or is attributable to any neglect on the part of, any director, manager, secretary or other officer of the company, such director, manager, secretary or other officer shall also be deemed to be guilty of that offence and shall be liable to be proceeded against and punished accordingly.

Explanation—For the purposes of this section:

(*a*) "Company" means any body corporate and includes a firm or other association of individuals, and

(*b*) "Director", in relation to a firm means a partner in the firm.

35. If any difficulty arises in giving effect to the provisions of this Act or the rules, schemes or orders made thereunder, the Central Government may, by notification, remove the difficulty:

Provided that no such notification shall be made by the Central Government after the expiry of a period of three years from the date on which this Act receives the assent of the President.

36. (1) The Central Government may, by notification, make rules for carrying out the provisions of this Act.

(2) In particular and without prejudice to the generality of the foregoing power, such rules may provide for all or any of the following matters, namely:

(*a*) the salaries and allowances payable to and other terms and conditions of service of the Chairman and other Members under sub-section (7) of section 6;

(*b*) the powers which may be exercised and the duties

which may be performed by the Secretary to the Board or the Appellate Authority under sub-section (1) of section 8;

(*c*) the restrictions and conditions subject to which officers and employees may be appointed to the Board or the Appellate Authority under sub-section (2) of section 8;

(*d*) the salaries and allowances and other conditions of service of the Secretary of the Board or the Appellate Authority under sub-section (2) of section 8;

(*e*) the additional matters referred to in sub-section (3) of section 13; and

(*f*) any other matter which is required to be, or may be prescribed.

(3) Every rule made under this Act shall be laid, as soon as may be after it is made, before each House of Parliament, while it is in session, for a total period of thirty days which may be comprised in one session or in two or more successive sessions, and if, before the expiry of the session immediately following the session or the successive sessions aforesaid, both Houses agree in making any modification in the rule or both Houses agree that the rule should not be made, the rule shall thereafter have effect only in such modified form or be of no effect, as the case may be, so, however, that any such modification of annulment shall be without prejudice to the validity of anything previously done under that rule.

11.2 Some Features of the Sick Companies Bill. 1985

11.2.1 Objectives

The objective of the Sick Companies Bill, 1985, is to carry out early detection of sickness in an industrial unit and then to evolve a package of measures to remove uncertainty about the working of the sick unit.

The sickness of the unit in the Bill has been appraised at two levels: (1) When the erosion of the net worth is of the order of 50 per cent, the Board of Directors of the sick unit have been asked to bring this fact to the notice of the shareholders and depending on their recommendations in a general body

meeting carry out their directives. (2) When the erosion of the net worth is 100 per cent and more and the unit continues to show cash losses for the next 2 years, the management of the unit is required to report to the newly constituted Board under the Bill who would then take appropriate actions which may involve merging, rehabilitation or even mercy killing after a fresh appraisal through an operating agency.

11.2.2 Level of sickness

A unit likely to be sick starts showing cash losses in the initial years leading to the loss of working capital which it tries to manipulate by borrowings. The erosion of net worth is a slow process. It may take several years of sickness before 50 per cent erosion of the net worth may take place and it is likely that from the appearance of first signal and symptoms of sickness to 100 per cent erosion of net worth, it may be 6 to 10 years of continuing sickness. Analysis of some of the sick units is given in Table 11.1 to support this fact.

11.2.3 Early detection of sickness

The mode of early detection of sickness as outlined in the Bill is not adequate. In fact, according to the standards laid down, a unit would be sick at 50 per cent level of the erosion of net worth and gravely sick (in fact nearing collapsing), at 100 per cent erosion of its net worth. Thus the objective of the Bill in respect of early detection is not met.

The early detection of sickness can only be made through a process of monitoring the sickness for which symptoms start appearing in various forms at very early stages. The signals and symptoms of early stages of sickness have been outlined in Chapter 2 and methods of detecting sickness in Chapters 5 and 6. In an analysis of over 200 projects, poor management has been identified to be the most important element which causes maximum sickness in industry. Poor management is that management which lacks requisite personnel, expertise, skills, and adequate information and reporting system. As discussed in Chapter 2, if the top management does not contain expertise and requisite skills, and have no

TABLE 11.1: **The time gap between first appearance of sickness and 100 per cent erosion of net worth**

Name of companies	Year of negative working capital	Year of cash loss	Year of 50% erosion of net worth	Year of 100% erosion of net worth
1. Mysore Spg. & Mfg. Co. Ltd.	1964	1965	1971	1972
2. The Elphinstone Spg. & Wvg. Mills Ltd.	1963	1967	1975	1976
3. The Ahmedabad Jupiter Spg., Wvg. & Mfg. Co. Ltd.	1963	1967	1970	1971
4. The Aurangabad Mills Ltd.	1963	1962	1970	1971
5. The Azam-jahi Mills Ltd.	1962	1963	1968	1969
6. The Himabai Mfg. Co. Ltd.	1962	1965	1967	1968
7. The Jehangir Vakil Mills Co. Ltd.	1961	1966	1969	1970
8. The Tata Mills Ltd.	1963	1968	1977	1980
9. The Indore Malwa United Mills Ltd.	1963	1965	1968	1969
10. The Cannanore Spg. & Wvg. Mills Ltd.	1964	1966	1969	1971
11. India Paper Pulp Co. Ltd.	1968	1967	1970	1973

proper information reporting system especially accounting information, the management is unaware of the approaching disaster which causes sickness. Poor management information system results in the management's inability to respond to changes which cause sickness. The cause of sickness may be technical, economic, social or even poor marketing. Identification of causes of sickness becomes difficult when there is no reporting system. If sickness is not detected in early stages it tends to grow and makes it difficult if not impossible to rehabilitate the unit. It will also cost much more. There should be, therefore, an emphasis on having a proper management information reporting system (Chapter 8) within every company and the Board of Directors given a mandate to report the incipient sickness when a unit shows cash losses and negative working capital and take appropriate measures when net worth starts eroding to 10 per cent.

APPENDIX 1

MICRO-COMPUTERS AVAILABLE IN INDIA

1. DCM	
(*i*) Spectrum 7	60 KB; 4 FDD (243 KB each); VDU; 165 cps Printer
(*ii*) Galaxy 9 (16 bit)	64 KB; 20 MB H.D., VDU; 600 Lpm Printer, 2 FDD (243 KB each); 1-Mag Tape, 2-DATEN 9
(*iii*) Galaxy 21 (16 bit)	128 KB; 2×20 MB H.D., VDU; 600 Lpm Printer, 2 FDD (243 KB), Mag Tape, DATEN 9 Multi-terminal
2. HCL	
(*i*) Systems 2	64 KB; 2 FDD (256 KB each); 1 MFD (80 KB) VDU; 200 Lpm Printer, 2-Application Packages
3. ORG	
(*i*) ORG 80 (16 bit)	128 KB; 2 FDD; VDU; 600 Lpm Printer, 80 MB H.D.; 1 Mag Tape (2400)
4. ECIL	
(*i*) TDC 312 (12 bit)	32 K Words, Teletype; 2 FDD 300 Lpm; 2×13 MB H.D. Off-line data entry
(*ii*) TDC 316 (16 bit)	128 KB; VDU; 2 FDD 300 Lpm Printer, 12 MB H.D. 2400 tape, Off-line data entry
5. UPTRON	
(*i*) S-800	64 KB; 2 FDD; VDU, 60 cps Printer

6. NELCO/IDM	
NELCO System 4000 (16 bit)	64 KB; 2 DSDD (1.2 MB each) 2 VDUs; 165 cps Printer
7. TELEVISTA	
Cosmos	64 KB; 2 FDD, VDU, 150 cps Printer
8. ZENITH ELECTRONICS	
Orion 8000 (16 bit)	64 KB; 2 FDD (266 KB), VDU, 180 cps Printer
9. ICIM	
ICIM-101	160 KB; MB H.D.; VDU; 1 Tape Drive (2400); 300 Lpm Printer, 1 FDD

APPENDIX 2

STRUCTURAL COMPONENTS OF MAIN FRAME, MINI AND MICRO-COMPUTERS

Main Frame [Cyber 170/Model 72(12)]—large computer system.

The main frame of the computer system is composed of the following:

		Nos.
1.	C.P.U.	2
2.	Master storage controller	4
3.	Disk storage unit—237 M Bytes	5
4.	Magnetic tape controller	2
5.	Magnetic tape—9 tracks 1600 bpi	4
6.	Magnetic tape—7 tracks 800 bits per inch	1
7.	Line printer —1600 lines per minute	4
8.	Card reader—1200 cards per minute	2

9. Network processing unit--can handle 24 data channels
10. Can have several mini computer hooks with it like HP 1000/20 and LSI 2/10 which can work as a terminal
11. Network operation system and remote batch facility
12. Software—PL/1, Algol, Fortran 4, Cobol, Basic. GPSS

LSI—2/10 Terminal System consists of

1. (*a*) Processor 16 bit word
   (*b*) 8 bit status register
   (*c*) 1.6 Micro Sec. cycle time
   (*d*) 188 instructions
2. Memory 32 K (semi-conductor)
3. Floppy disk drive 256 K bytes
4. Magnetic tape drive 25/Sec., 800 bpi, 9 track
5. Card reader 600 cards/minute
6. Line Printer 300 lines/minute
7. Teletypewriter speed 10 characters/sec.

Particulars		Mini Computer Galaxy 21-03	Microcomputer Workhorse Level 2
1. System Configuration	(*a*)	CPU+FP Processor 512 KB+1 console Terminal Floppy Disk Drive and Controller for LMD controller for Printer	Workhorse level 2 System of 64 KB RAM with VDU and 2×200 KB Floppy drives each and one 120 cps dot. matrix printer and one letter quality printer
	(*b*)	2 Additional Terminals—Spectrum workstation+1 Terminal keyboard+CRT	
	(*c*)	80/132 Col. Dot. Matrix Printer	
	(*d*)	200 cps Dot. Matrix Printer (Galaxy)	
	(*e*)	Cartridge Disk Drive (6 MB Fixed+6 removable)	
2. CPU		16 bit (Microprocessor)	8 bit (Microprocessor)
3. Facility		Multi-programming	NA
4. Disks		One Floppy Disk Drive One Cartridge Disk	2×200 KB Floppy drives
5. Line Printer		One 200 cps Dot. Matrix Printer Two 80/132 Dot. Matrix Printer	120 cps Dot Matrix Printer
6. User Chanels	(*a*)	Multi-terminal	NA
	(*b*)	Console+3 additional Terminals can take up	A terminal is a complete work-

Particulars	Mini Computer Galaxy 21-03	Microcomputer Workhorse Level 2
	to 16 Terminals	horse station. These can be added as independent units or integrated
	(*c*) Off line Data Entry	
7. Software	Supports Basic/21 Cobol/21 Converse/21 Fortran 77	HICOS BASIC FORTRAN Word Processing Software
8. Application software	20 applications include Scientific, Statistical, Network, LP	
9. Cost	Rs. 6,77,454.50 Rs. 25,000.00 for Fortran Compiler	
10. Flexibility	Memory and additional Spectrum workstations can be added up to 16 in numbers	(*a*) Each terminal means a separate workhorse station level 2 (*b*) More printers can be added (*c*) More Floppy Drives can be added
11. Space required	400 sq. ft. Air-conditioned, dust free	120 to 240 sq. ft. Air-conditioned space
12. Power requirement	3 phase 220V 50 Cycle Servo controlled Voltage Stabilizers-3	Single phase 220V 50 Cycle with Stabilizer

REFERENCES

1. Finance Minister's speech in the Lok Sabha on IRBI Bill, *Times of India*, August 8, 1984.
2. Reserve Bank of India Report on Currency and Finance, 1978-79 to 1983-84.
3. Ambika, 'Liquidation in Indian Corporate Sector', *The Economic Times*, August 4, 1984.
4. Walter, J.E., 'Determination of Technical Solvency', *Journal of Business*, 31st January, 1957, pp. 30-43.
5. Donaldson, G., 'New Framework for Corporate Debt Policy', *Harvard Business Review*, Vol. 40, March-April 1962, pp. 117-31.
6. Donaldson, G., 'Strategy for Financial Emergencies', *Harvard Business Review*, Nov.-Dec. 1969, pp. 67-69.
7. Altman, E.I., 'Corporate Bankruptcy in America', Lexington, Mass, D.C., Heath and Co., 1971, pp. 2-4.
8. Reserve Bank of India Report on 'Trend and Progress of Banking in India, 1977-78', p. 25.
9. Chairman's speech on 33rd Annual General Meeting of Industrial Finance Corporation of India (IFCI), Bombay.
10. Baruch Lev, *Financial Statement Analysis: A New Approach*, Prentice Hall, Inc., New Jersey, 1974, p. 134.
11. John Argenti, *Corporate Collapse—the Causes and Symptoms*, McGraw Hill, London, 1976.
12. Ross, J.E. and Kami, M.J., *Corporate Management in Crisis*, Prentice Hall, 1973.
13. Isadore Barmash, 'Great Business Disasters', Ballantine Books, 1973.
14. R.A. Smith, 'Corporations in Crisis', Doubleday, 1966.
15. Rajinder S., 'Causes of Sickness, its Prevention and Cure', *Indian Textiles Journal*, January 1979.
16. Robertson Andrew, 'The Lessons of Failure', Macdonald, 1973.
17. Deeson, A.F.L., 'Great Company Crashes', W. Foulsham, 1972.
18. Daughen, J.R., and P. Bin Jen, *The Wreck of the Penn Central*, Little Brown and Company, 1971.
19. Altman, E.I., 'Corporate Financial Distress', Wiley Interscience.
20. Altman, E.I. and Arnold W. Smetz, *Financial Crisis Institutions and Markets in a Fragile Environment*, John Wiley and Sons, New York, 1977.
21. Srivastava, S.S., 'Management of Industrial Sickness', *Productivity*, Oct.-Dec. 1983.

22. Yalaguresh B., Yalawar and Ramu P. Iyer, 'Timely Assessment of Key Symptoms', *The Economic Times*, August 2, 1984.
23. John Argenti, 'The Anatomy of Company Failures: The classical syndrome', *The Accountant*, May 1976.
24. John Argenti, 'Symptoms of Sickness', *Accounting*, 1977, pp. 46-54.
25. Kuchal, S.C., 'Success and Sickness of New Projects', *IIM*, Ahmedabad, 1984.
26. Laurant, L.R., 'Improving the Efficiency and Effectiveness of Financial Ratio Analysis', *Journal of Business Finance and Accounting*, 1979, p. 401.
27. Beaver, W.H., Kennelly, J.W. and Voss, V.M., 'Predictive Ability as a Criterion for the Evaluation of Accounting', *The Accounting Review*, 43 (October 1968).
28. P.J. Fitz Patrick, 'A Comparison of Ratios of Successful Industrial Enterprises with those of Failed Firms', *Certified Public Accountant*, 12 (October, November and December, 1932).
29. A. Winakor and R.F. Smith, 'Changes in Financial Structure of Unsuccessful Industrial Companies', *Bureau of Business Research Bulletin*, No. 51, University of Illinois Press, 1935.
30. Ramser, J.R. and Foster, L.O., 'A Demonstration of Ratio Analysis', *Bulletin No. 4* (Urbana: University of Illinois, Bureau of Business Research, 1931).
31. Merwin, C.L., 'Financing Small Corporations in Five Manufacturing Industries, 1926-36' (New York: National Bureau of Economic Research, 1942).
32. W. Braddock Hickman, 'Corporate Bond Quality and Investors Experience' (Princeton University Press, 1958), pp. 390-421.
33. Saulinier, R.J., Halcrow, H.G. and Jacoby, N.H., *Federal Lending and Loan Insurance* (Princeton University Press, 1938), pp. 456-81.
34. Moore, G.H. and Atkinson, 'Risk and Returns in Small Business Financing—Towards a Firmer Basis of Economic Policy', 41st Annual Report (National Bureau of Economic Research, 1961), pp. 66-67.
35. Seiden, M.H., 'Trade Credit: A Quantitative and Qualitative Analysis', Tested Knowledge of Business Cycles, 42nd Annual Report (National Bureau of Economic Research, 1962), pp. 86-88.
36. Beaver, W.H., 'Financial Ratios as Predictors of Failures', Empirical Research in Accounting Selected Studies, 1966, Supplement to Vol. 4, *Journal of Accounting Research*, pp. 71-127.
37. Beaver, W.H., 'Market Prices, Financial Ratios and the Prediction of Failure', *Journal of Accounting Research*, 6 (Autumn, 1968), pp. 179-92.
38. Tamari, M., 'Financial Ratios as Measure of Forecasting Bankruptcy', *Management International Review*, Vol. 4, 1966, pp. 15-21.

39. Altman, E.I., 'Financial Ratios, Discriminant Analysis and the Prediction of Corporate Bankruptcy' *Journal of Einance*, Vol. XXIII, September 1968, pp. 589-609.
40. Altman, E.I., Haldeman, R.G. and Narayanan, P., 'Zeta Analysis: A New Model to Identify Bankruptcy Risk of Corporations', *Journal of Banking and Finance*. Spring 1977.
41. Deakins, E.B., 'A Discriminant Analysis of Predictors of Failure', *Journal of Accounting Research*, Vol. I, No. 10, Spring, 1972, pp. 167-179.
42. Myer, P.A. and Pifer, H.W., 'Prediction of Bank Failures', *Journal of Finance*, Vol. XXV (Sept. 1970), pp. 853-68.
43. Blum, M., 'Failing Company Discriminant Analysis', *Journal of Accounting Research*, Spring, 1974, pp. 1-25.
44. Edmister, R.O., 'An Empirical Test of Financial Ratio Analysis for Small Business Failure', *Journal of Financial and Quantitative Analysis*, Vol. 7 (March 1972), pp. 1477-93.
45. Libby, R., 'The Use of Simulated Decision Makers in Information Evaluation', *The Accounting Review*, July 1975.
46. Elam, Rick 'The Effect of Lease Data on the Predictive Ability of Financial Ratios', *Accounting Review*, January 1975, pp. 25-43.
47. Richard Taffler and Howard Tishaw. 'Going, Going, Gone--Four Factors which Predict Failure', *Accountancy*, March, 1977, pp. 50-54.
48. Ohlson, James A., 'Financial Ratios and the Probabilistic Prediction of Bankruptcy, *Journal of Accounting Research*, Spring 1980, pp. 109-131.
49. Demolena, I.G. and Khoury, S.J., 'Ratio Stability and Corporate Failure', *Journal of Finance*, September 1980, pp. 1020-71.
50. Wilcox, J.W., 'Gambler's Ruin Approach to Business', *Sloan Management Review*, Vol. 18, 1976, pp. 33-46.
51. Delton Chesser, 'Predicting Loan Compliance', *Journal of Commercial Bank Lending*, August 1974.
52. R.A.I. Van Frederikslust, 'Predictability of Corporate Failure', Martinus Nyhoff Social Science Division, Leiden/Boston, 1978.
53. Baruch Lev, 'Financial Failures and Informational Decomposition Measures', Accounting in Perspective: Contributions to Accounting Thought by other Disciplines, R.R. Sterling and W.F. Bentz (South Western Publishing Co , 1971), pp. 102-111.
54. Aharony, J., Charles, P.J. and Swary, I , 'An Analysis of Risk and Return Characteristics of Corporate Bankruptcy Using Market Data', *Journal of Finance*, September 1980, pp. 1001-1017.
55. Walker, M.C. and Stowe, J.D. and Moriarty, S., 'Decomposition Analysis of Financial Statement', *Journal of Business and Accounting*, Summer 1979, pp. 173-186.

56. Argenti, John, 'Company Failure—Long Range Prediction not Enough', *Accountancy*, August 1977, pp. 40-48, 50, 52.
57. Kaveri, V.S., 'Financial Ratios as Predictors of Borrower's Health', Sultan Chand and Sons, New Delhi, 1980.
58. Chatterjee, S. and Roy, S., 'Forecasting Sickness: A Quantitative Approach', 20th All India Cost Conference, Calcutta, January, 1978.
59. NCAER—A Study of Industrial Sickness, 1979.
60. Sarama, L.V.L.N. and Rao, G.B., 'Financial Ratios as Predictors of Failure: A Multivariate Approach', *Indian Manager*, Vol. 7 (April-June 1976), pp. 175-189.
61. Bhattacharya, C.D. and Pande, K.M., 'Corporate Financial Strength: Application of Discriminant Analysis', *Jodhpur Management Journal* (Published by Faculty of Commerce, University of Jodhpur), Vol. 3, pp. 23-26.
62. Gupta, L.C., 'Financial Ratios as Forewarning Indicators of Corporate Sickness', A Study sponsored by ICICI, 1979.
63. Srivastava, S.S., 'Design and Development of Information Systems for Development Banks: A System Approach', Second IFCI Lecture, Faculty of Management Studies, University of Delhi, Feb. 1981, pp. 11-27.
64. Samuels, J.M. and Smyth, D.J., 'Profit, Variability of Profits and Firm Size', *Econometrica*, 1968, pp. 127-139.
65. Horrigan, J.O., 'Some Empirical Bases of Financial Ratio Analysis', *Accounting Review*, July 1965, Vol. 40, pp. 558-568.
66. Horrigan, J.O., 'The Determination of Long-Term Credit Standing with Financial Ratios', Empirical Research in Accounting: Selected Studies, 1966, Supplement to Vol. 4, *Journal of Accounting Research*, pp. 44-62.
67. Ball, R. and Brown, P., 'Some Preliminary Findings on the Association between the Earning of the Firm, its Industry and the Eeonomy', Empirial Research in Accounting: Selected Studies, 1967, Supplement to *Jonrnal of Accounting Research*, 1967, pp. 55-77.
68. James, H. Bliss, 'Financial and Operating Ratios in Management' (New York: The Ronald Press Co., 1923), p. 59.
69. Littleton, A.C., 'The 2 to 1 Ratio Analyzed', *Certified Public Accountant*, August 1926, pp. 244-246.
70. Sidney, Alexander, 'The Effect of Size of Manufacturing Corporation on the Distribution of the Rate of Return', *Review of Economics and Statistics*, August 1919, pp. 229-235.
71. Gilman, Stephen, 'Analyzing Financial Statements', The Ronald Press Company, New York, 1925.
72. Guthmann, Harry, 'Analysis of Financial Statements', Prentice Hall, Inc., New York.

73. Foulke, Roy A., 'Practical Financial Statement Analysis', 6th Ed., McGraw Hill Book Company, 1968.
74. Spencer, A. Tucker, 'Successful Managerial Control by Ratio Analysis', McGraw Hill Book Company, Inc., New York, 1961.
75. Irving, Kelogg, 'How to use Financial Statements', McGraw Hill Book Company, New York, 1969.
76. Myer, John M., 'Financial Statement Analysis', Prentice Hall, Fourth Ed., 1969.
77. Eric, A. Helfert, 'Techniques of Financial Analysis', Richard D. Irwin, Inc., 1972.
78. Kennedy, R.D. and McMullen, S.Y., 'Financial Statements, Forms, Analysis and Interpretation', Homewood, Illinois, Richard D. Irwin, Inc., 1973.
79. Bernstein, L.A. 'Financial Statement Analysis: Theory, Application and Interpretation', Homewood, Illinois, Irwin, 1974.
80. Slater, S.D., 'The Strategy of Cash: A Liquidity Approach to Maximising the Company's Profit', London, Wiley, 1974.
81. Tennent, M., 'Practical Liquidity Management', Epping Gower Press, 1976.
82. Foster George, 'Financial Statement Analysis', Prentice Hall, Inc., New Jersey, 1978.
83. Theil, 'Principles of Econometrices', John Wiley and Sons, New York, 1971.
84. Chudson, W.A., 'The Pattern of Corporate Financial Structure: A Cross Section View of Manufacturing Mining, Trade and Construction Corporations', 1937, New York, National Bureau of Economic Research, 1945.
85. Baruch Lev, 'Industry Averages as Targets for Financial Ratios', *Journal of Accounting Research*, 7 (Autumn, 1969), pp. 290-299.
86. Harry, H. Harman, 'Modern Factor Analysis', The University of Chicago Press, 1977.
87. Hofstede, G.H., 'The Game of Budget Control (Van Gorcum, 1967), p. 313.
88. Rummel, R.J., 'Applied Factor Analysis', Evanston, North Western University Press, 1970.
89. Fruchter, B., 'Introduction to Factor Analysis', D. Van Nostrand Company, Inc., pp. 44-50.
90. Overall John E. and Klett, James, C., 'Applied Multivariate Analysis', McGraw Hill, 1972, pp. 243-279.
91. Fisher R.A., 'The Use of Multiple Measurements in Taxonomic Problems', *Annals of Eugencies* No. 7, September 1936, pp. 179-188.
92. Cochran, W.G., 'On the Performance of the Linear Discriminant Function', *Technometrics*, Vol. 6, May 1964, pp. 179-190.

93. Travers, R.M.W., 'The Use of a Discriminant Function in Treatment of Psychological Group of Differences', *Psochometrica*' Vol. 4, No. 1, March 1939.
94. Henry, E. Ganet, 'The Discriminant Function and its Use in Psychology', *Psychometrica,* Vol. 8, No. 2, June 1983, pp. 65-79.
95. Durand, D.D., 'Risk Elements in Consumer Instalment Financing' (New York: National Bureau of Economic Research, 1941), pp. 105-142.
96. Myers, H. and Forgy, E.W., 'Development of Numercial Credit Evaluation Systems', *Journal of American Statistical Association,* Vol. 50, September, 1963, pp, 797-806.
97. Walter, J.E., 'A Discriminant Function for Earnings Price Ratios of Large Industrial Corporation', *Review of Economics and Statistics,* Vol. XLI, February, 1959), pp. 44-52.
98. Smith, K.V., 'Classification of Investment Securities using MDA', Institute Paper 101 (Purdue Univ., Institute for Research in the Behavioral, Economic and Management Sciences, 1965).
99. Roenfeldt, Rohney L. and Cooley Philip L., 'Predicting Corporate Profitability for Investment Selection', *Journal of Business Finance and Accounting,* Spring, 1978, pp. 57-65.
100. Bird, R.G. and McHugh, 'Financial Ratios: An Empirical Study', *Journal of Business Finance and Accounting,* Spring, 1977, pp. 29-45.
101. Deakin, E.B., 'Distributions of Financial Accounting Ratios: Some Empirical Evidence', *The Accounting Review,* 1976, pp. 90-96.
102. Guthman and Dougall, 'Corporate Financial Policy', Prentice Hall of India Ltd., New Delhi, 1969, p. 65.
103. Sidney Davidson, G.H. Sorter and Homer Kalle, 'Measuring the Defensive Position of a Firm', *Financial Analysts Journal,* 20 (January-February, 1964), pp. 23-29.
104. G.H. Sorter and G. Benston, 'Appraising the Defensive Position of a Firm: The Internal Measure', *According Review* (October, 1960), pp. 633-40.
105. Donald D. Morrison, 'On the Interpretation of Discriminant Analysis', *Journal of Marketing Research,* 6 (May, 1969), p. 156.
106. Smith, K.V., 'Management of Working Capital' (New York), West Publishing Company, 1974.
107. Walker, Earnest, W., 'Essentials of Financial Management', Prentice Hall, Inc., Englewood Cliffs, New Jersy, 1971.
108. Ramamoorthy, V.E., 'Working Capital Management', Institute for Financial Management and Research. Madras, 1976.
109. Weston, J. Fred and Evgene, F. Brigham, 'Managerial Finance', The Dryden Press, Illinois, 1975.

110. Reserve Bank of India Bulletin, 'Finances of Medium and Large Public Limited Companies', 1975-76, September, 1977, p. 556.
111. Keynes, John Maynard, 'The General Theory of Employment, Interest and Money', New York, Harcourt Brace Jovanovish, Inc., 1936, pp. 170-174.
112. Van Horne, James C., 'Financial Management and Policy', Prentice Hall of India Pvt. Ltd., New Delhi, 1973.
113. Bolten, S.E., 'Managerial Finance' (Boston), Houghton, Miffln Co., 1976.
114. Veinott, Arthur F. Jr., 'The Status of Mathematical Inventory Control', *Management Science*, 12th July, 1966, pp. 745-777.
115. Bhattacharyaa, S.K., Determinants of Effective Working Capital Management', Indian Institute of Management, Ahmedabad, April, 1977, p. 15.
116. Tandon Committee Report—Study Group to Frame Guidelines for Follow up of Bank Credit, Reserve Bank of India, 1975.
117. Padwal, S.M., and Bandopadhyay R., 'Information System Design in a Commercial Bank', *Operational Research Quarterly*, Volume 26, 1977 p. 99.
118. Padwal, S.M. and Bandopadhyay R., 'Concepts and Framework for information', *Mauagement Accountant*, Feb., 1979.
119. Srivastava, S.S., 'Management Information System and Computers', Atma Ram & Sons, Delhi-6, 1984.
120. RBI Report on Currency and Finance, 1983-84.
121. IDBI Annual Report, 1982-83, pp. 61-62.
122. RBI Report on Currency and Finance, 1982-83, p. 328.
123. The Union Budget, 1985-86.
124. IDBI Annual Report, 1983-84, p. 80.
125. IRCI Annual Report, 1982-83, 1983-84.
126. IFCI Annual Report, 1983-84, p. 81.
127. Ashok Dutta, 'Revival of Sick Units', *The Chartered Acconntant*, April, 1980, pp. 907-909.
128. Pratir Chakravarty, 'Revival of a Sick Unit—A case study of an Engineering Unit of West Bengal', *The Management Accountant*, Feb., 1985.
129. V.V. Desai. 'Rehabilitation of Sick Units', *The Chartered Accountant*', July, 1980, pp. 11-14.
130. K.N. Perumal Pillai, 'Turning round a Sick Unit—A practical approach', *The Economic Times*, June 6, 1984.
131. Yalaguresh B. Yalawar and Ramu P. Iyer, 'Revival is Management Responsibility', *The Economic Times*, Aug. 3, 1984.
132. Rajendra Prabhu, 'How Sick Units regain Health', *The Hindustan Times*, Sept. 24, 1984.

INDEX

LIST OF TABLES

LIST OF FIGURES

SIDC	=State Industrial Development Corporation
TD	=Total Debt
TLTA	=Total Liabilities divided by Total Assets
TOE	=Total Operating Expenditures
TTA	=Total Tangible Assets
UNIVAC	=Universal Automatic Computer
VDU	=Visual Display Unit
WCTA	=Working Capital divided by Total Assets

HD =Hard Disk
IBM =International Business Machine
ICICI =Industrial Credit and Investment Corporation of India Limited
IDBI =Industrial Development Bank of India Limited
IFCI =Industrial Finance Corporation of India Limited
IIM =Inter Institutional Meetings
IRCI =Industrial Reconstruction Corporation of India Limited
IRBI =Industrial Reconstruction Bank of India Limited
KB =Kilo bytes
Lpm =Lines per minutes
LSI =Large Scale Integration
LTD =Long-term Debt
MDA =Multiple Discriminant Analysis
MIDAS =Management Information and Decision Analsis System
MIS =Management Information System
MRTP =Monopolies Restrictive Trade Practices
NA =Not Available
NCAER =National Council of Applied Economic Research
NI =Net Income
NITA =Net Income divided by Total Assets
NOP =Net Operating Income
NS =Net Sales
NW =Net Worth
NWC =Net Working Capital
OCF =Operating Cash Flow
OR =Operation Research
PCD =Problem Cases Department
QA =Quick Assets
R&D =Research and Development
RBI =Reserve Bank of India
RFD =Rehabilitation Finance Division
SFC =State Financial Corporation
SIC =Standard Industrial Classification

ABBREVIATIONS

ALGOL	=Algorithmic Language
BARC	=Bhaba Atomic Research Centre
BASIC	=Beginners All-Purpose Symbolic Instruction Code
bpi	=bits per inch
BSE	=Bombay Stock Exchange
B/S	=Balance Sheet
CA	=Current Assets
CF	=Cash Flow
CD	=Current Debt
CL	=Current Liabilities
CLCA	=Current Liabilities divided by Current Assets
Co.	=Company
COBOL	=Common Business Oriented Language
CORAL	=Class Oriented Ring Associated Language—for handling certain ring types of lists
Cps	=Characters per Second
CPU	=Central Processing Unit
CRT	=Cattrode Ray Tube
CSIR	=Council of Scientific Industrial Research
DA	=Defensive Assets
DBMS	=Data Base Management System
DJSC	=Directory of Joint Stock Companies
EBDIT	=Earning Before Depreciation, Interest and Taxes
EBIT	=Earning Before Interest and Taxes
FA	=Fixed Assets
FDD	=Floppy Disk Drive
FERA	=Foreign Exchange Regulation Act
FORTRAN	=Formula Translator Language
FUTL	=Funds provided by operations divided by Total Liabilities
GR	=Group

CONTENTS

Director, Management Development Institute, New Delhi, Prof. R.S. Nigam, Head of the Department of Commerce, University of Delhi and Prof. B.S. Sharma of the Faculty of Management Studies and to the Dean, Faculty of Management Studies, University of Delhi for very useful discussions and encouragement. The help of Shri Anand Makkar is also acknowledged in carrying out several computer programmes of extendend MDA Model. The authors are also very thankful to Shri J.C. Sehgal for typing the manuscript. The authors will feel gratified if the book is found useful to the managers in Indian Industries and also to researchers in this important area of industrial sickness.

NEW DELHI
June 20, 1985

S. S. SRIVASTAVA
R.A. YADAV

onset of sickness in various industrial groups so that managerial actions could be taken well in time. Lot of research work has been carried out in recent years and various techniques have been developed to predict industrial sickness in India and abroad. Some of these techniques and models can be usefully employed in Indian situation. If sickness can be predicted, the process of decision-making can be made prompt and responsive. To predict sickness, an efficient and computerised management information system has to be employed which can effectively monitor the on-going operations and should even assess the usefulness of a rehabilitation programme if given to a sick unit.

The present book is an effort to meet the requirement of Indian industries of managing and monitoring industrial sickness. The book has 11 chapters which deal with growth and causes of sickness in Indian industries, signals and symptoms which can be identified as symptoms of sickness, the role of financial ratios and other technical parameters which can be used as indicators of sickness and can then be used in various computerised models for predicting the sickness. The indicators dealt with are physical indicators, graphical indicators, and multiple discriminant score index. The latter has been enlarged to include data from non-financial parameters also which has considerably enhanced the prediction accuracy of the industrialincknes. There is a chapter on management of working capital, and on management information system for monitoring industrial sickness. Chapters 9 and 10 deal with the prevention of sickness and rehabilitation of sick industries. The various measures adopted by the Government, financial institutions and state level financial corporations in rehabilitating the sick industry have been reviewed and an effective approach for monitoring and managing the sickness has been brought out in the book. It is hoped that the book would prove useful to the managers of industries in effectively developing a monitoring system on the on-going operations in an industry, and thus help in assessing the actual state of health of the industry.

The authors are grateful to the Industrial Finance Corporation of India for help and to Dr. T.N. Kapoor, Executive

PREFACE

THE SICKNESS in Indian industry is spreading at an alarming rate. The malady is now extensively spread in large and medium size units with credit facilities of more than Rs. 1 crore. A large percentage of small scale industries is usually sick but in some states this number exceeds more than 60 per cent of the total installed units. The locked up capital in industrial sickness today exceeds Rs. 10,000 crores if rescheduling of payment is also considered as inability to meet the obligations in time. Every year a large number of sick units are being taken over by the Government specially in industries like jute, paper, textiles and engineering. As more units are becoming sick every year even the Government finds it difficult to place experienced managers for takeover of these sick units.

There has been a number of suggestions made from various quarters regarding the measures which should be adopted to combat sickness. The rehabilitation programmes and soft loan schemes of the Government have not made much dent. The anxiety about increasing sickness is reflected in various statements made at the highest levels in Government and Parliament. Recently the Government has introduced a new bill "Sick Industrial Companies (Special Provisions) Bill, 1985" in Parliament in August 1985 which would ensure timely dectection of sick units and make arrangements for managing them.

Sickness in industry is an organic process. Although there are several reasons including some beyond the control of industries, mismanagement is considered to be a general malady. Poor performance may arise because of poor operations in any of the areas like finance, technical, labour and plant & equipment operations. Obsolete technology as time passes also leads to poor performance. But causes of sickness are not the same in different industries; these have to be diagnosed in each case. In fact, there is a need to predict

FOREWORD

I am very happy to find that a comprehensive book on *Management and Monitoring of Industrial Sickness* has been written by the authors. It has been an important subject in the present environment where sickness in Indian industry has spread at all levels. The book makes a comprehensive review of various factors which lead to sickness including some of the environmental factors not always within the control of the industry. The signals and symptoms though fairly well known, have been methodically identified and related with various stages of sickness. What is more impressive about the book is that it deals with various approaches in identifying and predicting the onset of sickness with a high degree of accuracy. The book also provides a survey of research work carried out in recent years of various techniques and models devoloped in this area and is thus very useful to research scholars and academicians in universities, industrial corporations and financial and industrial institutions. Chapters on Management of Working Capital and on Management Information System (MIS) for monitoring industrial sickness are likely to attract the attention of bankers and executives dealing with this important area. MIS is very important and will be very useful in stemming sickness and in measuring the effectiveness of the rehabilitation programmes being organised at various levels in government and financial institutions.

I am sure the book will prove useful to managers and executives of Indian industries and to the researchers in this field.

New Delhi
15th October, 1985

D.N. Davar
Chairman

Industrial Finance Corporation
of India, New Delhi

Dedicated to
Executives and Managers
of
Industries

First Published 1986

Shambhu Saran Srivastava (*b.* 1919-)
Ram Avtar Yadav (*b.* 1949-)

Published by
Naurang Rai
Concept Publishing Company
H-13, Bali Nagar
NEW DELHI-110015 (India)

Printed in India by
Ajit Singh, Printco India
Maujpur, Delhi-110053.

MANAGEMENT AND MONITORING OF INDUSTRIAL SICKNESS

Dr. S.S. SRIVASTAVA
M.Sc., Ph.D., D.I.C. (LONDON), J.S.S.C., C. ENG., MIERE
Formerly Professor of Management, Faculty of Management Studies,
University of Delhi, Delhi

Dr. R.A. YADAV
M.Com., Ph.D.
Senior Faculty Member, Shri Ram College of Commerce,
University of Delhi, Delhi

CONCEPT PUBLISHING COMPANY, NEW DELHI

MANAGEMENT AND MONITORING OF INDUSTRIAL SICKNESS